AMERICAN BAR ASSOCIATION
Public Contract Law Section

BEST PRACTICES IN THE ACQUISITION OF A GOVERNMENT CONTRACTOR

Second Edition

EDITORS

Todd R. Overman and Damien Specht

Cover design by Kelly Book/ABA Design

Printed in the United States of America.

25 24 23 22 21   5 4 3 2 1

Library of Congress Cataloging-in-Publication Data

Names: Overman, Todd R., editor. | Specht, Damien, editor. | American Bar Association. Section of Public Contract Law, sponsoring body.
Title: Best practices in the acquisition of a government contractor.
Description: Second edition. | Chicago, Illinois : American Bar Association, [2021] | "2nd Edition Editors: Todd R. Overman, Bass, Berry & Sims; Damien Specht, Morrison & Foerster"--ECIP galley. | Includes bibliographical references. | Summary: "The purpose of this manual is not to summarize all aspects of the law or to opine on what the law should be. Our purpose is also not to teach government contracts lawyers all they need to know about corporate law or, alternatively, to make corporate lawyers experts in government contracts. Instead, this guide is written to identify key transactional issues that arise in transactions involving government contractors across corporate, antitrust, political, foreign investment and other areas of law. Our goal is to provide audiences with targeted, and most importantly, useful advice from practitioners who have been involved in hundreds of transactions (often on opposite sides of each other). It is our hope that readers will learn from our hard-earned experience in the form of bold "Best Practice Tips" and this volume's highly structured, easy to reference format. Each page is designed to allow a reader to quickly grasp a key issue to readily deploy in their practice. This volume also includes detailed appendices and forms that will help practitioners to supplement their existing forms, gather key documents and perform comprehensive government contracts due diligence"--Provided by publisher.
Identifiers: LCCN 2021028096 (print) | LCCN 2021028097 (ebook) | ISBN 9781641059602 (paperback) | ISBN 9781641059619 (ebook)
Subjects: LCSH: Government purchasing--Law and legislation--United States. | Public contracts--United States.
Classification: LCC KF849 .B494 2021 (print) | LCC KF849 (ebook) | DDC 346.73/023--dc23
LC record available at https://lccn.loc.gov/2021028096
LC ebook record available at https://lccn.loc.gov/2021028097

2nd Edition Editors

Todd R. Overman, Bass, Berry & Sims

Damien Specht, Morrison & Foerster

2nd Edition Authors

Rachel J. Adcox, Axinn, Veltrop & Harkrider

Ata Akiner, White & Case

Michael Anstett, Fried, Frank, Harris, Shriver & Jacobson

Mary Beth Bosco, Holland & Knight

Ian Brekke, Covington & Burling

Stacie Soohyun Cho, Axinn, Veltrop & Harkrider

Steve Diamond, Arnold & Porter

Michael Elliot, Lockheed Martin

Jay Fraude, Defense Counterintelligence and Security Agency

Scott A. Freling, Covington & Burling

Alexander B. Hastings, Covington & Burling

Lauren Horneffer, King & Spalding

Farhad Jalinous, White & Case

Sajeev D. Malaveetil, EY

Karalyn D. Mildorf, White & Case

Kimi N. Murakami, MELE Associates

Cedric Powell, Sheppard Mullin

John Prairie, Wiley Rein

Lucantonio Salvi, Sheppard Mullin

Michael E. Samuels, Crowell and Moring

Varnitha Siva, Axinn, Veltrop & Harkrider

Jay Stine, Northrop Grumman

Sonia Tabriz, Arnold & Porter

Sylvia Yi, Bass, Berry & Sims

1st Edition Editors and Authors

Antitrust: Raymond Jacobsen, John Dubrow, Andrea Hamilton, Carla Hine, and Rachel Lewis

Classified Contracts, CFIUS, and Exon-Florio: Chris Griner, Farhad Jalinous, Christopher Brewer, and Jay Fraude

Corporate Structure and Practice: Marian Block, Kathryn G. Simpson, Paul T. Porrini, and Paul Shinn

Government Contracts: Steven S. Diamond, Joan Ochs, Brian Kingston, Joseph Barsalona, Richard Meene, Philip Koos, Allan Joseph, Suhani Kamdar, and Aaron Silberman

Contents

CHAPTER 1

Introduction

More than a decade ago, the original authors of this volume brought together leading practitioners from various disciplines to develop the *Best Practices in the Acquisition of a Government Contractor.* Since that time both the law and the market have changed. For example, we have seen the explosion of representation and warranty insurance and a significant uptick in asset transactions involving government contractors. It is also no surprise that the regulations that form the basis for our practice (and thus impact acquisitions) have continued to change. As a result, the authors of this volume fully expect that it too will be followed in a decade by an updated version reflecting our ever-changing industry.

In this new volume, we maintain the same focus as the original. The purpose of this manual is not to summarize all aspects of the law or to opine on what the law should be. Neither is our purpose to teach government contracts lawyers all they need to know about corporate law or, alternatively, to make corporate lawyers experts in government contracts. Instead, this guide is written to identify key transactional issues that arise in transactions involving government contractors across corporate, antitrust, political, foreign investment, and other areas of law. Our goal is to provide audiences with targeted and, most importantly, useful advice from practitioners who have been involved in hundreds of transactions (often on opposite sides). It is our hope that readers will learn from our hard-earned experience in the form of bold "Best Practice Tips" and this volume's highly structured, easy-to-reference format. Each page is designed to allow a reader to quickly grasp a key issue to readily deploy in their practice. This volume also includes detailed appendices and forms that will help practitioners to supplement their existing forms, gather key documents, and perform comprehensive government contracts due diligence.

This work was initiated by the American Bar Association Section of Public Contract Law, Mergers & Acquisition Committee, but the Section went beyond its membership to include top practitioners on all of the topics covered in this manual. Recognizing our debt to the original authors, we have identified the committee members that developed the prior volume as well. This manual represents the work of the listed authors but should not be considered to represent the views of their respective government agencies, companies, or firms.

CHAPTER 2

The Due Diligence Process

OUTLINE

A. Confidentiality Agreements
  1. Process Issues
    a. When to Put a Confidentiality Agreement in Place
    b. Battle of the Forms and Negotiations
    c. Timing of Negotiation
    d. Administrative Matters
      1. Administration by Target
      2. Administration by Acquirer
  2. Types of Nondisclosure Agreements
    a. Target and Acquirer
    b. Internal with Employees
    c. Third-Party Experts
  3. Substance of a Confidentiality Agreement
    a. Typical Provisions in Confidentiality Agreements
      1. Public vs. Private Deals
      2. What's Market and What's Not?
      3. Definition of Confidential Information
      4. Return or Destroy Provisions
      5. Employee Nonsolicitation Provisions
      6. Remedies for Breach and Equitable Relief
      7. Term
    b. How Acquisition Nondisclosure Agreements/Confidentiality Agreements Differ from Nondisclosure Agreements Used for Other Government Contracting Purposes
    c. How to Integrate Confidentiality Agreement Provisions into the Acquisition Agreement
    d. How Confidentiality Agreements Can Be Misused

This manual focuses on due diligence that an acquirer (the Acquirer) may perform on an acquisition target (the Target). Due diligence may be conducted on a formal or informal basis, and it is often conducted with varying processes and degrees of specificity, from the earliest stages of identification of a Target to immediately before or even after a transaction closes. The discussion below assumes the following general stages relevant to a due diligence process: (a) the identification of a Target by an Acquirer; (b) an initial approach and some level of discussion between the parties; and (c) an agreement in principle between the Acquirer and the Target that is appropriate to govern the sharing of confidential information and will allow the Acquirer access to information helpful to facilitate an acquisition decision.

A government contracts due diligence investigation assesses the Target's government business, including its value, sustainability, potential liabilities, and risks. For both the strategic and financial acquirer, a comprehensive and thorough due diligence process is intended to elicit documentation and information needed to:

- Identify key issues that may facilitate a more realistic valuation of the Target and an assessment of the Target's viability as a going concern.
- Identify critical transition and integration issues, including business processes and internal controls, and potential deficiencies in these and other areas.
- Identify agencies and contact points for required government or third-party approvals.
- Identify and assess risks of noncompliance with legal, regulatory, or contractual requirements (including adherence to internal policies and procedures) and specific instances of such noncompliance.
- Provide information necessary to negotiate representations and warranties, indemnification, and other contractual covenants and conditions.
- Support the issuance of representation and warranty insurance (if applicable).
- Identify any litigations, audits, investigations, disputes, and claims that may result in cost adjustments, disallowances under current contracts, or contractual terminations, or which may present other potential risks to the Target's business.

A. Confidentiality Agreements

1. Process Issues

This section reviews certain process and administrative issues attendant to the use of nondisclosure and confidentiality agreements (hereinafter referred to as a Confidentiality Agreement or a CA) in the context of mergers and acquisitions (M&A). These issues are not unique to transactions involving government contractors, but the competition in this industry places special emphasis on protecting proprietary information.

a. When to Put a Confidentiality Agreement in Place

Entering into a nondisclosure or Confidentiality Agreement is often an initial formally documented step of an acquisition process.

Before a CA is put in place, there are typically no contractual restrictions or procedures required for one side of a potential transaction to communicate with another. CAs, however, often contain provisions on this subject, and post-signing communication may be restricted to specifically designated individuals who serve as communication channels for the respective parties to an M&A transaction. Restricting communication obviously facilitates the protection of confidential and proprietary information, and when a Target is involved in an auction process, attempts to discipline the behavior of multiple bidders.

Whether a Target is conducting a formal auction process to market itself or its assets, or is approached by a unique potential Acquirer outside of a formal process, the Target should put a CA in place with all potential Acquirers before sharing any nonpublic or proprietary data regarding the company or the assets/business to be sold.

b. Battle of the Forms and Negotiations

Although there is no hard and fast rule, typically a Target asks an Acquirer to use a form of CA provided by the Target. This is nearly always the case in a formal auction process, in which multiple potential acquirers are bidding for the Target or its assets. In this case, advisors engaged to facilitate the auction process (typically an investment banker, broker, or investment advisor) will provide a standard form CA for the Target to review with its legal counsel. Once the CA is tailored to meet the needs of the particular Target, the form will be provided to each potential Acquirer, which in turn will negotiate the CA with either the Target's legal counsel or investment advisors. If the sales process is less formal, a Target may provide its own form to a potential Acquirer, or an Acquirer may provide a CA form for the Target to review and negotiate.

c. Timing of Negotiation

CAs are typically negotiated as one of the first steps in an acquisition process, before much, if any, substantive dialogue has occurred between the parties. While the substance of the negotiation is often simple, and a CA can be put in place quickly, the interaction between the parties offers insight into future relationships. The CA negotiations provide both Acquirers and Targets a valuable glimpse of their counterparties' negotiation tactics—whether they take aggressive or moderate positions, how easily they accommodate the counterparties' interests, and how knowledgeable they appear to be about the process. Relationships can be built or destroyed at this very early stage in a potential transaction. A difficult interaction over a CA may allow parties an early opportunity to evaluate how best to engage, who should be involved, and, if interactions are very contentious, whether the parties are, in fact committed to pursuing a deal.

d. Administrative Matters

Sound administration of CAs is crucial to the initial stages of a sales process. Lack of organization or excessive delay at the beginning of a transaction does not bode well for a smooth process.

1. Administration by Target

The very first step in administration is a decision on which CA form is used. A Target should develop its preferred CA form well in advance of dealing with any potential Acquirers. While many provisions are standard and may be found in the Target's standard CA, some provisions will need to be tailored. Experienced transactional counsel should be consulted to advise on which provisions are most important for the proposed transaction.

If multiple potential Acquirers are involved in a sales process, administrative and compliance reasons compel an attempt to maintain some level of consistency among the various CAs entered into with each potential Acquirer. Once a Target has decided on its standard form CA, counsel and bankers negotiating the documents with various bidders for a Target should ideally provide early guidance on which provisions are negotiable and which are not. Armed with this guidance, the team can often negotiate the CA quickly without the need to consult with the Target, except on particularly unique or sensitive issues. Advisors should be instructed to keep a log of all negotiated CAs, notated with any deviations from the approved form, for easy reference by the Target.

A Target should consider CA administration from two fundamental perspectives, the first with respect to the Acquirer with whom the Target actually enters into a transaction and the second with respect to potential Acquirers who receive diligence information but are not the successful Acquirer. For the successful Acquirer, the key administrative consideration is ensuring that CA provisions are properly incorporated into the definitive transaction documents. Because transaction documents often cover confidentiality obligations on a broader basis than confidentiality agreements, it is typical for definitive purchase agreement provisions to terminate the CA, with the definitive purchase agreement containing the surviving confidentiality provisions.

With respect to the unsuccessful potential Acquirers, a Target (or its successor) is well advised to require return or destruction of confidential information. The CA typically details procedures for return or destruction of confidential information and usually requires the receiving party to certify to its compliance with such provisions, post-transaction. Targets that do not follow through on these provisions risk breach (inadvertent or intentional) of the CA provisions by unsuccessful bidders.

2. Administration by Acquirer

An Acquirer must consider specific administrative issues.

First, because most CAs will require that an Acquirer only provide confidential information received from a Target to those of its directors, officers, employees, agents, and advisors with a "need to know," the Acquirer should keep track of all parties with whom it has shared the Target's information and ensure that those parties understand their (and the Acquirer's) obligations under the CA. Commonly, an Acquirer will fulfill these obligations with respect to its own employees through internal confidentiality certifications. Such certifications typically remind employees of their obligation to keep information received from the Target confidential; require the employees to keep information about the Acquirer's interest in the Target confidential; reiterate prohibitions against insider trading; and detail procedures for other transactional matters, such as Hart-Scott-Rodino (HSR) review, which may require employees to furnish certain internal documents to regulators.

Second, it is standard that obligations under CAs survive two to three years, and often indefinitely with respect to trade secret information. Therefore, an Acquirer should develop procedures for handling and storage of a Target's confidential information, both during the auction and definitive agreement negotiation process, and following the closing. These types of provisions may inform which individuals are given access to proprietary information in the first instance. For the successful Acquirer (who owns the information after the closing), the process may be relatively straightforward and require only the centralization of information received during the diligence process. Unsuccessful Acquirers, however, need to be especially mindful of future competitions that may involve the Target, as well as any contractual obligations to return or dispose of confidential information to avoid the potential for later breaches of the CA. Where a Target requests that information be returned or destroyed, an Acquirer should promptly comply with that request and keep complete, auditable records showing that each employee who may have had access to a Target's information has confirmed his or her return or destruction of such information. Even if a Target does not request return or destruction of its information, an Acquirer should require its employees to confirm return or destruction for internal record-keeping purposes. For both internal compliance and evidentiary purposes, an Acquirer should ensure that the CA allows it to retain, within its General Counsel's or outside counsel's office and in connection with such Acquirer's internal data backup or record retention policies, one copy of all information received from the Target.

2. Types of Nondisclosure Agreements

a. Target and Acquirer

The due diligence process typically involves a nondisclosure agreement between the Acquirer and the Target. Additional nondisclosure agreements (or joinder under existing agreements) may be required to obtain the assistance of external experts or to comply with specific requirements of the Target's nondisclosure agreement (such as, for example, disclosure of classified information or access to confidential information by a new representative of the Acquirer).

Most Target nondisclosure agreements require the Acquirer to limit use of the information to evaluation of the proposed transaction. The Target's nondisclosure agreement may require that the individuals to whom the Acquirer makes further disclosure either (a) generally agree to maintain the confidentiality of the due diligence material, or (b) agree to the exact terms of the nondisclosure agreement between the Acquirer and the Target. Typically, a nondisclosure agreement will state that the Acquirer is responsible for any unauthorized disclosure by anyone to whom the Acquirer provides the Target's confidential information.

✓ **Best Practice Tip:** To avoid future claims that the Acquirer or potential Acquirer breached the Target's nondisclosure agreement by disclosing information to third parties, a potential Acquirer should have an additional written nondisclosure agreement with anyone with whom the potential Acquirer shares the information (including employees). The form of such additional nondisclosure agreement will depend upon the terms of the potential Acquirer's nondisclosure agreement with the Target. For example, if the Target's nondisclosure agreement requires all recipients of information to agree to the terms of the Target's nondisclosure agreement, the potential Acquirer should provide each recipient with a copy of the nondisclosure agreement and obtain a written acknowledgement from each such recipient that they will abide by the terms of the agreement. If the Target's nondisclosure agreement requires only that the recipient agree to maintain the confidentiality of the information, the potential Acquirer can consider using its own form of nondisclosure agreement with the recipient rather than the Target's nondisclosure agreement. However, if the potential Acquirer's form of nondisclosure agreement is less rigorous than the Target's form, the Acquirer may be at risk of a third-party recipient having no obligation to comply with the terms of the agreement with the Target.

b. Internal with Employees

Although most companies have policies that restrict employees from disclosing confidential information obtained from the Target, it is still a good practice to obtain a written nondisclosure agreement from all employees who will be working on the transaction. Such employees should receive a copy of the nondisclosure agreement with the Target and should agree to comply with its terms. These agreements provide evidence of the Acquirer's efforts to comply with the terms of the Target's nondisclosure agreement and inform a due diligence team member who may be unfamiliar with nondisclosure agreements of the obligations imposed by the agreement. These agreements also require the potential Acquirer to give specific thought to which employees should be exposed to the Target's information.

> ✓ **Best Practice Tip:** Acquirers may also want to use an employee agreement as an opportunity to reaffirm compliance with regulatory requirements and internal policies that may come into play during the course of negotiating a deal, such as (a) compliance with insider trading rules with regard to both the Acquirer's and Target's securities; (b) handling of export control information; and (c) transaction administration policies regarding items such as rules on contacting the Target or the Target's employees, expectations about archiving or destruction of due diligence material, time frames, etc.

c. Third-Party Experts

A written nondisclosure agreement is not necessarily required of outside counsel, who are required by standards of practice and licensing requirements to maintain the confidentiality of materials supplied by their clients or obtained in the course of representing their clients. Regardless of whether outside counsel confirm in writing their agreement to comply with the Target's nondisclosure agreement, a copy of the nondisclosure agreement should be provided to outside counsel. Investment bankers, accountants, appraisers, actuaries, consultants, environmental experts, and other types of professionals understand that their livelihood depends on their ability to maintain the confidentiality of shared information. However, most professionals and experts are not subject to the rigorous practice standards and licensing requirements applicable to attorneys. As a result, an Acquirer should always have a nondisclosure agreement with any outside expert advising on the transaction that covers the disclosure of a Target's information. Most outside experts, investment banks, insurance brokers, and other consultants have their own form of nondisclosure agreement and may be reluctant to agree to the terms in the Target's nondisclosure agreement. The Acquirer will need to evaluate the acceptability of any such forms against the requirements imposed by the Target's form.

In transactions involving sensitive material, including classified material, export-controlled material, or competitively sensitive data, such as labor rates or business development contacts, additional confidentiality procedures may be necessary. Access to sensitive data of this sort is generally limited to a subset of the Acquirer's due diligence team that has the requisite clearances or is not in a position to use the material to the competitive disadvantage of the Target. The Target typically will segregate this information either in a password-protected access point online or by limiting access to paper copies in a secure facility.

> ✓ **Best Practice Tip:** The Acquirer should keep a list of those individuals who are permitted access to the sensitive material and document each such individual's agreement to comply with any special limitations on access, use, and disclosure.

3. Substance of a Confidentiality Agreement

This section discusses the following: (a) provisions typically included in CAs, (b) differences between CAs used for public company vs. private company transactions, (c) those provisions considered "market," and (d) the appropriate use of materials obtained under CAs. With a few exceptions, CAs used for acquisitions of government contractors do not differ from CAs used for other types of acquisitions. Note, however, that CAs used for transactional purposes typically do differ from "proprietary information agreements" or "nondisclosure agreements" used by government contractors for programmatic pursuits with teaming partners, vendors, suppliers, and other contractors. This issue is discussed further below. Appendix 2 contains examples of a typical CA.

a. Typical Provisions in Confidentiality Agreements

Most CAs cover the same basic provisions, with varying degrees of complexity based on the size and nature of the transaction and include:

1. Definition and scope of confidential information covered by the agreement;
2. Exceptions to the definition or instances in which information covered by the definition is carved out of the agreement;
3. Permitted use of confidential information and who may receive it;
4. Disclaimer of rights obtained by the receiving party and disclaimer of representations and warranties concerning the information by the disclosing party;
5. Procedures for return or destruction of information;
6. Procedures for compelled disclosure of confidential information subject to legal proceedings or applicable law or regulatory requirements;
7. A nonsolicitation provision applicable to the Target's employees, officers, and directors;
8. Acknowledgement that the CA does not imply any rights with respect to an ultimate transaction;
9. Remedies for breach;
10. Direction of information flow, or points of contact for the transaction; and
11. Governing law and other standard provisions.

CAs for government contractors also often include an acknowledgement of classified or export-controlled status of certain confidential information and agreement to comply with applicable law.

1. Public vs. Private Deals

Where a proposed transaction involves one or more public companies, other provisions will almost always be included in the CA. At a minimum, there will typically be a provision under which the Acquirer (or sometimes both parties) acknowledges that it is aware of US securities laws as they apply to trading while in the possession of material nonpublic information. Also, a public Target is well advised to include a "stand-still" provision under which the Acquirer will agree not to trade in the Target's securities for a certain period of time after execution of the CA. Although the basic purpose of a stand-still provision is to prevent an Acquirer from engaging in a hostile transaction, there are a number of caveats and other exceptions designed to provide some flexibility to an Acquirer; for instance, where other parties have received more favorable stand-still terms with the Target or where other parties initiate a hostile transaction. Stand-still provisions are often quite complex and heavily negotiated. Other provisions of CAs for public company transactions are generally very similar, if not identical, to CAs for private companies, although they may be more comprehensive given that public company deals are often larger than private company deals.

2. What's Market and What's Not?

Among sophisticated parties, CA negotiations tend to focus on a few key issues that often get resolved within a band of "market practices." These practices evolve over time, but the basic issues remain the same. The summary below highlights some of the more commonly negotiated provisions.

3. Definition of Confidential Information

Negotiations often center around defining confidential information by virtue of ***how*** and ***when*** it is received, and ***who*** produces or receives it. For instance, a Target will almost always attempt to include information that is transmitted orally within the definition of confidential information. Acquirers often resist this provision given its effect of broadening the scope of covered information and limiting the Acquirer's ability to track information that has been received and to monitor compliance with a CA in general. Resolution of this issue may depend on relative market power of the negotiating parties, although Acquirers are often successful in limiting the extent to which information provided orally is covered by the CA. For instance, CAs will often require that information provided orally be followed up with a written notice of confidentiality, or will state that certain types of information provided orally are assumed to be confidential regardless of subsequent written disclosure (e.g., information on proprietary technology, market share, strategic plans, financial matters, etc.), while other more general information is assumed not to be confidential unless followed up by written notice of confidentiality.

With respect to timing of disclosure, Targets sometimes attempt to cover information disclosed either before or after signature of the CA. However, Acquirers are generally successful in negotiating coverage to start as of the date of the CA.

The originator of confidential information is also often negotiated. Targets will almost always attempt to expand the definition of confidential information protected by a CA to include information that is produced by the Acquirer or its representatives based on, incorporating, or relating to confidential information of the Target. Acquirers will often resist such provisions because they may transfer ownership of the Acquirer's proprietary analysis to a Target, and because "return or destroy" provisions of a CA could require the Acquirer to deliver its analysis to the Target on the Target's request, if a transaction is not consummated.

> ✓ **Best Practice Tip:** The Target should consider limiting access to confidential information under CAs so that it is only provided to a designated recipient and not to *all* affiliates of large companies or financial sponsors (including portfolio companies of the Acquirer), unless specifically agreed to by the Target. This will mitigate the risk that confidential information will be shared with otherwise unknown or undisclosed direct competitors or other sensitive parties.

4. Return or Destroy Provisions

As noted, CAs will commonly require the Acquirer to return to the Target or destroy confidential information if the transaction is not consummated. Such provisions are often accompanied by a certification requirement from the Acquirer, affirming its diligent search for, and return or destruction of such information. Acquirers will often attempt to limit their obligations to the destruction of confidential information and will also ask for the ability to retain a copy of the confidential information solely for record-keeping purposes and otherwise subject to the terms of the CA. It is market practice for a Target to accept such changes; however, it is important to include language reaffirming the Acquirer's confidentiality obligations with respect to any confidential information included in any materials that have been retained or destroyed. Additionally, particularly for deals involving businesses in the same industry or a high volume of intellectual property rights, Acquirers often look to include a provision excluding from any such obligation to return or destroy information any confidential information that may be held in the residual memory of the Acquirer's deal professionals.

5. Employee Nonsolicitation Provisions

Targets will typically request a broad nonsolicitation provision, sometimes including a no-hire obligation, with respect to a Target's employees, representatives, and business partners. Requested terms range from two to five years in extreme cases, although it is market practice for an Acquirer to limit the term to one to two years and to limit the applicability to the Target's then-current key employees or executives that become known to the Acquirer in connection with its evaluation of the business. Additionally, it is market practice to include an exception to the covenant not to solicit for general advertisements not specifically directed at a Target's employees.

6. Remedies for Breach and Equitable Relief

CAs will commonly provide that equitable relief is available for a breach of the agreement. Targets will often attempt to limit relief provisions in their favor only and attempt to provide for the certainty of the relief by stating that it "will be available," often without the posting of a bond or proving actual damages. Occasionally, Target-friendly CAs will also provide for a breaching Acquirer to pay the Target's expenses in litigation or to indemnify the Target for breach. Acquirers are generally able to expand the provision to give them the ability to seek or obtain such relief in the event the CA contains obligations on the part of the Target (e.g., not to disclose to third parties that negotiations are ongoing with the particular Acquirer).

7. Term

CAs for acquisition purposes generally have relatively short terms. It is not uncommon for a Target to offer a CA with no stated term but to agree through negotiation to a term of eighteen months to three years. A two-year term is considered market practice in most cases; however, it is common for certain provisions to survive termination of the CA (e.g., trade secrets, remedies provisions, governing law, and venue selection provisions).

b. How Acquisition Nondisclosure Agreements/Confidentiality Agreements Differ from Nondisclosure Agreements Used for Other Government Contracting Purposes

Government contracting firms employ CAs in a number of contexts other than acquisitions. In those other contexts, a CA is often referred to as a nondisclosure agreement (NDA) or proprietary information agreement and is generally used to protect a party's information in connection with some form of collaboration with another party, such as a teaming agreement, joint venture, or subcontract relationship. There are several fundamental differences between the provisions of those NDAs and CAs intended for acquisition purposes. First, these NDAs typically contemplate that information is shared between parties over a longer term, with a "rolling" protection period starting from the date on which particular information is shared. Additionally, the term of the undertaking itself is often quite long, running five years or longer, depending on the program. Third, these NDAs often contemplate the reciprocal exchange of information and incorporate procedures through which ongoing exchange is administered. Finally, such NDAs tend not to incorporate provisions dealing with securities law compliance or other provisions dealing with issues arising uniquely in an acquisition context.

c. How to Integrate Confidentiality Agreement Provisions into the Acquisition Agreement

The provisions of a CA must be integrated into the acquisition agreement between the Target and the Acquirer. Although techniques can differ, often a CA is incorporated by reference into an acquisition agreement and made applicable to information of the Acquirer that the Target may have learned through the diligence and negotiation process. The CA provisions applicable to the Acquirer typically will expire on closing of the acquisition, while those applying to the sellers, if any, will continue to apply for some stated term or indefinitely after closing. It is also common, however, for the definitive transaction agreement to include confidentiality provisions applicable to the sellers post-closing. The latter point is particularly important where the Acquirer does not purchase the Target, but rather only certain assets of the Target, in an asset acquisition, or where the Target's equity holders may continue in a similar line of business post-closing.

d. How Confidentiality Agreements Can Be Misused

It is not uncommon for a potential Acquirer to be uncertain about its desire to acquire a particular Target when first considering the transaction. CAs are specifically intended to facilitate an Acquirer's diligence investigation of the strategic and financial value of an acquisition. They can be misused, however, where an Acquirer wants to conduct a "fishing expedition" for the purpose of learning how a potential Target does business, with no specific intent to consummate a deal. CAs are overtly breached where an Acquirer subsequently uses the information learned through a CA to enhance its own business. CAs typically contain specific language to prevent both intentional and inadvertent breach. However, given that the recipients of information obtained through a CA are often not familiar with the CA's terms, it is advisable to counsel Acquirers, especially those who have not been very acquisitive in the past, in the appropriate use of information received. The Acquirer should also institute a rigorous process of collecting and destroying information received from a potential Target, whether or not the Target requests the Acquirer to do so.

Additionally, Acquirers, in particular financial sponsors, should pay particular attention to issues involving investment professionals who may sit on the boards of multiple companies. Counsel for such Acquirers should be careful to include the appropriate carveouts from the Acquirer's and its representatives' confidentiality and non-use/nondisclosure obligations to ensure that the receipt of information by any such investment professionals will not constitute a breach of the Acquirer's nondisclosure obligations under the CA. To the extent there is any particular sensitivity at the Target with respect to certain investment professionals and their affiliation with specific entities, the parties may look to implement a "clean team" arrangement or some other process of segregating information to ensure that only preapproved representatives of the Acquirer are permitted access to competitively sensitive information. (See section C.4, "Review of Sensitive and Classified Information.") Similarly, counsel for the Acquirer and the Target should consider whether any other portfolio companies of the financial sponsor should be expressly permitted to access, or, conversely, prohibited from accessing, certain confidential information. (See section A.3.a.(3), "Definition of Confidential Information.")

B. Composition of the Due Diligence Team

1. Initial Diligence

Because conducting a due diligence investigation in connection with an acquisition can be a very resource-intensive exercise, even for relatively small acquisitions, it is often appropriate to conduct an initial, limited due diligence review of the Target prior to engaging in comprehensive diligence. Particularly in the context of an auction where full diligence may not be possible in advance of bidding, an Acquirer is well advised to prioritize its diligence review and to conduct a high-level review of the most important areas before undertaking comprehensive diligence. In a competitive auction process an

Acquirer may be under pressure to commit to a purchase price before completion of diligence. Therefore, an Acquirer may want to conduct a limited review of a Target's financial data to determine if certain metrics could be achieved by the acquisition and also to examine publicly available information on the Target.

A wealth of information on government contractors is publicly accessible in the System for Award Management (SAM), the US government's contractor database; in the Federal Awardee Performance and Integrity Information System (FAPIIS); on the General Services Administration Schedules e-Library; and on agency websites pertaining to mentor-protégé programs, such as active listings of current mentor-protégé agreements found on websites maintained by the US Small Business Administration, Department of Homeland Security, and Department of Defense. Information on veteran-owned businesses and certifications received by certain small businesses can be found on the Department of Veterans Affairs website. An Acquirer also might want to conduct a first-phase, high-level review of go/no go tax, accounting, legal, and compliance risks or specific programs or market opportunities before performing more detailed diligence.

✓ **Best Practice Tip:** For these purposes, an Acquirer is well advised to establish a small diligence team, tasked with discrete areas of inquiry and given a limited amount of time to conduct a "phase 1" review. Team members for initial diligence should be limited to essential disciplines for a focused review and may include one representative from each of the following departments: (a) Corporate or Business Development; (b) applicable business unit; (c) Legal Counsel; (d) Finance/Accounting; (e) outside advisors, such as outside counsel or financial advisors; and (f) other specialists, as appropriate.

It is important to note that an Acquirer's ability to conduct a phase 1 diligence review may be limited in an auction scenario where the Target's banker is tightly controlling the timing of the process and the nature and scope of the information made available to potential Acquirers. Even in this scenario, however, a disciplined diligence team can often undertake a high-level review within the Target's articulated timing. While it is hard to generalize, depending on the size of the Target and the scope of the phase 1 review, this exercise will generally take one to two weeks. Depending on the specific nature of the Target's business, the phase 1 diligence should focus on issues that may significantly change valuation or the viability of a transaction. Issues that may be worthy of focus may include risks related to the portfolio of the Target's customer contracts (e.g., fixed fee, time, and materials, etc.); contract performance issues (e.g., terminations for default or for convenience of the government; show-cause letters, cure or deficiency notices; suspension of work or stop work orders; notice of nonexercise of options); litigations, investigations or disputes; any voluntary or mandatory disclosures; cost accounting issues; cost overruns; small business or other preferred status relating to contract awards; Defense Contract Audit Agency (DCAA) or other agency audits; and organizational conflicts of interest (OCI) issues.

2. Comprehensive Diligence

When an Acquirer determines that a full due diligence investigation is warranted, either after a favorable phase 1 review or because of timing constraints, it will move to a comprehensive diligence review involving all relevant disciplines within the Acquirer's and Target's companies. Such reviews are generally extremely time-intensive exercises, involving review of all fundamental aspects of a Target's business. (See the sample Due Diligence Checklist in Appendix 4). This standard list will, of course, need to be tailored for the particular Target at issue. Team members for comprehensive diligence may include one or more representatives from each of the following departments:

a. Corporate and/or business development
b. Corporate and/or business unit legal counsel—specialists may be required for corporate/securities matters, litigation, environmental, real estate, human resources (HR) and employee benefits, intellectual property (IP), regulatory matters, tax, data privacy and security, antitrust, etc.
c. Contracts
d. Programs management
e. Supply chain
f. Engineering/technology, including information technology
g. Treasury
h. Finance and accounting, including government accounting
i. Tax
j. Ethics/compliance
k. Data privacy and security
l. National security
m. Communications
n. Insurance
o. Environmental, health, and safety
p. Export/import—including the Foreign Corrupt Practices Act (FCPA) and the Committee on Foreign Investment in the United States (CFIUS)
q. Internal audit

3. Additional Team Members for Government Contracts

A due diligence team assessing the acquisition of a US government contractor should include members with specialties unique, or of special concern, to government contractors, including:

- Counsel or contracts personnel familiar with the Federal Acquisition Regulations (the FAR) and agency supplements.
- Counsel or accounting consultants familiar with the government contracts cost principles and the Cost Accounting Standards (CAS).
- Subcontracts personnel familiar with the FAR and flow-down requirements.
- Organizational conflicts of interest (OCI).

- Protection of intellectual property.
- Export control requirements.
- Small business or other special designations for contract awards.
- FCPA compliance.
- Security expertise, including cleared personnel and personnel familiar with the National Industrial Security Program Operating Manual.
- Acquirer's in-house attorneys knowledgeable about the Target's claims, disputes, litigations, investigations, audits, and any voluntary or mandatory disclosures.

4. Organizing the Diligence Team

Organization and discipline within the diligence team is crucial to obtaining appropriate and useful information through the diligence exercise. Wherever possible, diligence teams should be led by experienced professionals with both strong transactional and leadership skills. Typically, a senior member of an Acquirer's corporate or business development staff or legal department will serve as the diligence team leader. Especially when undertaking a comprehensive diligence exercise, it is advisable to subdivide the diligence team by functional areas, roles, or responsibilities. The diligence team leader should establish which documents will be reviewed by each team (often by data room folder reference) so that nothing falls through the cracks. The team leader is also charged with determining the schedule, pace, and expected deliverables of each of the subteams or team members. Team deliverables should include a summary of findings in each diligence area, broken down by issues and potential risks that will affect contract negotiation and documentation, closing, integration, and post-closing operations.

5. Issues Concerning the Diligence Team

Acquirers should be sensitive to the deal dynamics that can be created by their diligence exercise and team members. The Target's first impressions of a potential Acquirer are often formed through the diligence process. Large diligence teams, with numerous or burdensome requests for information, or whose members lack sensitivity to the size, capabilities, and culture of a Target, can negatively influence a Target's view of its potential new owner. Diligence teams that are sensitive to these issues and actively help the Target to manage its time and resources efficiently, help "sell the Acquirer" to the Target, which can be particularly important in an auction context.

For these reasons, it is important that deal counsel for the Acquirer coordinate the due diligence efforts of the legal subject matter experts and the nonlegal advisors (e.g., tax, accounting, benefits, insurance, environmental, etc.). Given the number of reviewers, a specific point of contact for the Acquirer and each review team will help to ensure continuity between the due diligence process and the negotiation of the definitive transaction agreements. Part of this coordination process should involve establishing clear guidelines for performing the due diligence review and how follow-up requests will be coordinated, including considering whether any reports generated will need to be provided to the Acquirer's lenders and/or insurers (e.g., in connection with obtaining a buyer representations and warranties policy). In particular, deal counsel for the Acquirer should be certain to involve knowledgeable government contracts counsel early in the due diligence process to ensure that the scope of the legal due diligence review includes specific risk areas involved in government contracting generally and those presented by the Target's government contracts profile, in particular.

6. Performing Diligence on the Acquirer

Except in the context of mergers of equals, diligence exercises typically focus on the Target's business. There are a number of situations, however, in which it is important for a Target to do reverse diligence on its Acquirer. For instance, where antitrust clearance may be an issue, a Target's counsel may want to conduct due diligence on competitive considerations early in the process to determine whether antitrust clearance through the HSR process is likely to be an issue (see chapter X, sections A to C). If so, the Target may choose to seek other potential Acquirers, or in an auction context, to disqualify a bidder based on antitrust concerns. Even where antitrust concerns are less severe, the Target's counsel will want to be involved in reviewing diligence material created by the Target's employees to ensure the material does not raise red flags on competitive issues that may need to be disclosed as "Section 4(C)" documents in the HSR clearance process. Additionally, where a transaction contemplates an earn-out based on postacquisition performance, where the sellers of the Target will be "rolling" a portion of their equity into the Acquirer or where a Target has concerns about integration with its Acquirer, the Target may seek to do early reverse diligence on its Acquirer.

Additionally, the Target should be sure to carry out diligence on the financial profile of the Acquirer to determine whether the Acquirer's obligations under the definitive agreement should be guaranteed by an affiliated party (e.g., a financial sponsor). Further, as noted above, in cases where the acquisition of a government contractor involves classified operations or a non-US Acquirer, the Target review any concerns about the ultimate ownership of the potential Acquirer. If the Acquirer has foreign ownership, the parties will need to consider FOCI (foreign ownership, control, and influence) regulations and contact the Defense Counterintelligence and Security Agency (DCSA, formerly the Defense Security Service) as early as possible to begin discussing the transaction and any potential mitigation measures that may be required. Foreign ownership may also warrant that a CFIUS analysis be performed by counsel for each of the Target and the Acquirer.

C. The Data Room

1. Electronic vs. Physical Data Rooms

Electronic data rooms (as described above) are now the norm rather than the exception. They allow an Acquirer to review documents on a rolling basis and to review key documents as needed. Reviewers rarely need to copy data in the data room, as access is typically provided throughout the acquisition process. There are a number of commercial service providers of electronic data rooms available to assist a Target in establishing an electronic data room. These services will often also provide data management services, allowing the Target to restrict access to certain groups of data, restricting or allowing copying of data as deemed appropriate, and providing information about who has viewed what data stored in the data room.

Physical data rooms are very cumbersome in contrast, as they require diligence teams to assemble in person to review data at a specific physical location. Typically, an Acquirer will have much more limited access to physical data rooms and will often not be allowed to copy data in the room. This would require the Acquirer's diligence team to take notes on material reviewed and thus may preclude the Acquirer from capturing all relevant information in the limited time available for data review.

2. Working with the Target's Data Room

Once a CA is signed, a Target will typically provide access to a "data room" in which all the Target's due diligence material is stored and made available for the Acquirer's review. Depending on the size of the transaction and the sophistication of the Target, data rooms are more or less formal and may be physical (meaning hard copies of documents are stored in a room or rooms for viewing by an Acquirer) or, more typically, electronic (meaning that data is stored electronically and made available to Acquirers through limited access to the electronic site). Data rooms generally contain a wide range of information on the Target, and cover items on the due diligence checklist. It is very common for items to be added to a data room on a rolling basis.

3. Restricted Material

Either in the context of a physical or electronic data room, a Target may need to restrict access to certain documents. In an electronic data room, as stated above, this can be accomplished through the service provider and limited review folders. In a physical data room, this requires physical segregation of data and may also necessitate personnel to monitor access to the restricted data.

4. Review of Sensitive and Classified Information

In performing due diligence, it may be necessary to review sensitive information such as classified material; competitively sensitive data such as intellectual property, pricing information, employee lists, customer lists/names, labor rates or business development contacts, export-controlled material, prior acquisition agreements or documents identifying the names of other potential acquirers of the Target (e.g., auction process NDAs). If the acquisition involves sensitive information, the Target may resist providing it to the Acquirer until late in the negotiation process, when there is an executed transaction agreement. Meetings to discuss classified information, including classified contracts, may be held in the Target's Sensitive Compartmented Information Facility (SCIF), and classified briefings held at the SCIF will be limited to Target and Acquirer representatives that have personnel security clearances at the required clearance levels. Delaying due diligence on sensitive material until after the parties have negotiated key terms may weaken the Acquirer's bargaining position with regard to issues uncovered once the sensitive material is reviewed. Further, if the existence of these materials is only disclosed late in the process, it may undermine the Acquirer's trust in the Target. Other approaches include:

- Designation of a subteam of the Acquirer (a "Clean Team") to perform due diligence that is subject to additional restrictions on use and disclosure of the sensitive material. If the sensitive material is competitively sensitive material, the restrictions could include limitations on the ability of Clean Team members to be involved in business development or competitive efforts that relate to the Target's information for some period of time after the completion of due diligence (assuming the transaction does not go forward—often this is an appropriate role for outside counsel). If the sensitive information is classified material, the restrictions would be those required under law. For classified information, it is generally necessary to obtain the consent of the relevant governmental agency prior to permitting the review of the material by the Acquirer's diligence team. If this is the case, such a request should be made in time to allow for review of cleared individuals and performance of diligence.
- Partial due diligence—It may be possible to perform some due diligence without implicating competitively sensitive or classified information. Competitively sensitive information can be provided on an aggregated basis without disclosing competitively sensitive labor, profit, or other rates or may be redacted so that the remainder of the document may be reviewed by the Acquirer. In addition, the financial results of classified programs are typically not classified and may be disclosed. Further, many documents are only classified or sensitive in part and other portions can be released.
- Reporting out—A further issue with sensitive due diligence is reporting results to management. Assuming some form of limited access is permitted, the Acquirer then must determine how the Clean Team can report to management on the results of the due diligence without disclosing classified or other sensitive information. One possible mechanism used for such reports is use of a color-coded summary chart, which assigns red/yellow/green color ratings only to broad categories of contract information, such as performance, schedule, quality, deliveries, and costs.

5. Follow-up Inquiries

In most cases, the Target will establish a process for dealing with follow-up questions and additional data requests. An Acquirer will typically be asked to submit follow-up questions in writing, with the Target responding through posting of the additional data to the data room (if electronic) or providing it directly to the Acquirer (if a physical data room). Acquirers are well advised to create their own running check lists to keep track of the questions asked and the answers received. Such "due diligence trackers" are frequently created as a way of monitoring the Target's responses to supplemental data and information requests. Better organization in the diligence review stage (for example, reducing duplication or irrelevant requests) will allow the Acquirer's diligence team to create a more focused and useful diligence report.

6. Interviews as Part of the Diligence Process

In addition to follow-up written questions, it is common for an Acquirer to request interviews or question and answer sessions with key Target personnel from various functional areas. This method of acquiring information is particularly valuable in that it allows an Acquirer to make qualitative judgments about the strength of the Target's personnel and their views on the Target's business. A Target will typically attempt to limit the interviews both to preserve resources and to limit the number of a Target's personnel that need to be involved in the diligence process. Acquirers are well advised to seek a number of interviews with key personnel, as they often provide the best source of information that an Acquirer can obtain.

An Acquirer may also seek interviews with third parties, such as customers, key partners, or subcontractors, as part of its diligence process. For confidentiality reasons, Targets are often very resistant to such interviews prior to signing of the purchase agreement.

7. The Diligence Report

As stated above, the output of a diligence review is typically a diligence report, created by the various members of the Acquirer's diligence team. Many Acquirers develop a form for all members of the due diligence team to follow in preparing their individual reports, including highlighting particular issues that might make or break the deal. This form will typically include an executive summary of the most material issues noted as part of the due diligence review (e.g., third-party consents, material litigation, material risk exposure due to past operations false claims—including qui tam or whistleblower actions, suspension or debarment proceedings, employee misclassification, and severance or transaction-based payments). Additionally, the report will include a more detailed discussion of the various materials provided to and reviewed by the Acquirer's counsel, any potential areas of risk, recommendations for pre- or post-closing remedies or integration measures, and any requests that remain outstanding. Depending on deal specifics, alternative forms of diligence reports may be appropriate or desired. These could include reports based on publicly available diligence information, SWOT (strengths/weaknesses/opportunities/threats) analyses, or "red flags" diligence reports. Importantly, the diligence report should note any limits on the diligence review (e.g., contract review limited to top ten contracts) because of time, directions from the Acquirer, or restrictions imposed by the Target.

In today's marketplace, it has become market practice for Acquirers to share due diligence reports with their lenders (who will be financing all or a portion of the deal) and with their insurers (who will be providing representation and warranty insurance). To preserve attorney-client privilege, it is important to prepare the reports carefully and to share them only after the lenders and/or insurers have signed nonreliance letters. In this circumstance, it is typical for the lenders or insurers to have follow-up queries of their own based on the contents of the report and to confirm the scope of the due diligence review.)

✓ **Best Practice Tip:** Design the form of the report to allow the government contracts members of the due diligence team to provide attachments to describe particular issues that may not fit into the standard format for reporting issues on commercial contracts. If the report will be shared with third parties (e.g., lenders or insurers), the Acquirer should give special consideration to tailor the summaries in order to calibrate and assess any identified risks and to describe the scope of the diligence review, including a description of what was and was not reviewed.

8. How to Use a Diligence Report

Diligence reports have a number of functions, including (a) serving as a reporting device to decision makers; (b) facilitating go/no go decisions and deal valuation; (c) flagging items for remediation by the Target prior to deal signing/closure; (d) flagging items to be addressed in the acquisition agreement as representations, warranties, covenants, and/or special indemnities; (e) flagging items for attention by the Acquirer post-closing, as a matter of integration or remediation; (f) providing support for proposals to potential investors, lenders, and insurers.

D. Developing a Government Contracts Due Diligence Document Request

The government contracts due diligence team should prepare a document request as early as possible in the due diligence process. (See sample Government Contracts Document Request, Appendix 4). The document request should be comprehensive, covering a broad range of issues and a timeframe relating to the Target's government contracts, at both the prime contract and subcontract levels, and other contractual arrangements, such as joint ventures and teaming agreements. Typically, in its initial data room production, the Target may only provide copies of its contracts. This production may be adequate for commercial contracts, but it will not provide the Acquirer with the information needed to assess the Target's government contracting business. For that, the Target's contract files, including copies of correspondence with the customer agencies, as well as reports of government audits and investigations—to the extent available to the Target—will be critical. In a government procurement market where contract awards are based increasingly on assessment of contractors' "past performance" and determinations of the "best value" to the government, documentation that reflects the perceptions of the procuring and audit agencies may be particularly important. This includes requesting the Target's past performance reports, as set forth in final and interim Contractor Performance Assessment Reporting System (CPARS) documents, for specific contracts or periods of time.

If the Acquirer is pursuing a phased diligence approach, it may make sense to provide an initial high-priority diligence list focused on key compliance risks for businesses similar to the Target's. This may increase responsiveness on the part of the Target and the speed of initial review. Following the initial government contracts document request, the Acquirer can fill in any gaps in its standard list. Any follow-up requests after these initial lists should be tailored to the circumstances of a particular acquisition and demonstrate some level of knowledge of the Target's business and operations. Efficiency may require that these requests involve establishment of a dollar threshold, such as requesting all prime contracts and/or subcontracts over a certain dollar value or representing a significant portion or percentage of revenues, consistent with the nature and scope of the Target's government contracts business. Other alternatives might include identification of the Target's largest government contracts—for example, "Top 25" current government contracts by dollar value, customer, contract type, or other relevant factor. At the most basic level, the Acquirer should request the files and documents described in the sections that follow, the significance of which will depend on the volume and composition of the Target's government business. These documents should identify the principal areas of potential liabilities and risks and where further documentation, review, and analysis may be required.

1. Contracts and Related Information

a. Prime Contracts

The Acquirer should request the Target to provide contract files for all executory government contracts (including any modifications thereto) and any contracts that are currently the subject of government audits or investigations. The requested information should include all material correspondence between the Target and the government, encompassing communications to or from the contracting officer and/or contracting officer's technical representative, the DCAA or other administrative, audit, or investigative agency. The Acquirer should also seek all contracts and correspondence between the Target and its vendors and suppliers pertaining to any government prime contract. For such subcontracts, it will be important to review the Target's standard "flow down" forms and procedures for obtaining required government representations and certifications and other required provisions, consents, and approvals. The diligence team should review information for all subsidiaries, divisions, joint ventures, or operating entities that perform government contracts.

b. Subcontracts under Government Prime Contracts

The Acquirer should similarly request the Target to provide contract files for all government subcontracts awarded to the Target under government prime contracts, including all correspondence between the Target and the government and between the Target and its prime contractor relating to such subcontracts. Subcontract information is important in the context of identifying potential liabilities, notice and consent requirements, claims, and potential organizational conflicts of interest.

c. Specific Contract Documentation

1. Audits and Pricing Information

Contract documentation should include all draft and final audit reports and all correspondence relating to any audit, claim, or allegation of noncompliance with any pricing, disclosure, performance, statutory, or regulatory obligation arising from current or past government contracts. The diligence team should also review copies of any and all pre- and postaward audit reports by DCAA or any other agency inspector general's office. Depending on the Target's cost or pricing data disclosure and the government's recordkeeping and accounting requirements, significant documents may include (a) any rate agreements submitted to or approved by government agencies pertaining to forward pricing and provisional or final indirect cost rates; (b) any advance agreements covering FAR 31 cost issues, such as independent research and development or bid and proposal costs; (c) CASDisclosure Statements; and (d) any agreements relating to other special categories of costs allocated to or charged by the Target to its government contracts.

2. Documents Regarding Claims, Terminations, and Other Matters

The request should also include documentation of the following: (a) any and all existing or potential company, government, prime contractor, or subcontractor claims or disputes; (b) requests for equitable adjustment; (c) notices regarding existing or potential default terminations, terminations for convenience, letters of concern, show cause or deficiency notices, and cure notices; (d) pending or outstanding litigation matters, by forum, parties, and amount at issue, and the existence of any reserves established by the Target; (e) any False Claims Act matters, including *qui tam* actions; (f) liquidated damages assessments; (g) any suspension or debarment proceedings, and nonresponsibility or other ineligibility determination; (h) any cyber-incident reports or reports of data breaches; and (i) product liability claims or warranty claims. Large government contractors may maintain formal logs of all outstanding and recently resolved litigation claims, which provide valuable insight into the Target's overall litigation profile and the areas of significant legal risk to the Target's business. These logs often provide docketing and status information for the matters identified, as well as internal company contacts and information on outside counsel and total legal expenses to date.

Cost and schedule reviews, including any estimates to complete, should also be analyzed for important clues as to any past, current, or anticipated issues relating to performance, cost, or schedule. Program reviews, including any quarterly reviews, provided by Target representatives are also an important source of information on key programs, progress, and potential performance and legal issues.

In addition, if the Target produces or offers any "qualified anti-terrorism technology" to government customers, the diligence team should also review all documentation submitted in connection with the Support Anti-Terrorism by Fostering Effective Technologies Act of 2002 (SAFETY Act) protections.

2. Proposal Files

If the Target maintains proposal files separately from contract files, the Acquirer should also request proposal files. In general, Targets will be hesitant to provide proposal files because they include competitively sensitive information. At minimum, a request should be made for a list of pending proposals, identifying whether any are based on any preferred status (e.g., small business) category. If proposal files are produced, they should include: (a) all sales, cost, pricing, and discount information pertaining to or supporting government recordkeeping; (b) accounting and data disclosure requirements; (c) subcontractor sales, cost, pricing, and discount information; and (d) data supporting required representations and certifications (generally set forth in Section K of the RFP) pertaining to various business practices, contract performance, and socioeconomic requirements. These include, but are not limited to, compliance with Buy American/Trade Agreements Act certifications or representations and new material requirements; equal employment and affirmative action requirements; and any certifications regarding special contractor or subcontractor status, including small business, small disadvantaged business, veteran-owned small business, service-disabled veteran-owned small business, HUBZone small business, women-owned small business, or Section 8(a) contractors. Disclosures in individual proposals can be cross-checked using the Target's current registration in SAM, including review of the Target's representations and certifications.

3. Asset Lists

Asset lists, including identification of any liens, encumbrances, or security interests on assets used by the Target to perform government contracts and subcontracts should be reviewed. This would include documentation relating to the Target's facilities and equipment, whether leased or owned, utilized in the performance of government contracts and subcontracts. The diligence team should also identify any government-furnished property at the Target's facilities.

4. Claims, Disputes, Litigations, and Investigations

Any due diligence checklist must include information relating to any contract claims, disputes, appeals, or other litigation (and prelitigation disputes) that is asserted by or against the Target and arises under or relates to the Target's government contracts. Information also should be obtained on any pre- or postaward bid protests involving the Target (as a protester or as an intervenor), which have been filed at procuring agencies, the US Government Accountability Office, or the US Court of Federal Claims. The due diligence analysis will include an assessment of the impact of such protests on the Target's business operations or the sustainability of the business going forward, depending on the resolution of such matters in a manner favorable or adverse to the Target's interests.

The diligence team should also request any reports of investigations by audit agencies, agency inspector general offices, or criminal investigative agencies, such as the Defense Criminal Investigative Service, Navy Criminal Investigative Service, and Army Criminal Investigative Service, including any subpoenas issued to the Target or any of its officers, principals, or employees. Documents relating to any Public Law 85-804 requests for extraordinary relief should also be requested.

5. Government-Approved Systems

In addition to the audits mentioned above, the diligence team should request documentation relating to any system reviews conducted by the Defense Contract Management Agency. Such reviews could include, but are not limited to, purchasing, timekeeping, billing, pricing, and government property inventory systems. The reviews may cover the efficiency and effectiveness with which the Target spends government funds and complies with government policy when subcontracting.

6. Compliance Program Documentation

Evaluation of the Target's compliance program is important not only for assessing risks and potential liabilities, but also for determining the costs necessary to implement an "effective compliance program" to limit the risks of liability going forward. Requested documents should include the Target's government contracting compliance policies and procedures, including any internal compliance audits, monitoring reviews, logs, or other records relating to internal or external "hotlines" or other mechanisms established by the Target for reporting wrongdoing. In addition, the team should review ongoing internal investigations and management letters issued in connection with annual reports and financial statements (see chapter VI).

The Target's compliance policies and procedures will depend on the nature and scope of the Target's business and operations, including factors such as business size, industry involved, corporate structure, and compliance organization. While government contracting policies and procedures should be a particular focus, including areas such as government billing and time-charging, the diligence team should assess the breadth of the Target's compliance policies in critical areas of legal risk, such as (but not limited to) export controls, antibribery and Foreign Corrupt Practices Act, anti-kickbacks, revolving door, conflicts of interest, data and cyber-security, and antitrust. Minutes of board of director meetings pertaining to compliance reports and activities should be reviewed, including compliance committee meetings and meetings attended by corporate compliance officials. Finally, the team should review documentation pertaining to the Target's compliance with the FAR rules regarding mandatory disclosure and internal controls, including any mandatory or voluntary disclosures made to government agencies.

7. Environmental Issues

The diligence team should request documents relating to any environmental issues that may affect the Target's performance of government contracts and subcontracts (see chapter V, section C).

8. Employment Law Issues

The diligence team should request documents relating to a range of employment law issues, such as (a) percentages of employees fully dedicated to government contract or subcontract work; (b) workforce composition (number of full-time, part-time, or temporary employees); (c) collective bargaining agreements in force; (d) summary plan descriptions relating to employee or executive benefits, pensions, and severance; (e) security clearances; and (f) other employment contracts or agreements in effect. With labor category mapping becoming an increasingly challenging compliance issue, documentation related to policies and procedures for meeting labor requirements, such as education level and years of experience for service contracts, should also be requested.

The documents identified in this section should be supplemented with a request for documents relating to the Target's compliance with FAR labor and socioeconomic requirements. This would include compliance with equal opportunity/affirmative action program requirements (Executive Order 11246; FAR Subpart 22.8); equal opportunity for veterans (FAR Subpart 22.13); and employment of workers with disabilities and employment eligibility verification (FAR Subpart 22.18). Documents reflecting the Target's compliance with labor-related reporting requirements (EEO-1 and VETS-4212) should be identified. Documents relating to the Target's compliance with anti–human trafficking requirements (FAR Subpart 22.17) and with the Service Contract labor standards (FAR Subpart 22.10) should also be requested. The Target should be asked to provide information pertaining to any compliance evaluations or reviews being conducted by the U.S. Department of Labor, Office of Federal Contracts Compliance Programs (OFCCP).

9. Export Controls

Attorneys conducting the due diligence should request the Target's export control compliance program documentation covering compliance with US export control laws and regulations issued by the Departments of State, Commerce, and Treasury.[1] Documents to review in connection with the Target's export control compliance include:

[1] The State Department enforces the export control regime for items having primarily military use; the Commerce Department has jurisdiction over the export of so-called "dual-use" items (items that have both civilian and military application); and the Treasury Department regulates, among other things, financial transactions with prohibited persons and with persons in embargoed countries.

- Export control, trade sanctions, and anti-boycott policies and procedures; export control manuals, including any compliance audits, monitoring reviews, ongoing internal investigations, training materials, and management letters.
- Lists of international sales and countries in which goods and services are sold (for comparison against countries covered by Office of Foreign Asset Control (OFAC) regulations).
- Export control classification guides and matrices listing the U.S. government's export control classification numbers and categories for goods, services, and technology held by the Target.
- Nationalities of foreign nationals and any export authorizations necessary for their access to technology, or an explanation of why authorization is not necessary.[2]
- Corporate export control licenses, records, and shipping documentation, such as shipper's export declarations, which will allow the Acquirer to assess the items that the Target has exported and determine whether appropriate licenses were obtained prior to the export (for past exports and exports that are still in the process of shipment).
- Checklists that the Target uses as part of its export control compliance program (see chapter VI, section D).

10. National Security Issues

Documents relating to the nature and extent of classified work performed by the Target, including the number and level of security clearances held by the Target's facilities and personnel, should be reviewed. Any foreign nationals employed by the Target should be identified. If applicable, any internal procedures for the handling, control, and storage of classified information should also be reviewed (see chapter VI, section C and chapter XI).

11. Antitrust Issues

The diligence team should request documents that would customarily be sought by the government in any antitrust review of the transaction (see chapter X, section E.4).

---

[2] One often-overlooked type of export is the transfer within the United States of controlled technology to foreign nationals, that is, persons who are neither US citizens nor permanent residents. Attorneys conducting due diligence on an acquisition target must consider the possibility that "deemed exports" have been made by the Target without appropriate authorization. They must learn whether foreign nationals are employed by the Target—whether as employees, subcontractors, or consultants—and, if so, their nationalities and export-controlled activities.

CHAPTER 3

Scope of Government Contracts Review

OUTLINE

A. Methods of Selling to the Government
   1. Fixed-Price vs. Cost-Reimbursement Contracts
   2. Federal Acquisition Regulations (FAR) Part 15 vs. FAR Part 12
   3. Indefinite Delivery/Indefinite Quantity, Blanket Purchase Agreement, and Governmentwide Acquisition Contracting Vehicles
   4. Foreign Military Sales/Foreign Military Financing
   5. Other Transaction Authority Agreements

B. Contracting Parties
   1. US Government Prime Contracts
   2. Subcontracts under Government Prime Contracts
   3. Teaming Agreements
   4. State and Local Contracts

Any evaluation of a government contractor should begin with considering the nature of the market in which the company sells its goods or services. This portion of the manual examines the methods of selling to the government, the categories of government contracts, and the varying types of relationships surrounding government contracts.

A. Methods of Selling to the Government

1. Fixed-Price vs. Cost-Reimbursement Contracts

The type of contract defines the allocation of risk between the contractor and the government. If the contract is fixed-price, the contractor assumes the risk that the cost of performance will exceed the contract price. A slight variant is where the fixed-price contract includes an incentive-fee provision, by which the contractor's fee (profit) is usually determined by applying a formula based on the performance cost incurred by the contractor in performing as compared to a negotiated target.

In a cost-reimbursement contract, the government takes on the risk of cost overruns (assuming the contractor has given the proper notices as funds are expended). The contractor's fee may be: (a) a fixed amount, (b) subject to determination by application of an incentive formula based on the costs incurred, or (c) an award fee that is determined on a periodic basis by the government contracting officer. Contracting officials have been subject to increasing oversight in their determination of the proper award fee. This can have an adverse impact on the amount of award fee actually granted.

> ✓ **Best Practice Tip:** Types of contracts held by the Target will determine risk areas that need to be explored during diligence, such as applicability of the government contracts cost principles and CAS. Similarly, award-fee determinations on major procurements will identify trends over time in the government's assessment of the Target's performance.

2. Federal Acquisition Regulations (FAR) Part 15 vs. FAR Part 12

Most major government contractors are subject to an extensive array of statutes and regulations governing their rights and obligations from contract formation through performance of the contracts and beyond. Many of their products, particularly military items, are not sold outside of the government. Among other regulations, these procurements are subject to the provisions of FAR Part 15, which covers "Contracting by Negotiation." The scope and impact of those requirements are discussed below.

Part 12 of the FAR is titled "Acquisition of Commercial Items." In general, the government will attempt to rely on the commercial marketplace for the purchase of its goods and services to the extent it concludes that commercial practices will protect the interests of the government, particularly with respect to establishing a fair price.

FAR 2.101 includes a definition of "Commercial Item." The primary description is an item (other than real property) that is of a type customarily used by the general public or by nongovernmental entities for nongovernmental purposes, and has been sold, leased, licensed (or offered) to the general public. The term also covers products or services that include minor modifications to a commercial item or items "of a type" customarily combined and sold to the general public. Whether a particular product or service meets the definition often requires an extensive analysis, with the outcome not free from doubt.

General Services Administration (GSA) Schedule contracts, discussed in detail in chapter IV, section F, are one specialized form of commercial contracts. These contracts include unique compliance requirements.

Even where the acquisition is of a "commercial item," the regulations require compliance with significant requirements that are particular to doing business with the government. FAR 52.212-4 contains a simplified set of required terms and conditions for commercial items. A more limited set of required statutes, executive orders, and regulations also applies to the acquisition of commercial items. FAR 52.212-5.

The FAR encourages the use of commercial items for subcontracts and contains a mandatory clause incorporating flow-down provisions that must be included in a subcontract for commercial items. FAR 44.403 and FAR 52.244-6. These mandatory provisions include FAR 52.203-13, "Contractor Code of Business Ethics," and FAR 52.222-26, "Equal Opportunity."

Difficulties can arise when there is a mismatch between the contracting methods employed by the Acquirer and the Target. This can pose particular problems when the time comes to integrate the Target's activities into the operations of the combined company. For example, if the Target sells entirely commercial items, it might not be prepared to comply with the external and internal control processes that will apply if its activities are subject to the full range of government contract requirements, particularly in cost, price, and accounting areas. Conversely, if the Target fully participates in all types of government contracts, an Acquirer that has limited its activities to sales of commercial items might find it problematic to adopt the compliance and control procedures necessary to manage an entity exposed to the full range of government contracts requirements.

As a part of every potential acquisition, the Acquirer undertakes a financial analysis that seeks to model the anticipated efficiencies and synergies that will result from the combination of the acquiring and target companies. This financial modeling plays a key role in determining the price that the Acquirer is willing to pay for the Target, but financial analysts may not be aware that a lack of symmetry between the sales methods of the two companies for government contracts could create a major impediment to the planned integration.

> ✓ **Best Practice Tip:** During the due diligence process, focus on any differences in government sales, accounting, and contracting practices between the Target and Acquirer, and ensure that the financial modeling takes into account the possibility that those differences could impede the full integration of the two companies.

3. Indefinite Delivery/Indefinite Quantity, Blanket Purchase Agreement, and Governmentwide Acquisition Contracting Vehicles

Multiple-award indefinite delivery/indefinite quantity contracts (IDIQs) involving competition for task or delivery orders raise business and competitive issues regarding the sustainability of the business that differ from those raised by single-award IDIQs awarded to a Target. Similarly, traditional blanket purchase agreement (BPA) awards under FAR Subpart 13.3 raise concerns that are different than those presented by BPAs established under Federal Supply Schedule (FSS) program awards under FAR 8.405-3.

4. Foreign Military Sales/Foreign Military Financing

Defense articles and services sold to foreign countries or customers, either under the Foreign Military Sales (FMS) program, administered by the Defense Security Cooperation

Agency (DSCA) or through Foreign Military Financing (FMF), which is authorized by the State Department and administered through DSCA, raise unique compliance issues and requirements. For example, sales eligible for FMF funding include unique certification requirements for US and non-US content.

5. Other Transaction Authority Agreements

Other Transaction Authority (OTA) agreements (also called Other Transaction Agreements) are legal instruments *other than* contracts, grants, or cooperative agreements. The Department of Defense's (DOD's) use of OTAs has ramped up in recent years to obtain research, cutting edge technology, and even full production of military hardware. In the deal context, OTAs raise special concerns where small businesses and nontraditional defense contractors are involved. In particular, loss of status as a small business or as a nontraditional defense contractor could affect the sustainability of business awarded under OTAs.

B. Contracting Parties

The nature of the Target's obligations will depend in substantial part on the categories of parties with whom the Target has contracted. Therefore, it is often useful to organize the due diligence effort by categories that correspond to the Target's contracting parties.

1. US Government Prime Contracts

Contracts with the federal government are subject to a wide range of statutes and regulations that provide comprehensive coverage of the procurement process, contract terms, and performance obligations. The primary source of information is found in the FAR system that was adopted in 1984 in an effort to standardize procurement across all federal agencies. The principal regulation, the Federal Acquisition Regulation, is issued and maintained by the Office of Federal Procurement Policy located in the Office of Management and Budget (OMB). The FAR itself is more than one thousand pages long.[1] Each major procurement agency issues its own regulations supplementing the FAR. The Department of Defense Supplement, for example, is more than five hundred pages. The entire set of the FAR and the FAR supplements for all the agencies is more than four thousand pages. The FAR and its supplements are continuously evolving as new statutes and regulations are implemented.

The FAR is generally written in the form of direction and guidance to government procurement officials, and it also contains a comprehensive set of standard terms for solicitations and contracts and applicable forms. For contract professionals, the FAR is the starting point for researching any question that might arise on a pending procurement or on an existing contract.

---

[1] *See* http://farsite.hill.af.mil.

Federal prime contracts are largely governed by federal law. The Supreme Court has held that federal common law controls the interpretation of a federal contract, because all such contracts are issued ultimately pursuant to the United States Constitution (the Supremacy Clause) and federal statutes.[2] State law will only be consulted where there is no federal law on point, and even then the respective board of contract appeals or court will not look to the law of the place where the contract was made or performed. Instead, the board or court should turn to "the best in modern decision and discussion, including the general principles of contract . . . law."[3] This means that state law will be secondary in determining the Target's rights and obligations under federal prime contracts.

Most federal prime contracts are in a standard format in three parts. See FAR 14.201-1, Table 15-1. Part I is the "Contract Schedule," which is divided into Sections A through H. Part II lists standard contract clauses from the FAR system that are either spelled out or incorporated by reference. Part III, Sections I–J, contains the list of attachments to the contract.[4]

Diligence on prime government contracts can be divided into two major tasks. First, the standard government contracts provisions contained in Section I (and which are discussed extensively throughout this manual) largely do not change from contract to contract, and thus they can ordinarily be summarized once in the due diligence memorandum. The generic summary should be supplemented to identify whether a particular contract: (a) is cost-reimbursement or fixed-price, (b) is subject to the Truth in Negotiations Act or Cost Accounting Standards (see chapter IV, section D), (c) involves classified information, or (c) contains a standard FAR performance warranty.

The second portion of diligence is to evaluate clauses specific to each contract. Although there may be relevant information throughout the contract, the due diligence effort should concentrate on key data in several of the sections in the Contract Schedule (Part 1). Section B lists the supplies or services to be provided and the pricing for each contract line item number. Section B will disclose whether there are options yet to be exercised that could expose the Target to increased exposure, or which the Target may be including in its backlog of sales.

Section C contains the statement of work (SOW) for the Contract. This is often a lengthy document extending to many pages and even volumes on occasion. Counsel is usually not in a position to evaluate the SOW, but counsel may be asked to assist technical personnel in evaluating the risks assumed by the Target.

---

2 United States. v. Seckinger, 397 U.S. 203, 209–210 (1970). In so holding, the Supreme Court cited Clearfield Trust Co. v. U.S., 318 U.S. 363 (1943), in which the Court declined to follow the holding of Erie v. Tomkins Railroad applying state law to a diversity case, to a situation (forgery of a $24.20 check) where the Court deemed it desirable to maintain a uniform federal rule. *Id.* at 367. The *Clearfield Trust* Doctrine formed a significant underpinning for Boyle v. United Technologies Corp., 487 U.S. 500 (1988), in which the Supreme Court established the Government Contractor Defense to third-party tort claims to protect the uniquely federal interest in federal procurements.

3 Prudential Ins. Co. of America v. U.S., 801 F.2d 1295, 1298 (Fed. Cir. 1986).

4 Part IV is also included in the solicitation preceding contract award. It consists of: the standard representations, certifications, and other statements of offerors (Section K), the instruction to offerors (Section L), and the evaluation factors for award (Section M).

Critical information may also be found in Section H of the Contract, which contains the special, nonstandard government contract provisions. Thus, Section H may include items such as special award-fee or target-fee provisions, specific performance and data warranties, one-off agreements on intellectual property rights, and specially negotiated termination rights and obligations.

✓ **Best Practice Tip:** Prepare a section of the due diligence memorandum that explains the generic provisions in government contracts; this portion of the memorandum need not be restated for each contract. Carefully review the Section H provisions in each contract under evaluation to determine whether the Target has taken on obligations or obtained rights beyond those found in the standard government contract clauses.

2. Subcontracts under Government Prime Contracts

Subcontracts issued under federal prime contracts (sometimes referred to in the vernacular as "government subcontracts") are a hybrid of federal prime contracts and commercial transactions. Many of the clauses in the subcontracts are required flow-down provisions from the FAR and agency supplements to the FAR. In addition, the prime contractor will often utilize the government contract format for its major subcontracts. These subcontracts will include an extensive list of FAR (and FAR Supplement) clauses that are incorporated by reference, including clauses that are not mandatory flow-down provisions. The subcontract usually specifies that, in these incorporated clauses, the term "contractor" shall mean the subcontractor and the term "contracting officer" shall mean the prime. With respect to the work undertaken by the subcontractor, the prime's objective should be to assure that the subcontractor's obligations at least equal those of the prime under its contract with the government.

Because of the close alliance between federal prime contracts and the subcontracts issued thereunder, primes and subcontractors often administer government subcontracts as if they were subject to the same rules and processes as prime contracts. However, the rights may vary considerably.

There is a split in the circuits as to the law applicable to disputes under subcontracts that are issued under government prime contracts. The Ninth Circuit takes the view that federal contract law must be applied to subcontracts issued under prime contracts connected with national security.[5] Other circuits instruct that federal law should apply only where there is a unique federal interest in the outcome of the dispute.[6]

In part to avoid controversy over what law applies, many prime contractors include a provision in their standard form of subcontract stating that federal contract law will apply to a dispute arising under the subcontract, except with respect to conflict of interest

---

[5] *See* New SD, Inc. v. Rockwell Int'l Corp., 79 F. 3d 953 (9th Cir. 1996).

[6] *See, e.g.*, Woodward Governor Co. v. Curtiss Wright Flight Sys., Inc., 164 F.3d 123 (2nd Cir. 1999).

rules. Such a provision is likely to be given a broad reading by a court in deciding a subcontract dispute.[7]

> ✓ **Best Practice Tip:** Pay particular attention to the choice of law provisions in major subcontracts, since the applicable law can have a significant impact on the parties' rights and obligations.

During diligence, the Target's compliance with the small business subcontracting requirements set forth in FAR Subpart 19.7 also warrants careful review. This will include review of the Target's approved commercial or individual contract subcontracting plan and compliance with the subcontract reporting requirements in the government's Electronic Subcontracting Reporting System. Under the FAR, maximum practicable utilization of small business, veteran-owned small businesses, service-disabled veteran-owned small businesses, HUBZone small businesses, small disadvantaged businesses, and women-owned small business concerns as subcontractors in government contracting is considered a matter of "national interest with both social and economic benefits." A contractor's failure to make a good faith effort to comply with its subcontracting plan could subject the contractor to an assessment of liquidated damages, in an amount equal to the actual dollar amount by which the contractor failed to achieve each subcontracting goal.

3. Teaming Agreements

Companies enter into teaming agreements to present a joint proposal to the government on a prospective procurement or program. These teaming agreements are often quite elaborate and designate which entity will be the prime contractor and which entity or entities will serve in a subcontractor capacity. The expectation is that the prime will award subcontracts as described in the teaming agreement, subject to good faith negotiation after award of the prime contract. There are often serious disputes as to the applicability of the teaming agreement to a particular government procurement, the proper division of work share, enforceability obligations specified in the teaming agreement, and the duration of the teaming arrangement.

In addition, teaming agreement requirements should be taken into account in the premerger business case in assessing the extent to which future work can be obtained by the merged company. For example, the Target might have an existing teaming agreement requiring that certain designated work scope be awarded to a teaming partner. Post-merger, that agreement would preclude the acquired entity from transferring that designated work scope to another entity in the merged company, or could raise actual or potential organizational conflicts of interest for consideration, mitigation, or resolution under FAR Subpart 9.5. That restriction, if material, should be taken into account in

---

7 *See, e.g.*, Sulzer Bingham Pumps, Inc. v. Lockheed Missiles & Space Co., Inc., 947 F.2d 1362 (9th Cir. 1991) (stipulation of federal contract law incorporates full FAR requirements into the subcontract).

evaluating the intended benefit of the acquisition and whether any mitigation measures will be required, such as divestiture of certain contracts.

Similar risks may be encountered in connection with joint venture agreements. Although joint venture agreements ordinarily are more specific than teaming arrangements, disputes can arise between the joint venture parties, particularly as to allocation of responsibilities, liabilities, and other rights and obligations relating to performance. As a result of recent changes to Small Business Administration (SBA) regulations on its mentor-protégé programs, including development of the All Small Mentor Protégé Program, the recent increase in small business mentor protégé joint ventures has placed added importance on review of joint ventures during due diligence.

✓ **Best Practice Tip:** Determine whether the Target might encounter potential disputes with its teaming partners. Particularly, examine all of the Target's teaming agreements to identify areas where assignment of work may be restricted because of obligations to teaming partners.

4. State and Local Contracts

State and local contracts have some, but not all, of the features of federal contracts. Often, these contracts are of longer duration and are less standardized than federal contracts. Further, state and local entities often impose obligations that are not found in commercial contracts, such as audit access. In addition to state-specific laws, regulations, and contract provisions, such as those related to Minority Business Enterprises and liquidated damages, such contracts frequently contain required flow-down provisions where the funding is from federal sources. On occasion, state and local entities will place orders under the GSA Schedule and those contracts may incorporate the terms of the applicable schedule contract.

Because they are neither as standardized as federal contracts nor as heavily negotiated as commercial contracts, state and local government contracts should be subject to specific and careful review.

✓ **Best Practice Tip:** At the outset of the due diligence process, identify which counsel will be responsible for evaluating state and local contracts. In reviewing those contracts, identify the provisions that go beyond standard commercial terms. Specific emphasis should be put on socioeconomic preferences, which may extend beyond small business status to include various local preferences.

CHAPTER 4

Cost Issues Particular to Government Contracts

OUTLINE

A. "Cost-Disclosure" Contracts
B. Allowability Cost Principles under FAR Part 31
    1. Applicability of the Cost Principles
    2. General Requirements
        a. Reasonable
        b. Allocable
        c. Unallowable or Conditionally Allowable Costs
        d. Advance Agreements
    3. Certification of Indirect Costs
    4. Allowability Issues That Frequently Arise in Acquisitions
        a. Organizational Costs
        b. Goodwill
        c. Interest and Other Financial Costs
        d. Compensation Costs
        e. Relocation Costs
        f. Idle Facilities and Idle Capacity Costs
        g. Asset Valuations from Business Combinations
C. Allocation under Cost Accounting Standards
    1. List of Standards
    2. Applicability
        a. Full Coverage
        b. Modified Coverage
    3. Exemptions
    4. Cost Accounting Standards Board Disclosure Statements
        a. Requirements for Filing
        b. Content of the Cost Accounting Standards Disclosure Statement
        c. Revisions to Cost Accounting Standards Disclosure Statements
        d. Procedure for Government Audit for Adequacy

Government contractors are subject to unique cost accounting and cost allowability rules that can significantly affect the profitability of both their existing contracts and future government business. These rules are frequently critical to the valuation of a government contractor and must be considered in conducting a due diligence review and structuring an acquisition.

A. "Cost-Disclosure" Contracts

It is very important to understand that the government contract cost rules do not apply only to cost-reimbursement contracts. They also extend to fixed-price and time-and-material (T&M) contracts that are awarded noncompetitively to noncommercial item contracts and to contracts over specified thresholds. Thus, it is useful to adopt the phrase "cost-disclosure contracts" to encompass both cost-reimbursement and those fixed-price and T&M contracts that are subject to these rules. This will make clear to all involved in the due diligence that the investigation as to cost issues must go beyond cost-reimbursement contracts.

The substantive provisions applicable to cost-disclosure contracts are found primarily in the FAR Part 31 cost principles, dealing largely with cost allowability; the CAS, dealing primarily with cost allocation; and the requirements of the Truthful Cost or Pricing Data Statute (formerly known as Truth in Negotiations Act—TINA), dealing with contractor disclosures in pricing of its cost-disclosure contracts. There are also specific rules addressing the pricing of GSA schedule contracts. These subjects are discussed in sections B through E of this chapter. Section F then discusses the government's audit rights relating to these substantive requirements.

✓ **Best Practice Tip:** Define the universe of contracts that are subject to government contracts cost regulations as "cost-disclosure contracts," to include not only cost-reimbursement contracts, but also fixed-price and T&M contracts that are subject to FAR Part 31 cost principles, the Truthful Cost or Pricing Data Statute and, where applicable, the CAS.

B. Allowability Cost Principles under FAR Part 31

FAR Part 31 contains the contract-cost principles and procedures for the pricing of contracts, subcontracts and modifications whenever cost analysis is performed in accordance with FAR Part 15. FAR Part 31 provides general guidance on determining the allowability, reasonableness, and allowability of contract costs, as well as guidance on the treatment of forty-seven selected costs.

1. Applicability of the Cost Principles

In general, the cost principles would apply to all of the following contracts or contract-related actions:

1. Cost-reimbursable contracts
2. Time-and-material contracts
3. Fixed-price contracts where cost analysis is utilized, including contracts where offerors submit certified cost or pricing data under the Truthful Cost or Pricing Data Statute
4. All contracts containing the "Allowable Cost and Payment Clause"
5. Contracts containing price redetermination provisions
6. Contracts where progress payments based on cost are requested
7. Forward-pricing rate agreements
8. Contract modifications where cost analysis is utilized

2. General Requirements

a. Reasonable

For a cost to be allowable, it must be both reasonable and allocable. FAR Part 31 defines a reasonable cost as one that "in its nature and amount . . . does not exceed that which would be incurred by a prudent person in the conduct of competitive business." The reasonableness of costs "must be examined with particular care in connection with firms or their separate divisions that may not be subject to effective competitive restraints." FAR 31.201–3. Whether a cost is reasonable depends on a variety of considerations and circumstances, including:

- Recognition of the cost as one that is ordinary and necessary for the conduct of the contractor's business or the contract performance
- Generally accepted sound business practices, arm's-length bargaining, and federal and state laws and regulations
- The contractor's responsibilities to the government, other customers, the owners of the business, employees, and the public at large
- Any significant deviations from the contractor's established practices

b. Allocable

For a cost to be allowable, it must also be allocable. FAR 31.201-4 instructs that a cost is allocable "if it is assignable or chargeable to one or more cost objectives on the basis of relative benefits received or other equitable relationship." A cost is allocable to a government contract if it is incurred specifically for the contract, benefits both the contract and other work, or if it is necessary to the overall operation of the business.[1] Specific rules as to allocability are contained in the Cost Accounting Standards (see section C).

c. Unallowable or Conditionally Allowable Costs

FAR 31.205 addresses the allowability of forty-seven categories of costs. Some costs, such as bad debts, donations, entertainment, fines, penalties, and losses on other contracts, are made expressly unallowable. Other costs, such as those incurred for travel, compensation, selling, and insurance, are made allowable if they meet certain criteria as set forth in the applicable FAR subsection. The allowability—or unallowability—of costs requires a careful analysis of these detailed regulations.

It should also be noted that FAR 31.204(c) provides that allowability of costs not specifically addressed by the FAR is to be based on general allowability principles plus the "treatment of similar or related . . . items" that are specifically addressed under the FAR. This concept has been applied recently to disallow costs that formerly were thought to be allowable.[2]

---

1 *Id.*

2 *See, e.g.*, Boeing North American Inc. v. Roche, 298 F.3d 1274 (Fed. Cir. 2002) (holding that the costs of unsuccessfully defending a private suit charging a contractor with wrongdoing were not allowable since "similar" costs would be disallowed under the FAR).

d. Advance Agreements

FAR 31.109 allows for the company and the government to negotiate advance agreements on the treatment of costs. These agreements may be employed to avoid subsequent disputes on the reasonableness, allocability, or allowability of costs, but they may not be used for the treatment of costs inconsistent with Part 31—that is, costs that are expressly unallowable cannot be made allowable with an advance agreement.

3. Certification of Indirect Costs

For contracts that contain the Allowable Cost and Payment clause (typically cost-reimbursement and T&M contracts) a contractor is required to obtain final indirect cost rates. Contractors must submit a proposal to the government to obtain these final indirect cost rates and FAR 52.242-4 requires the proposal to be certified by the contractor. The certification must be signed by a division vice-president, chief financial officer, or equivalent, stating under penalty of perjury that he or she has reviewed the claim and that all costs claimed are allowable in accordance with contract terms and the applicable cost principles.

Certain penalties may apply if unallowable costs are contained in any of the certified proposals for final indirect cost rates. FAR 42.709 describes the government's process for determining if a contractor should be assessed penalties for claiming unallowable costs. If the indirect cost is expressly unallowable under a cost principle in the FAR (or an executive agency supplement thereto), "the penalty is equal to the amount of the disallowed costs allocated to contracts that are subject to this section for which an indirect cost proposal has been submitted; plus interest on the paid portion."[3] If the indirect cost was determined to be unallowable before the proposal submission, the penalty is two times the amount of the unallowable cost.[4] These penalties are in addition to any other administrative, civil, and criminal penalties provided by law. The cognizant contracting officer determines whether the penalties should be assessed or waived. Strong internal controls in this area are critical to safeguard against cost mischarging.

> ✓ **Best Practice Tip:** The diligence team (often supplemented with accounting expertise) should review the internal controls over the preparation of certified rates to evaluate whether adequate procedures are in place to ensure the exclusion of unallowable costs from all indirect rate submissions.

4. Allowability Issues That Frequently Arise in Acquisitions

The following seven selected cost principles have specific relevance to businesses that are involved in mergers and acquisitions. For the most part, these costs are not allowable in

3 FAR 42.709-1(a)(1).

4 FAR 42.709-1(a)(2).

pricing government contracts. Some of these costs, however, may become allowable if the contractor enters into a special restructuring agreement (see section C).

a. Organizational Costs

Under FAR 31.205-27, all costs—both internal and external—associated with planning, executing, or resisting the organization or reorganization of the corporate structure of a business are unallowable. These include (a) the costs of performing due diligence activities; (b) legal and other professional costs incurred in the due diligence or acquisition process, including such activities as reviewing or preparing contracts, assisting in raising capital or financing; (c) incorporation fees; (d) costs of investment advisors or brokers; and (e) costs incurred for resisting a change in controlling interest.

b. Goodwill

FAR 31.205-49 makes any amortization, expensing, write-off, or write-down of goodwill unallowable.

c. Interest and Other Financial Costs

Interest and other financial costs such as interest on borrowings, bond discounts, and costs of financing capital are unallowable under FAR 31.205-20. This can have a significant impact on leveraged transactions through debt.

✓ **Best Practice Tip:** For transactions financed through debt, ensure that cash-flow projections consider the fact that interest on the debt cannot be included in pricing government contracts subject to the cost principles.

d. Compensation Costs

FAR 31.205-6(l) identifies a number of compensation costs incidental to business acquisitions that are unallowable. These include: (a) payments to employees under agreements in which they receive special compensation in excess of the contractor's normal severance pay practice, if their employment terminates following a change in management control; and (b) payments to employees under plans introduced in connection with a change (whether actual or prospective) in the management control in which those employees receive special compensation, contingent upon the employee remaining with the contractor for a specified period of time.

FAR 31.205-6 also includes several other compensation costs that may impact businesses post-merger, including any compensation that is calculated based on changes in the price of corporate securities and any compensation represented by dividend payments. Further, payments to an employee in lieu of the employee receiving or exercising a right, option, or benefit that would have been unallowable under (a) or (b) above are also unallowable. It should also be noted that FAR 31.205-6(p) imposes compensation limits on employees. The compensation limits, and the population of employees to which it applies, changed significantly in 2014. For contracts awarded after June 24, 2014, the compensation limit applies to all employees unless an exemption is obtained for scientists, engineers, or other specialists.

> ✓ **Best Practice Tip:** In its review of existing or planned compensation arrangements, the diligence team should consider any potential negative cost impacts of these compensation restrictions.

e. Relocation Costs

FAR 31.205-35 addresses the allowability of relocation costs. In general, the cost of relocating employees is an allowable cost, with certain limits. For example, closing costs on the sale of a former residence, combined with any continuing costs of ownership of a vacant former residence after the closing date on a new home, may not exceed 14 percent of the sales price of the home. Also, the allowable portion of a lump-sum relocation payment is limited to $15,000.

> ✓ **Best Practice Tip:** If a significant number of relocations are anticipated, the diligence team should carefully review the relocation plan along with this cost principle.

f. Idle Facilities and Idle Capacity Costs

FAR 31.205-17 generally treats idle facilities and idle capacity costs as allowable, with the following limitation: "Costs of idle facilities are allowable for a reasonable period, ordinarily not to exceed 1 year, depending upon the initiative taken to use, lease, or dispose of the idle facilities."

> ✓ **Best Practice Tip:** Since the consolidation of facilities is not uncommon following a merger or acquisition, the Acquirer's diligence team should implement a formal plan to address how any idle facilities or capacity costs will be treated. The team should also consider entering into an advance agreement on the treatment of these costs with the appropriate cognizant contracting officer.

g. Asset Valuations from Business Combinations

FAR 31.205-52 addresses the step-up or step-down of tangible or intangible capital assets resulting from business combinations. For tangible capital assets, when the purchase method of accounting for a business combination is used (whether or not the contract or subcontract is subject to CAS), "the allowable depreciation and cost of money shall be based on the capitalized asset values measured and assigned in accordance with 48 CFR 9904.404-50(d), if allocable, reasonable, and not otherwise unallowable."[5] For intangible

[5] FAR 31.205-52.

capital assets, when the same method of accounting is used, "allowable amortization and cost of money shall be limited to the total of the amounts that would have been allowed had the combination not taken place."[6] To meet the requirements of this cost principle, companies will have to maintain two sets of records to allow for the difference in accounting under FAR and GAAP.

> ✓ **Best Practice Tip:** Companies should properly identify and segregate asset revaluation costs so that they may be excluded from the pricing, costing, and billing on government contracts.

C. Allocation under Cost Accounting Standards

The CAS are designed "to achieve uniformity and consistency in the cost accounting practices governing measurement, assignment, and allocation of costs to contracts with the United States Government." The Cost Accounting Standards Board (CASB) administers CAS and is an independent board within the Office of Federal Procurement Policy of the OMB. The CAS rules and regulations impose major accounting requirements on contractors. The rules are promulgated by the CASB and are periodically modified by regulation. In addition, the courts have interpreted most of the standards. If deemed to result in increased costs to the government, violations of these accounting principles can result in repricing contracts, including fixed-price contracts.

Government contracts and subcontracts may be subject to the CAS (as discussed in section C.2) pertaining to estimation, accumulation, and allocation of costs, unless one of the exemptions in 9903.201-1 applies or CAS coverage is waived. A complete list of the exemptions is provided below, with some of the most common exemptions being negotiated contracts and subcontracts less than the Truthful Cost or Pricing Data threshold (currently $2,000,000), contracts and subcontracts with small businesses, fixed-price and T&M contracts and subcontracts for commercial items, and fixed-price contracts and subcontracts awarded on the basis of adequate price competition without submission of cost or pricing data.

1. List of Standards

The CASB has adopted nineteen separate standards, listed here:

CAS 401	Consistency in Estimating, Accumulating and Reporting Costs
CAS 402	Consistency in Allocating Costs Incurred for the Same Purpose
CAS 403	Allocation of Home Office Expenses to Segments
CAS 404	Capitalization of Tangible Assets
CAS 405	Accounting for Unallowable Costs
CAS 406	Cost Accounting Standard—Cost Accounting Period

[6] *Id.*

CAS 407	Use of Standard Costs for Direct Material and Direct Labor
CAS 408	Accounting for Costs of Compensated Personal Absence
CAS 409	Cost Accounting Standard—Depreciation of Tangible Capital Assets
CAS 410	Allocation of Business Unit General and Administrative Expenses to Final Cost Objectives
CAS 411	Cost Accounting Standard—Accounting for Acquisition Costs of Material
CAS 412	Cost Accounting Standard for Composition and Measurement of Pension Cost
CAS 413	Adjustment and Allocation of Pension Cost
CAS 414	Cost of Money as an Element of the Cost of Facilities Capital
CAS 415	Accounting for the Cost of Deferred Compensation
CAS 416	Accounting for Insurance Costs
CAS 417	Cost of Money as an Element of the Cost of Capital Assets under Construction
CAS 418	Allocation of Direct and Indirect Costs
CAS 420	Accounting for Independent Research and Development

2. Applicability

a. Full Coverage

Full coverage applies to business units that receive a single CAS-covered contract award of $50 million or more or that received $50 million or more in net CAS-covered awards during its preceding cost accounting period. The clause applicable to full coverage ("CAS," FAR 52.230-2) requires a contractor to:

1. Describe in writing its cost accounting practices when a business unit is part of a company that is required to submit a disclosure statement.
2. Follow its cost accounting practices consistently.
3. Comply with all standards in effect either on the contract award date or on the date of the signed "Certificate of Current Cost or Pricing Data."
4. Comply prospectively with all standards that become applicable during contract performance.
5. Agree to an adjustment of the contract price or cost allowance (as described below), where it fails to comply with existing standards or fails to follow its cost accounting practices.[7]

b. Modified Coverage

Modified coverage applies to a covered contract of less than $50 million awarded to a business unit that received less than $50 million in net CAS-covered awards in the immediately preceding cost accounting period. The clause applicable to modified coverage

[7] FAR 52.230-2.

("Disclosure and Consistency of Cost Accounting Practices," FAR 52.230-3) requires a contractor not otherwise exempt to:

1. Comply with CAS 401, 402, 405, and 406.
2. Describe in writing its cost accounting practices when a business unit is part of a company that is required to submit a "CASB Disclosure Statement."
3. Consistently follow its cost accounting practices.
4. Agree to an adjustment of the contract price or cost allowance (as described below) in those situations when it fails to comply with applicable standards or to follow its cost accounting practices.[8]

3. Exemptions

The following contracts and subcontracts are exempt from CAS:

- Sealed bid contracts
- Negotiated contracts or subcontracts under $2,000,000 (the Truthful Cost or Pricing Data Statute)
- Any contract or subcontract awarded to a small business concern, as defined by Small Business Administration regulations
- Any contract or subcontract in which price is set by law or regulations
- Firm-fixed-priced, fixed-priced-with-economic-price-adjustment (provided the price adjustment is not based on actual costs), T&M, and labor-hour contracts or subcontracts for the acquisition of commercial items
- Any contract or subcontract awarded to a foreign government or its agencies or instrumentalities
- Any contract or subcontract awarded to a foreign concern, except for CAS 401 and 402
- Contracts or subcontracts less than $7.5 million, provided that, at the time of award, the business unit is not currently performing any CAS-covered contracts or subcontracts valued at $7.5 million or greater
- Any firm-fixed-price contract or subcontract awarded on the basis of adequate price competition without submission of cost or pricing data
- Contracts under the NATO PHM Ship Program to be performed entirely outside the United States by a foreign concern[9]

4. Cost Accounting Standards Board Disclosure Statements

The CASB Disclosure Statement describes a company's cost accounting practices that are used to estimate and accumulate costs under CAS covered contracts.

---

8 FAR 52.230-3.

9 North Atlantic Treaty Organization Patrol Craft Hydrofoil Missile Ship Program.

a. Requirements for Filing

Currently, a company seeking award of a negotiated government prime or subcontract in excess of $50 million that has not previously submitted a disclosure statement must file a disclosure statement prior to award of the contract. In addition, a company that has received CAS-covered negotiated prime or subcontracts in excess of $50 million during its most recently completed cost accounting period, generally the fiscal year, must submit a disclosure statement within ninety days after the close of the fiscal year. A contractor must submit a disclosure statement for each of its segments with a CAS-covered contract unless, in the most recently completed cost accounting period, a respective segment's CAS-covered awards were less than 30 percent of total segment sales *and* less than $10 million. If two segments of a single company have identical cost accounting practices, then a single disclosure statement may be filed.

A foreign contractor or subcontractor that is required to submit a disclosure statement may, in lieu of filing a Form No. CASB-DS-1, file a disclosure form prescribed by an agency of its own government, provided that the CASB determines the information disclosed by such means will satisfy the objectives of Public Law 100-679. The use of alternative forms has been approved for contractors from Canada, the Federal Republic of Germany, and the United Kingdom.

b. Content of the Cost Accounting Standards Disclosure Statement

The disclosure statement form is quite detailed and includes the following general subjects:

1. Certification and general information
2. Direct costs
3. Direct versus indirect costs
4. Indirect costs
5. Depreciation and capitalization practices
6. Other costs and credits
7. Pension costs, deferred compensation, and insurance costs
8. Corporate or group expenses

c. Revisions to Cost Accounting Standards Disclosure Statements

A company must revise its disclosure statement to implement requirements imposed by any new standards, correct noncompliant practices, and reflect "changes in cost accounting practices" agreed to by the contracting parties. The FAR indicates a description of changes to cost accounting practices should be submitted sixty days prior to implementing the changes, or such a date mutually agreed to by the government.

In addition to submitting a description of the change a company must also submit a proposal that identifies the change in costs on their CAS covered contracts as a result of the change. There are two types of proposals that could be required to be submitted: a general dollar magnitude (GDM) or a detailed cost-impact (DCI).

d. Procedure for Government Audit for Adequacy

FAR Part 30 provides for review and approval of the disclosure statement by the cognizant federal agency official, based on the advice of the DCAA. The auditor's review is confined to a determination of whether the statement adequately describes the contractor's cost accounting practices and is current, accurate, and complete. The DCAA audit for adequacy must be completed before contract award.

5. Noncompliance and Voluntary Changes

a. Cost Accounting Standards Noncompliance

CAS-covered contracts and subcontracts are subject to adjustment to account for the cost impact of a contractor's failure to comply with applicable standards or its disclosed accounting practices. FAR Part 30.6 provides guidance on how to determine the cost impact of any noncompliance with CAS. Adjustments arising from a noncompliance are made only in favor of the government; thus, contract prices can only be adjusted downward. However, the CAS rules do allow for offsets where noncompliance results in a lower cost to the government on some contracts and higher costs on others. As an example, if the noncompliance resulted in a $1,000,000 reduction in one contract and an increase of $800,000 in another contract, the impact can be netted resulting in a $200,000 downward price adjustment.

b. Voluntary Changes

CAS-covered contracts and subcontracts are also subject to adjustment to account for the cost impact of changes made in an accounting practice by a company during the performance of CAS-covered contracts. These adjustments are applied prospectively from the change date to covered prime contracts and subcontracts awarded before the accounting change occurred. FAR Part 30 provides guidance on establishing the cost impact for voluntary and desirable changes, including how to determine whether a change is "desirable." As with noncompliance, unless the change is determined to be desirable and not detrimental to the government's interests, any adjustments arising from a voluntary change are made only in favor of the government—that is, contract prices can only be adjusted downward. The CAS rules do allow for offsets when one voluntary change results in a lower cost to the government on some contracts and higher costs on others (as the example in section C.5.a above illustrates). If a voluntary change is deemed "desirable," then upward price adjustments may be allowed, or the contracting officer may waive downward price adjustments.

✓ **Best Practice Tip:** During diligence steps should be performed to identify any changes to cost accounting practices made by the target company. If changes have been made, confirm a GDM or DCI proposal has been submitted and identify potential reductions to contract values as a result of the change.

6. Consideration of Changes in Applicability

An acquisition raises particular issues concerning CAS application.

a. Large CAS-Covered Business Purchase of a Small Business Acquisition Target

When a CAS-covered contractor acquires a small business whose contracts were exempt from CAS, contracts executed with the small business prior to the acquisition will remain exempt from CAS. However, for all contracts awarded subsequent to the acquisition, the small business exemption may no longer be claimed.

> ✓ **Best Practice Tip:** To avoid disagreement as to CAS coverage at a later date, maintain a complete list of small business set-aside contracts/grants in backlog as of the date of acquisition.

b. Non-CAS-Covered Contractor Acquisition of a CAS-Covered Target

If a non-CAS-covered contractor acquires a contractor with CAS-covered contracts, the event may trigger the application of CAS to future contracts of the combined entity. This would occur if the acquired segments are merged with the Acquirer's segments.

> ✓ **Best Practice Tip:** By maintaining the acquired business as a separate segment, a contractor may be able to avoid the need to apply CAS to its existing business. A critical issue will be the level of interdependencies between the existing and acquired businesses.

7. Post-Closing Changes to the Acquiring and the Acquired Companies' CAS Disclosure Statements

As a result of a merger or acquisition, disclosure statements will need to be revised in the event of changes of accounting practices; creation, elimination, or consolidation of home offices; or creation, elimination, or consolidation of any segments

D. The Truthful Cost or Pricing Data Act—Overview

The Truthful Cost or Pricing Data Act (for decades known as the Truth in Negotiations Act, or TINA, and referred to as TINA here), 10 U.S.C. § 2306a and 41 U.S.C. § 254b, requires the contractor to submit cost or pricing data in support of the award of a contract in excess of the threshold—currently $2,000,000 for contracts awarded after June 30, 2018—unless the contract is for a commercial item or the product or service is being obtained in a competitive procurement.[10] The contractor is required to certify that the

10 FAR 15.403.

data are current, accurate, and complete as of the date the parties reached agreement on price (the "handshake" date).[11] To comply with these requirements, government contractors should conduct a "sweep" to secure and disclose updated information just prior to certifying the data that has been submitted.

Even where the conditions do not require submission of certified cost or pricing data, the government may require the contractor to submit "data other than certified cost or pricing data." This is information the contracting officer believes necessary to support the fairness and reasonableness of the price, and can include such information as prior prices at which the items have been sold or even, in some cases, limited cost data.[12] "Data other than certified cost or pricing data" are, as the name indicates, not certified, and "defects" in that data (lack of currency, accuracy, or completeness) will not ordinarily result in defective pricing liability. However, a contractor could be liable under fraud statutes for knowingly submitting inaccurate information. When certified cost or pricing data is required, the contractor must disclose facts but need not disclose judgments. The line between facts and judgments can be hard to locate, and prudence dictates that contractors not stray too close to that line.

Where TINA applies, if the contractor's certified data is later determined to be "defective"—that is, not current, accurate, and complete—the government is entitled to a price adjustment to the extent that the price was increased because of the defective data.[13]

Government auditors usually raise allegations of TINA violations during defective pricing audits that may take place long after the contract has been negotiated. Defective pricing claims can run into many millions of dollars. Defending such actions requires the contractor to present evidence of what was available on the handshake date and what was disclosed.

> ✓ **Best Practice Tip:** Determine whether the Target's practices, including its process for maintaining the records of contract pricing negotiations, enable it to comply with TINA. Also examine any outstanding allegations of defective pricing against the Target.

1. Disclosure of the Potential Acquisition

The TINA requirements may well have an impact on the due diligence process, and the acquisition may have an impact on the organization and accounting structure of the Target, the Acquirer, or both. For example, the planned combination of the Target with the Acquirer would likely cause a change in the indirect cost pool and cost bases of one or both entities, resulting in a change in the indirect cost rate currently being used in cost projections for pricing of future government contracts. The question to be assessed is: When do the acquisition and the plans for integration become "facts" that must be

---

11 FAR 15.406-3.

12 FAR 15.403-3.

13 FAR 15.407-1.

disclosed under TINA? The difficulty in making this determination is compounded by the confidential nature of the discussions between the Acquirer and the Target.

While there is no clear dividing line, many practitioners adopt the standard that disclosure under TINA should be made when a "management decision" to go forward with the acquisition has been made. In some instances, this management decision might be made only a few days before a public announcement is made. That timing will allow disclosure to be made to the cognizant government officials at the time of the announcement, without violating confidentiality requirements. The disclosure should provide the information available at that time as to the impact on the costs of both the Target and the Acquirer for government contracts pricing purposes.

✓ **Best Practice Tip:** Early in the due diligence process, both the Target and the Acquirer should identify the potential need for TINA disclosure. Each should maintain documentation establishing the date on which management approved the transaction. The transaction should be disclosed to the government immediately after the public announcement of the transaction. If the Target or Acquirer have information on the anticipated impact of the transaction, that information must be disclosed as well.

E. Government Audit Rights

1. Nature and Scope of Government Audit Activities

The government has broad statutory and contractual audit rights with respect to government contracts, both prior to award and post-award. The government generally has the right to audit a contractor's books and records at any time up to three years after final payment under a contract.

The due diligence team should undertake a thorough analysis of all audits conducted by government agencies to determine potential liabilities and costs that may potentially be recovered under the Target's government contracts. Post-award audits, in particular, may provide valuable insight into the Target's cost, pricing, and accounting practices, and whether government auditors have identified problems that could be potential deal breakers. For example, post-award audit reports may highlight certain problematic direct costs (such as labor charges, executive compensation, or travel expenses) or indirect costs, which may be included in overhead or G&A.[14] The diligence team should also assess the Target's procedures for responding to government audits and its relationship with government auditors.

Government audits to be evaluated during the due diligence review include those relating to: (a) cost or pricing data under TINA; (b) government-specific cost and accounting rules, including the FAR Part 31 cost principles; and (c) the CAS. Liability for audit issues potentially can include unilateral price adjustments and interest assessments

[14] General and Administrative Expense.

on government cost recoveries under existing contracts and contracts closed during the preceding six years (the generally applicable statute of limitations).

2. Types of Government Audits

During the due diligence review, the following types of government audit reports, among others, should be reviewed carefully for relevant information about the Target's cost and accounting practices, with an eye toward identifying actual and potential liabilities. This information will assist the Acquirer in evaluating and negotiating how contracts, liabilities, and potential liabilities should be accounted for in negotiating the purchase price.

a. Pre-Award Audits

Government auditors are often called in by procurement officials to conduct an audit of the contractor's proposed contract costs to assist the government in negotiations with the contractor.

b. Incurred Cost Audits

Audits to determine projected costs based on historical incurred costs represent the largest category of audits performed by DCAA. These audits are often used to assist the contractor and government in establishing billing and pricing rates, pending the establishment of final rates.

Incurred cost audits are particularly valuable to the due diligence team because they provide information concerning the reasonableness, allocability, and allowability of direct and indirect costs charged by the Target to its government contracts. They also shed light on whether the Target's cost charging and accounting practices comply with the FAR cost principles and CAS. Information learned from incurred cost audits can identify isolated and systemic problems and risk areas, as well as other deficiencies inherent in the contractor's accounting system. In the context of a merger or acquisition, these types of audits are important in assessing potential legal risks and financial exposure, and in negotiating representations and warranties, indemnifications, and other contract covenants and conditions.

c. Defective Pricing Audits

Defective pricing occurs when a contractor fails to submit to the government cost or pricing data that is current, accurate, and complete prior to reaching agreement on price, as required under TINA (see section D). Generally, the auditor identifies defective pricing in a post-award audit through an analysis of the records and data available to a contractor as of the date of agreement on the contract price (the "handshake date," as noted above) and by comparing them with submitted cost or pricing data. The types of records reviewed include historical unit cost records, cost estimates, vendor quotes, purchase orders, supplier credits/refunds, cost trend records, sales and manufacturing volume projections, profit and loss statements, and product cost and profit analyses.[15] Based on that review, the auditor may

[15] DCAA Audit Manual ¶ 14-117.

recommend a price adjustment to the contracting officer, who in turn can seek a reduction in the contract price pursuant to the Price Reduction for Defective Pricing clause of the contract. Identification of potential defective pricing by the Target, as well as any systemic problems or deficiencies that may have led to the defective pricing, will be important in assessing potential legal risks and financial exposure to the Acquirer.

d. Cost Accounting Standards Audits

CAS audits include review of the Target's CAS disclosure statement for adequacy and compliance with specific CAS standards. As with other audits, identification of any CAS noncompliance issues will be important for assessing potential legal risks and financial exposure, as well as for negotiating representations and warranties, indemnifications, and other contract covenants and conditions.

e. Audits of Contract Terminations, Delay and Disruption Claims, and Other Price Adjustment Proposals

Government audits involving a broad range of adjustments to contract pricing—from contract termination settlement proposals to contractor requests for equitable adjustments—are critical to evaluating the sustainability of the Target's contracts, profits and losses, revenues, and actual and potential liabilities. Audits in any of these areas are important to the Acquirer not only to determine a reasonable price, but also to assess the continuing viability of the business it is purchasing.

> ✓ **Best Practice Tip:** Although the Target may push back, insist on production of audit reports or, at minimum, internal summaries of potential liabilities reflected in audit reports and related correspondence. The reports may also be critical in evaluating systemic weaknesses and related risk.

3. Role of the Defense Contract Audit Agency

The Department of Defense (DOD) relies for its auditing requirements on the DCAA. Many other agencies house their auditing function within the agency Office of Inspector General (OIG). Still others utilize the services of DCAA through interagency agreements with DOD.

The DCAA was established by a directive of the DOD as a separate agency, under the authority, direction, and control of the DOD Comptroller. Its mission is to:

> Perform all necessary contract audit for the Department of Defense and provide accounting and financial advisory services regarding contracts and subcontracts to all DOD Components responsible for procurement and contract administration. These services will be performed in connection with negotiation, administration, and settlement of contracts and subcontracts.[16]

[16] DOD Directive 5105.36 (2/28/02).

While DCAA performs many types of pre- and post-award audits, along with reviews of contractors' internal control systems, DCAA's role is generally advisory only. Final determinations on matters such as pricing proposals, cost allowability issues, defective pricing, CAS compliance, forward pricing rates, final indirect rates, and contractor purchasing system adequacy, to name a few, are made by the contracting officer, who draws on information from DCAA or other audit reports.

The DCAA is authorized by its charter to cooperate with and provide audit support to various agencies of the government that oversee government contractors. These include the Department of Justice (DOJ), the DOD Inspector General (DOD IG), the Defense Criminal Investigative Service, agency suspension and debarment offices, as well as the various military service investigatory agencies. The DCAA Contract Audit Manual provides extensive information on audit policies and procedures. DCAA pamphlet 7641.90, "Information for Contractors," is also a reference source on DCAA practices. These materials can be found on the agency's website at www.dcaa.mil.

a. Subjects of DCAA Audit

As stated in chapter 1 of its Manual and Pamphlet 7641.90, the major areas of emphasis for the auditor include:

1. A contractor's internal control systems
2. Management policies
3. Accuracy and reasonableness of cost representations
4. Adequacy and reliability of records and accounting systems
5. Financial capability
6. Contractor compliance with contract provisions having accounting or financial significance, such as the Cost Principles (FAR Part 31), the CAS Clause (FAR 52.230-2), and the clauses pertaining to TINA (FAR 52.215-10, -11, -12, and -13)

To assist the DCAA in making determinations regarding the foregoing areas, certain FAR clauses in government contracts require contractors to provide the procuring agencies with access to their records. If contractors deny access to their records, the DCAA may invoke its subpoena authority for "any records" relative to government contract or subcontract costs.[17]

A contract auditor who determines that costs charged to a government contract are unallowable may issue to the contractor a Form 1, "Notice of Contract Costs Suspended or Disapproved." The contractor may challenge this notice by writing to the contracting officer who administers the contract or filing a claim under the Contract Disputes Act.

The role of the DCAA in government contracting also includes responsibility for detection and reporting of suspected irregularities.[18] Upon forming a "reasonable suspicion" of fraud, corruption, or unlawful activity relating to a government contract, the auditor prepares a Form 2000, "Suspected Irregularity Referral," that is sent to the appropriate DOD investigatory agency. Form 2000 is used to address a number of

---

[17] 10 U.S.C. § 2313(b).

[18] Contract Audit Manual, chapter 4, section 7.

irregularity categories, such as defective pricing, billing, labor or material mischarging, product substitution, cost accounting, false certifications, subcontracts, ethical matters, and obstruction of audit.

✓ **Best Practice Tip:** Ascertain whether the DCAA has issued any Form 1s to the Target regarding disallowed contract costs and determine the status of any issued Form 1s.

b. Sarbanes-Oxley Considerations

There is an ongoing debate regarding DCAA auditor access to contractor records—in particular, access to internal audit reports and work papers related to Sarbanes-Oxley (SOX) internal controls. Contractors have taken the view that the DCAA's access to records is limited to those documents necessary to support actual costs and document estimating methods used to calculate actual or proposed costs within the scope of the DCAA's audit. This includes records such as receipts and invoices from vendors and subcontractors, as well as bases of estimates.

However, DCAA audit guidance instructs auditors to consider company SOX information, if available or if access can be attained, because such contractor information may enhance the quality of the audit or avoid the duplication of efforts already performed by the contractor's internal or external auditors. Moreover, DCAA audit guidance states that auditors should in the course of their field work "inquire" regarding the SOX executive certification, which includes significant disclosures for deficiencies and material weaknesses. Auditors are also instructed to request access to SOX work papers that support disclosures and determinations of controls issues. Accordingly, the DCAA will likely request access to information such as that contained in internal audit programs, controls requirements, internal audit reports, and internal audit work papers, and may also request access to sensitive company materials (e.g., management assessment of internal controls, including internal audit and other outside professional consultant reports; audit committee documents or meeting minutes; and reports from external auditors on company internal controls or management's assessment of internal controls).

When a company receives a DCAA request for such sensitive company documents, it faces particular challenges in denying the DCAA access to SOX and internal audit work papers. For example, the DCAA can claim that denial of access to SOX records is grounds for questioning costs. In addition, denying work papers can make it difficult for companies that place a high value on a cordial relationship with the DCAA. These problems are elevated by the "Full Cooperation with Audits and Investigations" provision under the new Ethics and Business Conduct and Mandatory Disclosure rules.

4. Role of Inspectors General and Investigative Organizations

The Inspector General Act of 1978 established an Office of Inspector General at each executive agency of the government.[19] Among the many functions of the Inspector

19 5 U.S.C. Appendix 3.

General offices are audits and investigations relating to the operations of their agencies, including acquisitions.

Within the DOD, the Inspector General Act assigns responsibility to the DOD IG to investigate fraud, waste, and abuse uncovered as a result of internal audits. For DOD contracting, the Office of the Deputy Inspector General for Auditing has oversight of acquisition and contract management. DOD IG auditors review areas such as allegations of fraud, waste and abuse, hotline complaints, and information on alleged violations of laws and regulations. This oversight encompasses all types of contracting, including research and development, weapons acquisition, information technology, and construction.

In 2008, the DOD IG instructed all defense components to ensure coordination of remedies for fraud and corruption related to procurement activities.[20] Each component is to establish a centralized organization to coordinate criminal, civil, contractual, and administrative remedies with respect to DOD contracts.

Investigations of criminal matters on behalf of the DOD IG are conducted by Defense Criminal Investigative Organizations (DCIO). These include the Defense Criminal Investigative Service (DCIS), Navy Criminal Investigative Service (NCIS), Air Force Office of Special Investigations (AFOSI), and Army Criminal Investigation Division (Army CID). The Procurement Fraud unit plays a major role in DCIS investigative programs. Investigations include defective or substituted products, environmental contract fraud, defective pricing, progress payment fraud, fast pay fraud, and antitrust violations. NCIS, AFOSI, and Army CID also have procurement fraud units covering contracts with their military branches.

The Defense Contract Management Agency (DCMA) administers the majority of contracts awarded by the military services. Within DCMA's Office of General Counsel, the Contract Integrity Center provides legal services to DCMA personnel on the detection and reporting of fraud and corruption involving defense contractors. The Contract Integrity Center also coordinates with DOD investigatory agencies and the Justice Department on fraud and integrity matters affecting military contracts.

✓ **Best Practice Tip:** Until public disclosure occurs, information about a pending investigation of the Target by a government agency is not available. Even if the Target is aware of the investigation, government personnel will not discuss an investigation with any party outside of the government, except in unusual circumstances.

5. Role of the Department of Justice

The Civil and Criminal Divisions of the Justice Department are responsible for enforcement of the civil and criminal statutes involving fraud against the United States.

The Criminal Division prosecutes cases under fraud statutes such as 18 U.S.C. § 1001 (False Statements Act), 18 U.S.C. § 287 (Criminal False Claims Act), and 18 U.S.C. § 371

[20] DOD Instruction 7050.05 (6/4/08).

(Conspiracy). The various US Attorney offices throughout the country play a major role in these prosecutions.

In 2006, the Justice Department created the National Procurement Fraud Task Force. It is chaired by the Assistant Attorney General for the Criminal Division and includes the Federal Bureau of Investigation, the Inspectors General of the federal agencies, Defense Department investigative agencies, US Attorney offices, and other government entities. The Task Force detects, investigates, and prosecutes procurement fraud, grant fraud, and associated corruption.

The Commercial Litigation Branch of the Civil Division, Fraud Section, also works with the US Attorney offices to litigate cases involving financial fraud against the government. Actions are brought under the False Claims Act and other civil fraud statutes. These include *qui tam* suits where private citizens allege wrongdoing by government contractors and share in any monetary recoveries.

F. General Services Administration (GSA) Schedule

The GSA is responsible for the award and administration of the Federal Supply Schedule (FSS) program, which provides federal agencies with a simplified process for obtaining commercial products and services at prices associated with volume buying.[21] GSA awards FSS and Multiple Award Schedule (MAS) contracts, often referred to simply as "Schedule contracts," on a governmentwide basis to multiple companies to supply commercial products and services at stated prices for specified time periods.

Under the Schedule program, federal agencies place orders directly with a Schedule contractor through the issuance of delivery orders or task orders, and deliveries are made directly to the ordering agency. Schedule contracts have a base period of five years, with three five-year option periods.

As of September 30, 2017, there were more than 14,000 Schedule contracts under the GSA's procurement program that generated nearly $32 billion in sales.[22] For fiscal year 2017, the top GSA Schedule in terms of sales was the Information Technology (IT) Schedule 70, with approximately $15 billion in sales to 5,142 companies.[23] Other top GSA Schedules include the Professional Services Schedule (PSS) Schedule 00CORP (approximately $9 billion in sales), Security Schedule 84 (approximately $1 billion in sales), Furniture Schedule 71 (approximately $800 million in sales), and Scientific Equipment and Services Schedule 66 (approximately $600 million in sales).[24]

---

[21] *See* FAR Subpart 8.4, "Federal Supply Schedules"; FAR Part 38, "Federal Supply Schedule Contracting"; and 41 U.S.C. § 259(b)(3)(A). Although the GSA awards most FSS contracts, it may authorize other agencies to award Schedule contracts and publish schedules. FAR 38.101(d). For example, the Department of Veterans Affairs awards schedule contracts for certain medical and nonperishable subsistence items via the VA Federal Supply Schedule Service. *See* https://www.fss.va.gov/.

[22] https://www.gsaig.gov/sites/default/files/semiannual-reports/GSA-OIG-SAR-11-2017.pdf.

[23] http://gsa.federalschedules.com/resources/gsa-schedule-sales-fiscal-year-2017/.

[24] *See id.*

1. Principal Risks of General Services Administration Schedule Contracts

The principal types of risks presented by Schedule contracts relate to the pre-award disclosures of pricing and discount practices, which present the risk of potential liability for pre-award defective pricing and noncompliance with the ongoing pricing and disclosure requirements imposed under the "Price Reductions" clause during the performance period. Although Schedule contracts purport to be modeled on commercial buying practices, in fact, they contain a number of requirements and clauses that are inconsistent with commercial practices and unique to the government. In the context of a merger or acquisition, the pricing and discount obligations undertaken by a Target in its Schedule contracts will require careful review. On a going-forward basis, and absent any changes to the Target's accounting system, the Acquirer will need to implement controls to ensure adherence to the Target's disclosed commercial pricing and discount practices, based on its published commercial price lists and standard commercial pricing practices. Problems may arise based on discounts to commercial customers generally and specifically to customers identified as the Target's "most favored customer" or customer(s) and used as the basis for award. During the performance period, the Target's commercial pricing and discount practices could present risk of potential liability under the "Price Reductions" clause.

a. Pre-Award Pricing Disclosures to the General Services Administration and Defective Pricing Risk

GSA Schedule contracts are negotiated by the government with the intent of achieving the contractor's "most favored customer" pricing and discounts under similar terms and conditions.[25] As part of its offer, a prospective Schedule contractor must provide detailed information about its commercial sales, pricing, discounts, concessions, and other data related to the products and services offered to enable the government to determine whether the prices offered are fair and reasonable.[26] This information is provided on a standard GSA form CSP-1, known as the "Commercial Sales Practices Format."[27] The contractor must aver on the CSP form that the information provided is current, accurate, and complete, and is responsible for updating the information as necessary prior to contract award.[28]

The GSA utilizes the commercial pricing information and data provided by the offeror to establish its negotiation objectives and to determine price reasonableness. The GSA compares the terms and conditions of the solicitation with the terms and conditions of the offeror's commercial customer contracts. The GSA will also consider other distinguishing factors, including, but not limited to, aggregate volume of anticipated

25 *See* https://www.gsa.gov/acquisition/purchasing-programs/gsa-schedules/gsa-schedules-frequently-asked-questions.

26 *See* GSA Acquisition Manual ("GSAM") 515.408.

27 *Id.*

28 *Id.*

purchases, pattern of historic purchases and prices, guaranteed quantity commitment, value-added services provided by the commercial customers, length of the contact period, ordering and delivery practices, as well as any combination of discounts and concessions offered to commercial customers.[29] The GSA further reserves the right to consider "[a]ny other relevant information," including differences between the solicitation and commercial terms and conditions that "may warrant differentials between the offer and the discounts offered to the most favored commercial customer(s)."[30] The GSA therefore recognizes that the terms and conditions of commercial sales may vary and that there could be legitimate reasons why it may not be entitled to the best price.[31] The GSA may award a contract containing pricing that is less favorable than the best or actual lowest price the contractor extends to any commercial customer for similar purchases, if it determines that (a) the prices offered to the government are fair and reasonable, even though comparable discounts were not negotiated; and (b) award is otherwise in the best interests of the government.[32] The documentation submitted by the offeror will be critical to the GSA's determination.

Defective pricing occurs when a contractor neither submits nor discloses to the government cost or pricing data that is current, accurate, and complete. If the contractor's certified data (CSP form) is later determined to be "defective," the government is entitled to a price adjustment to the extent that the price was increased because of the defective data.[33] If the contractor intentionally provided inaccurate information or failed to disclose necessary information, the contractor may be subject to civil or even criminal penalties and damages under the False Claims statutes, potential civil and criminal liability under federal fraud statutes, and potential administrative sanctions, such as suspension or debarment.

b. The Price Reductions Clause

The GSA 552.238-75 Price Reductions clause imposes ongoing disclosure, pricing, and discount obligations during the contract performance period. Essentially, it operates as an ongoing most-favored customer pricing provision. Prior to contract award, the GSA and the contractor will agree on the customer or category of customers which will be the Basis of Award (BOA) and the GSA's price or discount relationship to the identified customer(s). The Price Reductions clause requires that this relationship be maintained throughout the contract period. Any change to the contractor's commercial pricing or discount arrangement applicable to the identified BOA customer(s), which alters the negotiated pricing/discount relationship, constitutes a price reduction, which the contractor must report promptly and offer to the government.[34]

---

29 *See* GSAM 538.270(c).

30 *Id.*

31 *Id.*

32 GSAM 538.270(d).

33 *See* GSAR 552.215-72.

34 *See also* GSAM 538.272 (MAS Price Reductions).

Price reduction liability can be triggered where, during the term of the contract, a contractor fails to disclose price reductions to the government, including any discounts, rebates, special promotions, or other special pricing arrangements. Failure to report such price reductions to the contracting officer constitutes a violation of the Price Reductions clause.

To comply with the obligations imposed by the Price Reductions clause, a contractor must have an accounting and tracking system (along with pricing policies) in place that can monitor sales to the commercial customer or category of customers upon which award is based, and more generally to other commercial customers, to ensure that the government continues to receive the negotiated prices and discounts. In the context of a merger or acquisition, the Acquirer will need to evaluate the Target's internal accounting and tracking system and procedures for monitoring commercial and government sales to ensure compliance with its obligations under the Price Reductions clause. Lax tracking systems and internal controls over commercial pricing are red flags for potential defective pricing and price reductions liability.

GSA Schedule contracts have long been a focus of government enforcement activity, ranging from defective pricing claims to civil false claims, civil and criminal fraud claims, and potential suspension and debarment. Accordingly, a diligence team reviewing any Target that conducts a significant volume of Schedule business should focus on pricing and discount practices, and disclosure and reporting requirements, including the IT and accounting systems that provide the data to support these requirements. If there are any indications of defective pricing or price reductions, the diligence team should consider whether a disclosure to the GSA would be prudent, or whether a mandatory disclosure to the GSA OIG under FAR 52.203-13(b) may be required.

c. Industrial Funding Fee and Sales Reporting Clause

Schedule contracts also include an "Industrial Funding Fee and Sales Reporting" clause.[35] The clause requires contractors to report all contract sales to the GSA on a quarterly basis and to pay a fee known as the Industrial Funding Fee (IFF). The IFF represents a percentage of the total quarterly sales reported and is set at the discretion of the GSA. Failure to remit the IFF after the end of the applicable reporting period constitutes a contract debt to the government, subject to the government's rights under the Debt Collection Improvement Act of 1996, including withholding or setting off payments and interest on the debt.[36] A contractor's failure to submit the required sales reports, to submit accurate reports, or to timely pay the IFF, may provide a basis for the government to terminate the Schedule contract for cause.[37] Similar to the pricing of Schedule contracts, a contractor's compliance with the sales reporting and IFF requirements of Schedule contracts is tied to the ability of its systems to accurately track and report FSS sales.

---

[35] *See* GSAM 552.238-74, "Industrial Funding Fee and Sales Reporting" (July 2003). According to the clause, "[t]he IFF reimburses [the General Services Administration's Federal Supply Service] for the costs of operating the Federal Supply Schedule Program" and "recoups its operating costs from ordering activities." Offerors must include the IFF in their prices. The fee is included in the award price(s) and reflected in the total amount charged to ordering activities. Most recently, the IFF was 0.75 percent of sales. *See* https://72a.gsa.gov/iffrates.cfm.

[36] GSAM 552.238-74(d).

[37] *Id.*

d. General Services Administration Office of Inspector General Audits

The GSA Office of Inspector General (OIG) provides oversight of GSA operations and programs, including GSA's contracts. The OIG has three primary offices that perform oversight functions: the Offices of Audits, Inspections and Forensic Auditing, and Investigations.[38] The Office of Audits is generally responsible for conducting routine audits of GSA Schedule proposals and contracts.

The GSA retains broad audit rights relating to Schedule contracts. The GSA may perform pre-award audits before initial awards or extensions of the contract to provide GSA contracting officials with information to use when negotiating fair and reasonable GSA contract prices. The review generally covers the contractor's historical data, commercial price lists, and information on prices and discounts offered to commercial customers and to the government.

In addition, the GSA OIG performs post-award audits that examine GSA contractors' compliance with contract terms and conditions. A post-award audit by the GSA OIG may encompass both pre-award pricing and discount disclosures made to the GSA, as well as post-award compliance with Price Reductions and IFF requirements. Contracting officers typically use the audit report findings to recover money through contract price adjustments or to reopen contract negotiations. The government has the right to audit the contractor's compliance with its disclosure requirements for up to two years after contract award. Additionally, the government has the right to audit a Schedule contractor's compliance with contract requirements, including the Price Reductions clause, for three years after final payment under the contract.

The OIG typically audits forty to fifty contracts each year.[39] The OIG develops a contract audit plan on an annual basis after receiving input from and collaborating with both GSA and OIG management officials. Some factors that the OIG considers while developing the contract audit plan include the dollar value of annual sales for each Schedule contract, contract audit requests from GSA officials, recent OIG reviews of Schedule contracts, and GSA industrial operations analyst reports. The OIG typically seeks to audit a mix of contracts that offer products and services throughout the Schedule. Post-award audits tend to be performed after a problem has been identified in a contract, and may also be initiated in advance of a contract extension based on pre-award audit findings, at the request of a contracting officer, and to assist in False Claims Act investigations.[40]

Common issues found by the OIG auditors include instances where the contractor:

- Did not submit current, accurate, and complete information.
- Did not maintain sales monitoring and billing systems that ensure proper administration of the price reduction and billing provisions of their MAS contract.

---

[38] *See* https://www.gsaig.gov/content/about-oig.

[39] Between 2014 and 2017, the OIG issued 237 contract audit reports. See https://www.gsaig.gov/sites/default/files/misc-reports/ABA%20Article%20-%20GSA%20OIG.pdf.

[40] *See* https://www.gsaig.gov/sites/default/files/misc-reports/ABA%20Article%20-%20GSA%20OIG.pdf.

- Did not adequately accumulate and report Schedule sales for IFF payment purposes or correctly calculate and submit either IFF payments.
- Overcharged or overbilled the GSA's federal government customers.
- Did not comply with price reduction provisions.
- Did not comply with the Buy American Act or Trade Agreement Act.
- Assigned employees who were unqualified for the labor categories properly billable under GSA Schedule task orders.
- Did not adequately segregate and accumulate labor hours, material costs, and other direct costs on time and material task orders.[41]

An investigation by the GSA OIG may result in a referral to the DOJ for criminal prosecution or civil action and to agency suspension and debarment officials for administrative action.

Any audits conducted by the GSA OIG (or standard GSA report cards) should therefore be scrutinized carefully during the due diligence review for potential issues or deficiencies in the areas of pricing, discounting, reporting, recordkeeping, or sales tracking.

2. Transferring the General Services Administration Schedule Contract to the Acquiring Company

There are unique concerns with the process of transferring a GSA Schedule contract to the acquiring company.

First, and as discussed in detail in chapter XI, the regulatory requirements of FAR Subpart 42.12 on contract novation apply to GSA Schedule contracts and task and delivery orders issued under the Schedule. The transaction documents or schedules should include GSA Schedule contracts, Blanket Purchase Agreements, and outstanding task and delivery orders on the list of contracts to be transferred. In addition to working through the administrative contracting officers as directed by the FAR, the Target should contact both the GSA contracting officer for the specific GSA Schedule contract(s) regarding any GSA-specific novation requirements and the agency contracting officer(s) issuing any task or delivery orders under the Schedule contract regarding any agency-specific requirements.

When both the acquiring company and the target have GSA Schedule contracts, the Modification Clause, 552.243-72, can be used to add or delete products, change payment information, and make other administrative changes. This clause provides common information that is required to be submitted to the GSA when requesting to add products or services to the contract, add Special Item Numbers to the contract, delete products or services from the contract, increase or decrease pricing, and trigger price reductions requirements. The clause also discusses updating the contract electronic files and pricelists after a modification has been implemented. Each GSA Schedule has specific modification instructions and document requirements that a company should consult and discuss with the contracting officer prior to submitting any modification request.[42]

---

[41] *See Id.*

[42] *See* https://vsc.gsa.gov/administration/modOptions.cfm.

In addition, there may be instances where both the target and acquiring company have the same multiple-award schedule contract (i.e., IT Schedule 70). The acquiring company should consult with the GSA as to recommended next steps. The GSA has previously articulated that contractors that have more than one Schedule contract as a result of a merger should select one contract to continue and allow the other to expire or be cancelled.

✓ **Best Practice Tips:** The due diligence team should evaluate the answers to the following questions:

- Which agencies, or other prime contractors, have issued task orders to the Target under the Target's GSA Schedule contracts?
- Does the Target have adequate documentation to support its pre-award CSP disclosures?
- Does the Target have standard written commercial pricing and discount policies in place supporting its proposed Schedule prices?
- What systems does the Target have in place for compiling commercial sales data, including historical data, commercial price lists, discount policies, and other information on the prices and discounts that the company offers to its commercial customers?
- How are pricing and discount practices to both commercial and government customers administered and monitored within the company?
- What training is provided to contract and sales employees of the Target who are involved with award and administration of Schedule contracts and sales to commercial customers?
- For service Schedule contracts, does the Target have a system in place to ensure that the labor provided meets the contract-stipulated minimum education, experience, and other qualifications?
- Are the Target's accounting systems adequate to track and report FSS sales, IFF payments, and commercial sales more generally?

CHAPTER 5

Claims, Disputes, and Bid Protests

OUTLINE

A. Contractor Claims Against the Government
  1. Requests for Equitable Adjustment
  2. Claims
  3. Risks of Requests for Equitable Adjustment and Claims
B. Government Claims Against the Contractor
  1. Claims under the Contracts Disputes Act
  2. The False Claims Act
    a. False Claims Act—Overview
    b. Government Investigations
    c. Mandatory Disclosures
  3. Criminal Matters
    a. Criminal False Claims Act
    b. False Statements Act
    c. Mail and Wire Fraud
    d. Bribery
    e. Kickbacks
    f. Procurement Integrity Act
C. Labor and Employment Obligations
  1. Service Contract Act
  2. Equal Employment Opportunity
D. Disputes Arising Out of Subcontracts
E. Bid Protests

Although most government contracts are performed and paid for in satisfactory fashion, it is not uncommon for disputes to arise between a contractor and the government. Disputes may involve routine contract administration matters concerning a contractor's request for schedule relief or payment for performing extra work. Disputes may also involve a contractor's noncompliance with material contract terms or allegations of fraud or misconduct by the contractor or its employees. Such matters can result in administrative, civil, or even criminal penalties against a contractor. This chapter covers common types of claims and disputes that can arise under government contracts, and which should be identified and evaluated in any acquisition involving a government contractor.

A. Contractor Claims Against the Government

1. Requests for Equitable Adjustment

A Request for Equitable Adjustment (REA) is an informal way for a contractor to assert a claim for relief under a government contract. Although not required to submit an REA, some FAR clauses specifically contemplate an equitable adjustment under certain circumstances, such as when the government makes changes to the contract[1] or the contractor encounters a differing site condition.[2] REAs can seek various forms of relief from the government, but in most cases the contractor seeks additional compensation.

Most REAs are resolved through negotiations with the contracting officer. Where the negotiation is unsuccessful, the contractor's next step is to submit a formal claim.

2. Claims

Contractor claims against the government are governed by the Contracts Disputes Act (CDA).[3] The disputes process begins with the presentation of a claim by the contractor to the contracting officer. Although the CDA contains no definition of a "claim," it does require that the claim be (a) in writing, (b) submitted to the contracting officer, and (c) certified if it exceeds $100,000.[4] The "Disputes" clause defines a claim as "a written demand or written assertion by one of the contracting parties seeking, as a matter of right, the payment of money in a sum certain, the adjustment or interpretation of contract terms, or other relief arising under or relating to this contract."[5] Claims must be submitted within six years after the accrual of the claim.[6]

For claims of more than $100,000, the contractor must certify that the claim is made in good faith, the supporting data are accurate and complete to the best of the contractor's knowledge and belief, and the amount requested accurately reflects the contract

---

1 FAR 52.243-1.

2 FAR 52.236-2.

3 41 U.S.C. §§ 7101–7109. As discussed below, the CDA also governs government claims against the contractor.

4 *Id.* § 7103(a)(1), (a)(3), (b).

5 FAR 52.233-1(c).

6 41 U.S.C. § 7103(a)(4)(A).

adjustment for which the contractor believes the government is liable.[7] The certification must be executed by an individual authorized to bind the contractor with respect to the claim.[8] A contractor claim begins to accrue interest at the US Treasury rate from the date it is submitted to the contracting officer.[9]

If the contracting officer and contractor are unable to resolve their dispute through a negotiated settlement, the contracting officer must issue a "final decision" on the contractor's claim.[10] If the claim exceeds $100,000, the contracting officer must issue a final decision within sixty days of receiving the claim or notify the contractor of the time within which a decision will be issued.[11] If the contracting officer fails to act within the specified period or a reasonable time thereafter, the contractor can treat the undue delay as a "deemed denial" of its claim and pursue an appeal or suit on the claim.[12]

The contractor has a choice of forum for challenging a contracting officer's final decision. Within ninety days of receipt of the final decision, the contractor can file a notice of appeal with the relevant board of contract appeals—that is, the Armed Services Board of Contract Appeals or the Civilian Board of Contract Appeals.[13] Alternatively, the contractor can file suit in the US Court of Federal Claims within one year of receiving the final decision.[14]

The Boards and the Court review the claim on a *de novo* basis.[15] A decision by a Board or the Court may be appealed to the US Court of Appeals for the Federal Circuit, which applies established appellate review standards.[16]

It is common for the contracting parties to elect to resolve a contract dispute through alternative dispute resolution techniques before or after the initiation of a claim.

3. Risks of Requests for Equitable Adjustment and Claims

In addition to the risk that a contractor will not recover the full amount claimed, there are other risks associated with REAs and claims. Under the CDA, if a contractor is unable to support any part of its claim because of a misrepresentation of fact or fraud by the contractor, then the contractor is liable to the government for an amount equal to the unsupported part of the claim plus all of the federal government's costs attributable to reviewing the unsupported part of the claim.[17] Further, under the Forfeiture

---

[7] *Id.* § 7103(b)(1).

[8] *Id.* § 7103(b)(2).

[9] *Id.* § 7109.

[10] *Id.* § 7103(a)(3), (g).

[11] *Id.* § 7103(f)(2).

[12] FAR 33.211(g).

[13] 41 U.S.C. § 7104(a).

[14] *Id.* §§ 7104(b), 7105.

[15] *Id.* § 7104(b)(4).

[16] *Id.* § 7107.

[17] *Id.* § 7103(c)(2); *see also* Daewoo Eng'g and Constr. Co., Ltd. v. United States, 557 F.3d 1332 (Fed. Cir. 2009) (contractor liable for penalty of more than $50 million because that portion of its claim was unsupported and submitted only as a negotiation tactic).

of Fraudulent Claims Act, a contractor that commits fraud in connection with a claim against the government forfeits the claim.[18] From a diligence perspective, it is important to understand if the Target has submitted REAs or claims, particularly in circumstances where the situation that required the REA or claim might recur after acquisition.

B. Government Claims Against the Contractor

1. Claims under the Contracts Disputes Act

The government can submit contract claims against a contractor as well. Such claims are also governed by the CDA.[19] The definition of a government "claim" is the same as a contractor claim.[20] The same six-year statute of limitations applies to government claims.[21] Unlike contractors, the government is not required to certify its claims.

The interest-entitlement provisions of the CDA do not apply to government claims, but the government obtains interest on its claims by making a demand for payment.[22] If payment is not made within thirty days, interest begins to run at the Treasury rate.[23]

2. The False Claims Act

Potential liability under the civil False Claims Act (FCA)[24] poses perhaps the greatest risk of acquiring a government contractor. The FCA has become the government's primary tool against fraud in connection with government contracts, and the financial consequences of an FCA matter can be staggering. Government investigations of FCA and similar matters also present unique challenges during due diligence.

a. False Claims Act—Overview

The FCA imposes civil liability on a person that "knowingly presents, or causes to be presented, a false or fraudulent claim for payment or approval[.]"[25] Similarly, the FCA imposes liability where a person "knowingly makes, uses or causes to be made or used, a false record or statement material to a false or fraudulent claim[.]"[26]

For purposes of the FCA, a person acts "knowingly" if he or she has actual knowledge of the information, acts in deliberate ignorance of the truth or falsity of the information,

---

18 28 U.S.C. § 2514; *see also* Long Island Savings Bank, FSB v. United States, 503 F.3d 1234 (Fed. Cir. 2007) (overturning $435 million award to bank for breach of contract because the bank had obtained the contracts through false statements).

19 41 U.S.C. § 7103(a)(3).

20 FAR 52.233-1(c).

21 41 U.S.C. § 7103(a)(1)(A).

22 FAR 32.604.

23 FAR 32.604(b)(4)(ii).

24 31 U.S.C. §§ 3729-33.

25 *Id.* § 3729(a)(1)(A).

26 *Id.* § 3729(a)(1)(B).

or acts in reckless disregard of the truth or falsity of the information.[27] Proof of specific intent to defraud is not required, as reckless disregard can provide the necessary intent.[28] The reckless disregard standard has been interpreted to be "an extension of gross negligence."[29] Although the conduct must rise above the level of "mere negligence," the FCA "is intended not to permit artful defense counsel to require some form of intent as an essential ingredient of proof."[30] For example, courts have held that the failure to make a minimal review of records before submitting a claim to the government can constitute deliberate ignorance or reckless disregard.[31]

The FCA imposes liability even where a company does not directly submit a claim to the government. A company may be liable for causing a false claim to be presented or made.[32] Thus, a subcontractor can be liable under the FCA for submitting false invoices or reports to its prime contractor, which relies upon that information in submitting a claim for payment to the government, because the subcontractor *caused* the prime to submit a false claim. FCA liability can also be found under the theory of "*implied certification*." This theory holds that when a contractor submits a claim for payment, it is impliedly certifying that it is complying with relevant regulatory and contractual provisions. Therefore, the claim for payment can be actionably "false" even if the claim is itself accurate and no one made explicit certifications concerning compliance with the rules at issue.[33]

To create liability under the FCA, the false record or statement must be "material" to the false or fraudulent claim.[34] "Material" means "having a natural tendency to influence, or be capable of influencing, the payment or receipt of money or property."[35]

Liability under the FCA carries serious consequences. The FCA imposes treble damages for violations, plus penalties for each claim submitted.[36] In 2017 alone, the DOJ recovered more than $3.7 billion in FCA cases. Additionally, a private whistleblower may bring a civil suit under the FCA "in the name of the Government."[37] Known as "*qui tam* relator," the whistleblower can receive a percentage of the government's recovery plus his or her attorney's fees if the case results in a settlement or judgment against

---

27 *Id.* § 3729(b).

28 *Id.*

29 United States v. Krizek, 111 F.3d 934, 941 (D.C. Cir. 1997).

30 132 Cong. Rec. H9382-03.

31 *See, e.g.*, *Krizek*, 111 F.3d 934; UMC Elecs. Co. v. United States, 43 Fed. Cl. 776 (1999).

32 31 U.S.C. § 3729(a)(1)(A).

33 *See* Universal Health Servs., Inc. v. United States, 136 S. Ct. 1989, 2001 (2016) (holding that implied certification is a valid theory of liability under the FCA, "at least where two conditions are satisfied: first, the claim does not merely request payment, but also makes specific representations about the goods or services provided; and second, the defendant's failure to disclose noncompliance with material statutory, regulatory, or contractual requirements makes those representations misleading half-truths").

34 31 U.S.C. § 3729(a)(1)(B).

35 *Id.* § 3729(b)(4).

36 *Id.* § 3729(a); 28 C.F.R. § 85.3(a)(9).

37 31 U.S.C. § 3731(b).

the defendant.[38] More than 70 percent of FCA cases generating recoveries of damages are brought by whistleblowers. Facing such severe penalties, some contractors find it cheaper and safer to settle unmeritorious claims rather than risk a court finding that the contractor, or some combination of employees, committed fraud.

The FCA covers a broad range of misconduct, including but not limited to submission of claims for work not performed; misrepresentations of quality of goods produced; false, fraudulent or defective pricing; and falsified reports of testing or inspections performed.[39] All government contractors are subject to the FCA.

During the due diligence review, identification of any actual or threatened FCA actions involving the Target, or investigations or matters that could lead to FCA actions by the government, is critical to assessing the Acquirer's potential legal and financial exposure. The statute of limitations applicable to actions under the FCA is six years from the date of the violation, or three years from the date when facts material to the right of action are known, or reasonably should have been known, by the government official "charged with responsibility to act" in the circumstances, but in no event more than ten years after the violation was committed, whichever is later.[40] Because of the statute of limitations considerations, and the fact that potential FCA liability can survive years beyond the date of an acquisition, it is important to address the Target's potential FCA liability during the due diligence review.

b. Government Investigations

Most FCA actions are initially filed under seal so the government has an opportunity to investigate the allegations of fraud. Thus, a government contractor may be the subject of an FCA matter and not even know it. During the investigation, the government may take a number of steps to gather facts concerning the alleged misconduct, such as conferring with knowledgeable government personnel, issuing subpoenas and Civil Investigative Demands, and interviewing current and former contractor employees.

Government investigations of FCA matters or other alleged misconduct can have profound effects on a company. The mere initiation of an investigation can disrupt operations, discourage morale, and in some cases, trigger reporting obligations. If those investigations become public, the effects can be even more serious. Customers can question the integrity of the company, investors can dump shares or challenge management, and lenders can tighten credit. For government contractors, the exposure can multiply quickly. Government agencies often consider suspension or debarment based solely on the allegations in a complaint.

With the stakes so high, it is essential that the Acquirer closely scrutinize all known investigations involving the Target during due diligence to assess potential business and legal risk to the Target.

---

38 *Id.* § 3731(d).

39 In United States v. Neifert-White, 390 U.S. 228, 232 (1968), the U.S. Supreme Court stated that the FCA "was intended to reach all types of fraud, without qualification, that might result in financial loss to the Government."

40 31 U.S.C. § 3731(b).

c. Mandatory Disclosures

The Mandatory Disclosure Rule requires government contractors to establish a written code of business ethics and conduct and a business ethics awareness and compliance program and internal control system. The Rule is implemented through the clause at FAR 52.203-13, which must be inserted in all solicitations and contracts if the value of the contract is expected to exceed $5,000,000 and the performance period is 120 days or more.[41] The clause requires contractors' internal control systems to include certain mandatory elements, among them periodic reviews of company business practices and an internal reporting mechanism such as a hotline.[42]

One of the mandatory elements is that the internal control system provide for timely disclosure to the agency Office of the Inspector General (OIG), with a copy to the contracting officer, whenever the contractor possesses "credible evidence" of a violation of federal criminal law involving fraud, conflict of interest, bribery, or gratuity violations, or a violation of the civil FCA in connection with the performance of a government contract.[43] The relevant standard that triggers a contractor's obligation to report suspected violations under the Mandatory Disclosure Rule is "credible evidence." After initially using the phrase "reasonable grounds to believe" in the proposed rule, the standard was changed to "credible evidence" in the final rule to prevent overreporting.[44] The "credible evidence" standard is intended to reflect "a higher standard, implying that the contractor will have the opportunity to take some time for preliminary examination of the evidence to determine its credibility before deciding to disclose to the Government."[45]

Separate from the contractual requirement embodied in the clause at FAR 52.203-13, one of the causes for debarment or suspension is the knowing failure to make a required disclosure to the agency OIG under the Mandatory Disclosure Rule.[46] Thus, even if FAR 52.203-13 is not included in any of a contractor's government contracts, the contractor can still be suspended or debarred for failing to make a required disclosure.[47] The "look back" period is limited to three years after contract closeout.[48] As a result, contractors cannot be suspended or debarred for failing to disclose violations that occurred more than three years after closeout. It is common that government contracts are not formally closed until several years after performance ends, however, so the "look back" period often extends more than three years after contract performance is complete.

---

41 FAR 3.1004(a).

42 FAR 52.203-13(c)(2)(ii).

43 FAR 52.203-13(c)(2)(ii)(F); FAR 52.203-13(b)(3)(i).

44 73 Fed. Reg. 67073 (Nov. 12, 2008).

45 *Id.*

46 FAR 9.406-2(b)(1)(vi); FAR 9.407-2(a)(8).

47 FAR 3.1003(b) ("Whether or not the clause at 52.203–13 is applicable, a contractor may be suspended and/or debarred for knowing failure by a principal to timely disclose to the Government . . .").

48 FAR 9.406-2(b)(1)(vi); FAR 9.407-2(a)(8).

3. Criminal Matters

For each of the criminal matters that follow, a diligence review should ask about existing matters, test applicable policies and procedures, and determine general compliance.

a. Criminal False Claims Act

The criminal False Claims Act makes liable "whoever" presents any claim upon the United States "knowing such claim to be false, fictitious or fraudulent."[49] The criminal False Claims Act applies to any false claim submitted to the government and imposes both a fine and imprisonment for all convictions.

As with the civil False Claims Act, a "claim" comprises a request or demand for money or property, but there are significant differences between the two statutes: a party violating the criminal False Claims Act faces a jail sentence of up to five years; the government must prove a violation of the criminal False Claims Act beyond a reasonable doubt; only the DOJ may bring an action under the criminal False Claims Act, while *qui tam* actions may be brought under the civil False Claims Act; and the criminal statute imposes potentially staggering fines.

Any claim ultimately passed on to the government or reimbursed by the government may be subject to criminal prosecution; a contractor may be found guilty under the criminal False Claims Act by causing an intermediary like a subcontractor to submit a false claim.[50] Charges under the criminal statute may be brought in conjunction with the civil False Claims Act as well as the False Statements Act, discussed next.

b. False Statements Act

The False Statements Act prohibits the knowing and willful making of a false statement to the United States or any department or agency thereof.[51] Although Title 18 also contains more specific false statement statutes, prosecutors use section 1001 most often, because they can enforce it either alone or in tandem with more specific statutes such as the criminal False Claims Act.[52] During the past decade, the government prosecuted a wide variety of crimes under section 1001.

To illustrate: under the False Statements Act, a contractor was found liable on account of his reckless indifference for failure to read a form signed in connection with a certificate prepared for a bid on a government project.[53] Government contractors have also been found liable for submitting false invoices.[54] Causing another person to make a false statement also subjects a party to prosecution.[55] The government need not rely

---

49 18 U.S.C. § 287.

50 *See* United States v. Gumbs, 283 F.3d 128 (3rd Cir. 2002).

51 18 U.S.C. § 1001.

52 *See, e.g.*, United States v. Dedman, 527 F.3d 577, 603 (6th Cir. 2008) (in which defendant was indicted under both 18 U.S.C. §§ 286 and 1001). *See also* Halverson and Olson, *False Statements and False Claims*, 46 AM. CRIM. L. REV. 557.

53 *See* United States v. Puente, 982 F.2d 156, 159 (5th Cir. 1993).

54 *See* United States v. Brack, 747 F.2d 1142 (7th Cir. 1984).

55 *See* United States v. Kiefer, 799 F.2d 1115 (6th Cir. 1980).

specifically on the false statement in acting; the alleged activity must merely influence government action.[56]

c. Mail and Wire Fraud

The federal criminal statutes covering mail fraud and wire fraud prohibit the use of the mail or interstate (or foreign) telecommunications systems to further "a scheme to defraud."[57] These broadly worded statutes basically make illegal any activity that is covered by the false claims or false statements criminal statutes discussed above and involves the use of the mails (including email), telephone, telegraph, or the like.

d. Bribery

It is a criminal offense to directly or indirectly give, offer, or promise anything of value to any public official with the intent to (a) influence any official act, (b) influence the public official to commit or collude in any fraud, or (c) induce a public official to commit any act in violation of his or her lawful duty.[58]

e. Kickbacks

A "kickback" is defined as "any money, fee, commission, credit, gift, gratuity, thing of value, or compensation of any kind that is provided to a prime contractor, prime contractor employee, subcontractor, or subcontractor employee to improperly obtain or reward favorable treatment in connection with a prime contract or a subcontract relating to a prime contract."[59]

It is unlawful for any person to (a) provide, attempt to provide, or offer to provide a kickback, (b) solicit, accept, or attempt to accept a kickback, or (c) include the amount of a kickback in the contract price a subcontractor charges a prime contractor or a higher-tier subcontractor, or a prime contractor charges the federal government.[60]

f. Procurement Integrity Act

The Procurement Integrity Act (PIA) promotes fair competition by prohibiting government officials from disclosing and contractors from knowingly obtaining "contractor bid or proposal information or source selection information before the award of a Federal agency procurement contract to which the information relates."[61]

A contractor that violates the PIA or the implementing FAR prohibitions faces severe consequences. Where the contractor obtained bid or source selection information for the purpose of gaining a competitive advantage or something else of value, it may be

---

56 *See* United States v. Parsons, 967 F.2d 452 (10th Cir. 1992).

57 *See* 18 U.S.C. §§ 1341, 1343.

58 *Id.* § 201.

59 41 U.S.C. § 8701(2).

60 *Id.* § 8702.

61 41 U.S.C. § 423(a) and (b); *see also* FAR 3.104-3(a) and (b).

subject to criminal penalties.[62] Any violation may subject a contractor to civil penalties.[63] Depending on where the parties are in the procurement process, a contractor found to have violated procurement integrity requirements may be disqualified from bidding, its proposal may be rejected, an award to it may be cancelled or, if there is already a contract, that contract may be rescinded or voided, and the government may recoup all payments made to the contractor.[64]

C. Labor and Employment Obligations

Several labor and employment requirements apply to government contractors. During the due diligence review, the Acquirer should determine whether (a) the Target has appropriate policies and procedures in place to facilitate compliance with applicable labor and employment law requirements, and (b) the Target has actual or potential exposure—legal, financial, contractual, or administrative—for noncompliance with applicable labor and employment requirements. The two most common types of labor and employment issues encountered by government contractors are discussed below.

1. Service Contract Act

The Service Contract Act of 1965[65] ("SCA") and its implementing regulations provide wage and safety protection to contractor employees working under government contracts for services.[66] The SCA governs employment practices of service contractors and, in particular, the minimum wages and fringe benefits that they must pay to employees under government contracts. The SCA is also applicable to subcontracts awarded under prime government contracts.

The SCA requires that service contractor and subcontractor employees be paid not less than the "prevailing" wage rates and fringe benefits paid to private and public

---

62 41 U.S.C. § 423(e)(1).

63 *Id.* § 423(e)(2).

64 *Id.* § 423(c)(4), (d)(4), (e)(3); FAR 3.104-7.

65 In addition to the Service Contract Act discussed in this section, the Target's business may implicate the following statutes: The Walsh-Healey Public Contracts Act, which applies to federal contracts exceeding $10,000 for the manufacture or furnishing of materials, supplies, articles, or equipment, and establishes a minimum wage, maximum hours, and safety and health standards for work on such contracts. The Davis Bacon Act requires each federal contract over $2,000 for the construction, alteration, or repair of public buildings or public works to include a clause setting forth the minimum wages to be paid to various classes of laborers and mechanics employed under the contract.

66 41 U.S.C. § 351, *et seq.* The Department of Labor has issued regulations implementing the SCA, which are set forth in 29 C.F.R. Parts 4, 6 and 8, and Section 1925. Additionally, for government contractors, there are additional regulations implementing the SCA, which are set forth in FAR Subpart 22.10. FAR 22.1002-1 provides that "[s]ervice contracts over $2,500 shall contain mandatory provisions regarding minimum wages and fringe benefits, safe and sanitary working conditions, notification to employees of the minimum allowable compensation, and equivalent Federal employee classifications and wage rates." The mandatory contract provision is set forth in FAR 52.222-41, "Service Contract Act of 1965 (Nov. 2007)."

sector employees engaged in similar work in the same locality, as determined by the US Department of Labor, Wage and Hour Division (DOL). Unlike the Fair Labor Standards Act, which mandates a nationwide minimum wage rate established by Congress, the SCA relies on DOL determinations of wage rates for specific job categories, consistent with prevailing market rates in the locality (state, region, city) where the contract is being performed or, where the work force is unionized, consistent with the rates in any applicable collective bargaining agreement. Wage determinations establish the minimum monetary wages and fringe benefits that a service contractor or subcontractor must pay covered service employees working under an SCA-covered contract. As noted above, there are two types of wage determinations under the SCA: (a) prevailing wage determinations published by the DOL,[67] and (b) wage determinations based on collective bargaining agreements.[68]

A contract is covered by the SCA if it exceeds a $2,500 threshold, is performed in the United States, and its "principal purpose" is to furnish services. There are statutory and administrative exemptions for certain types of contracts, such as construction, transportation services, and communications services.[69] However, the SCA is applicable to contracts with a supply or construction component as well, so long as the principal purpose of the contract is to furnish services. DOL is responsible for enforcement of the SCA and has the authority to conduct investigations, make findings related to alleged violations, and impose penalties for violations, including recovery of wage and fringe benefit underpayments through legal action or administrative withholding of contract payments, contract termination, and debarment.[70] From a diligence perspective, it is important to understand whether a Target understands the SCA's requirements and how it goes about categorizing its employees under the act.

2. Equal Employment Opportunity

Executive Order 11246, as amended, requires a government contractor meeting the threshold requirements to comply with nondiscrimination requirements and to develop and implement a written affirmative action program. Executive Order 11246 and the

67 FAR 22.1002-2.

68 FAR 22.1002-3.

69 FAR 22.1003.

70 FAR 52.222-41(k) provides that the contracting officer "shall withhold or cause to be withheld from the Government Prime Contractor under this or any other Government contract with the Prime Contractor such sums as an appropriate official of the Department of Labor requests or such sums as the Contracting Officer decides may be necessary to pay underpaid employees employed by the Contractor or subcontractor. In the event of failure to pay any employees subject to the Act all or part of the wages or fringe benefits due under the Act, the Contracting Officer may, after authorization or by direction of the Department of Labor and written notification to the Contractor, take action to cause suspension of any further payment or advance of funds until such violations have ceased. Additionally, any failure to comply with the requirements of this clause may be grounds for termination of the right to proceed with the contract work. In such event, the Government may enter into other contracts or arrangements for completion of the work, charging the Contractor in default with any additional cost."

implementing regulations issued by DOL and in the FAR[71] apply to nonconstruction (supply and service) contractors or subcontractors with fifty or more employees and (a) government contracts or subcontracts of $50,000 or more, or (b) government bills of lading that in a twelve-month period amount to $50,000 or more.[72]

Under Executive Order 11246 and the implementing regulations, covered contractors or subcontractors are required to refrain from discrimination and to engage in affirmative steps to ensure that applicants and employees receive equal employment opportunity regardless of race, color, religion, sex, or national origin. All aspects of the hiring and employment process are covered: employment; promotion and upgrading; demotion; transfer; recruitment or recruitment advertising; layoff or termination; rates of pay or other forms of compensation; and selection for training, including apprenticeship. In addition, Executive Order 11246 requires all covered contractors and subcontractors to include a mandatory equal opportunity clause in each of their nonexempt contracts and subcontracts, FAR 52.222-26, Equal Opportunity (MAR 2007).

Covered contractors and subcontractors are required to develop a written affirmative action program (AAP) for each of its establishments. In general, the AAP will describe the policies, practices, and procedures that the contractor or subcontractor uses to ensure that all qualified applicants and employees receive equal opportunities for employment and advancement. The regulations establish that an AAP must include an analysis of workforce composition; an analysis of all major job groups within the company, with identification of job groups where minorities or women are underutilized; and goals and timetables for correcting this underutilization. The regulations also set forth recommendations on how to develop or reaffirm a company's policy regarding equal employment opportunity, how to disseminate that policy and who in the company should be responsible for implementing it. The AAP must be updated annually.

A covered contractor's or subcontractor's compliance obligations with respect to equal opportunity and affirmative action also include annual reporting requirements. The Employment Information Report, known as Standard Form 100 (EEO-1), must be filed with the Equal Employment Opportunity Commission (EEOC) by September 30 of each year. The EEO-1 report includes employment data on all full-time and part-time employees by sex and race or ethnic category for each of the ten specified job categories and subcategories.

The Office of Federal Contract Compliance Programs (OFCCP) within DOL is charged with investigating violations of Executive Order 11246 through compliance evaluations or in response to complaints. If a violation is found, DOL can issue an order to the contractor or subcontractor to provide appropriate relief, which may include restoration of back pay and employment status and benefits for the victim(s) of discrimination. Depending on the circumstances, violations also may result in cancellation,

---

[71] *See* FAR Subpart 22.8, and regulations issued by DOL, which are set forth in 41 C.F.R. Parts 60-1, 60-2, 60-3, 60-20, and 60-50.

[72] *See* FAR 22.804-1. Certain contracts are exempt from all or part of the requirements of Executive Order 11246, such as national security contracts, transactions of $10,000 or less, and those for work performed outside the United States by employees who were not recruited in the United States. *See* FAR 22.804-1.

suspension, or termination of contracts; withholding of contract payments; debarment of the contractor or subcontractor; and other sanctions. From a diligence perspective, it is important to review AAP and EEO-1 documents to determine if the Target is in compliance with these requirements.

D. Disputes Arising Out of Subcontracts

Except in very unusual circumstances, claims brought by a party to a subcontract under a government prime contract are resolved outside of the prime government contracts disputes process.[73] If the subcontractor has a claim based on government action, the prime can agree to sponsor the subcontractor's claim and submit it to the contracting officer. In that instance, the claim is made in the name of the prime contractor, and the prime must certify the claim to obtain jurisdiction.[74] Recovery in this type of case is limited to the extent of the government's responsibility for the relief sought. Ordinarily, in exchange for this sponsorship, the prime insists that the subcontractor agree that its rights will be limited to the recovery obtained from the government. The prime should also insist on indemnification for any claims by the government due to an improper claim certification.

Except for sponsorship situations, disputes between prime contractors and subcontractors are typically handled like any other commercial suit. In many instances, the matter at issue between the prime and subcontractor involves conduct that was initiated by the government. In that case, the prime may file a separate claim under the CDA for recovery against the government at the same time that it is litigating against the subcontractor.

E. Bid Protests

A key issue in government contracts due diligence is evaluating the continuing viability and sustainability of the Target's government business. Government contracts have limited terms and are generally subject to ongoing competitive procurements. Following the expiration of contract base term and options, the contracts will be recompeted for and, win or lose for the Target, may be the subject of a bid protest at the Government Accountability Office (GAO) or the US Court of Federal Claims. Because of protective order requirements, the Acquirer's counsel may not be able to gain access to protest pleadings. To the extent possible, however, the Acquirer's counsel should request copies of any redacted filings related to protests. The objective is to assess the value of any ongoing contracts that may be lost, which could affect any assumed ongoing programs and any backlog identified in the Target's financial information and, ultimately, the value of the Target.

---

73 *See* United States v. Johnson Controls, Inc., 713 F.2d 1541 (Fed. Cir. 1983).

74 *See* United States v. Turner Constr. Co., 827 F.2d 1554, 1559–61 (Fed. Cir. 1987).

CHAPTER 6

Adequacy of The Target's Compliance Program

OUTLINE

A. Overall Company Compliance Program and Internal Controls
B. Present Responsibility
    1. Debarment and Suspension
    2. Past Performance on Competitive Procurements
        a. Types of Past Performance Records
        b. Past Performance as an Evaluation Factor and Indicator of Operational Concerns
        c. Past Performance Information of Predecessors and Affiliates
C. Existing Arrangements for Classified Contracts
    1. Assessing a Company's Existing Compliance Program
        a. Companies under Foreign Ownership, Control, or Influence
    2. Identification of Foreign Ownership, Control, or Influence and Security Issues Arising from the Acquisition
        a. Forms and Reports
        b. Deal Structure
    3. Integration of the Target into a Corporate Structure
D. Foreign Sales
E. Export Control Compliance

A. Overall Company Compliance Program and Internal Controls

Doing diligence on a Target's compliance program and internal controls is an important step in identifying historical risk areas, assessing the Target's compliance culture, and flagging post-closing integration issues.

Several factors impact the appropriate makeup of a Target's compliance program and internal controls. For instance, if the Target is a public company (or part of a public company), it must comply with the ethics, internal controls, and internal audit requirements under the Sarbanes-Oxley Act (and the compliance diligence should include a review of the Target's public filings to identify potential areas of concern). By contrast, if the Target is a privately held company, it may not need to comply with such requirements, but still will have compliance requirements imposed by its contracts and the FAR clauses incorporated into those contracts.

A Target's compliance program and internal controls will also likely reflect the age, size, and trajectory of the company. Young Targets with relatively few contracts or customers may have unsophisticated internal controls and compliance programs, particularly if the Target has limited legal resources or no internal counsel assigned to this task. Additionally, a Target that has quickly grown may not yet have a compliance program that matches the size and complexity of the expanding company and issues may still be dealt with in a reactive manner. Such an environment does not necessarily mean that there will be compliance issues; however, it means that satisfactory answers to due diligence questions may not come easily and that there may need to be a focus on post-closing compliance reviews.

Additionally, the content of the Target's compliance program may depend on the types of contracts involved in the business. For instance, a Target with primarily commercial-item, fixed-price contracts may not have the same need for a comprehensive compliance regime as would be expected for a contractor that is delivering customized solutions to the government under cost-reimbursement contracts. Indeed, the latter type of Target would likely need an advanced compliance system with the ability to manage accounting data and labor reporting practices. Additionally, a Target that holds controlled technical information, performs classified work, or maintains a facility security clearance will require unique and more detailed security procedures as compared to contractors that do not hold sensitive material and may be subject only to standard confidentiality clauses. Finally—although there are certainly a host of other criteria that can inform the makeup of a compliance system—a Target that performs work outside the United States should have adequate controls to ensure compliance with anti-corruption, anti-human trafficking, and export control laws, which are elements of a compliance system one would not expect to encounter on a purely US-focused Target.

Noting that the complexity and makeup of an appropriate compliance program may vary, in general, due diligence of a Target's compliance program should consider the following:

- Policies—Do policies exist that provide meaningful standards and guidance on compliance with regulatory requirements and standards for business conduct? What topics are included in the regulatory compliance and business conduct program? Are all appropriate areas of regulatory risk addressed?
- Training—What training programs exist on compliance with regulatory requirements and standards for business conduct? Are the training programs appropriately tailored to the business and the employees who receive the training? Are the training programs mandatory and are there records of employee attendance? What steps are taken to ensure that the training is effective?

- Personnel—Which personnel are charged with oversight of the compliance and business conduct program? Are the workload, background, and experience of the personnel assigned to the function appropriate for the size of the compliance program?
- Audit—Is there an internal audit function and, if so, how is it staffed and what is the scope of its responsibilities? Is there a regular process for collecting and assessing compliance information? By what methodology is compliance audited? What have the findings of internal audit been in the several years prior? How were such findings resolved? Who has oversight over the compliance and business conduct program (e.g., ethics function, board of directors, audit committee, compliance officer)? What is the role of external auditors?
- Disclosure procedures—What are the procedures for employees to ask questions and report concerns about regulatory compliance and business conduct issues? Do the procedures permit anonymous tips? What logs or records are kept of the process? Do the practices reflect the FAR mandatory compliance reporting requirements? Has the company made any disclosures in the prior several years?
- Access to compliance systems post-closing—If the Acquirer will fold in the Target, how does the compliance and business conduct program compare to the programs of the Acquirer? Will migration to the Acquirer's program be easy or difficult? If the Acquirer will not be migrating the Target into its own business, does the Target have what it needs to successfully maintain a compliance program and internal controls? If the Target previously relied on compliance policies and personnel of the parent entity, will it need to develop new policies tailored to its business or hire its own compliance personnel?

B. Present Responsibility

1. Debarment and Suspension

The government's acquisition policy is to purchase from and award contracts to "responsible prospective contractors," and unless the contracting officer makes an affirmative determination of contractor responsibility, no purchase or award can be made. Prospective contractors may also be required to demonstrate the responsibility of their proposed subcontractors.[1]

A contractor's debarment or suspension may be grounds for a determination of nonresponsibility. A contractor may be debarred or suspended by agency administrative action pursuant to FAR Subpart 9.4.[2] Each executive agency has a suspending and

1 FAR 9.103.

2 In addition to the procurement regulations governing suspension and debarment set forth at FAR Subpart 9.4, a parallel set of regulations governing suspension and debarment in the nonprocurement context (e.g., grants, cooperative agreements, leases, loans, etc.) is codified at 2 C.F.R. Part 180. These regulations governing suspension and debarment in the nonprocurement context, known as the Nonprocurement Common Rule ("NCR") largely—though not entirely—parallel the regulations at FAR Subpart 9.4. Actions taken under the FAR and NCR have reciprocal effect; exclusions issued under one system will result in ineligibility for all government procurement and nonprocurement programs.

debarring official (SDO). If a contractor is performing prime contracts or subcontracts at the time it is debarred or suspended, it will not be eligible for award of new federal contracts (or orders, options, or extensions under existing federal contracts), although it may continue performance on the contracts unless the agency directs their termination.[3]

The scope and effect of debarments and suspensions is broad, applying to all federal executive branch agencies and frequently (though not always) extending across a corporate family structure. A debarment or suspension generally will extend to all organizational elements of the contractor, unless limited by the agency SDO to specific corporate units. Debarments and suspensions may also be extended to any affiliates of the contractor.[4]

Causes for debarment are manifold but fall into three general categories: (a) conviction of or civil judgment for a legal violation involving fraud, theft, bribery, antitrust, or any other offense indicating a lack of business integrity; (b) violations of contract or subcontract terms, a history of unsatisfactory performance, or delinquent federal taxes; and (c) "any other cause of so serious or compelling a nature that it affects the present responsibility of the contractor."[5] This latter category of causes is particularly broad and highlights the apparently wide discretion afforded to SDOs to impose suspension and debarment actions.[6] When assessing whether any of these causes arise, the misconduct of any individual officer, director, shareholder, or employee may be imputed to a contractor, FAR 9.406-5(a), though courts have, in some cases, limited to the extent to which the conduct of former officers, directors, and employees can be imputed to a corporate entity.[7]

Contractors are afforded the opportunity to submit information and argument in opposition to a proposed debarment, though the exclusion from government contracting takes immediate effect upon issuance of a notice of proposed debarment. By default, the period of debarment is three years, though SDOs have wide discretion to tailor the period of debarment in accordance with the seriousness of the underlying causes.[8]

An offeror for a government contract is required to certify that it and/or any of its principals either are or are not presently debarred, suspended, proposed for debarment,

---

3 FAR 9.405-1.

4 FAR 9.406-5(a).

5 FAR 9.406-2.

6 A "suspension," as opposed to a debarment, is intended to be a temporary exclusion pending the completion of an investigation or legal proceeding. *See* FAR 9.407. The causes for suspension closely track the same three categories as the causes for debarment, FAR 9.407-2, with two exceptions. First, a cause for suspension can be established based on "adequate evidence," which is considered lower than the "preponderance of evidence" standard that applies to debarment. FAR 9.407-1(b). Second, a suspension also requires the SDO to make a finding that "immediate action is necessary to protect the Government's interest." *Id.*

7 *See, e.g.*, Impresa Construzioni Geom. Domenico Garufi v. United States, 238 F.3d 1324, 1336 (Fed. Cir. 2001) (recognizing that a former ownership group "no longer control [the company], and therefore any misconduct by them should not be imputed to the company"); John Carlo, Inc. v. Corps of Eng'rs of U. S. Army, 539 F. Supp. 1075, 1082 (N.D. Tex. 1982) ("It seems clear that prior delinquencies of any business entity should not be imputed to it after it is acquired by persons who had no prior connection with its management.").

8 FAR 9.406-4.

or otherwise ineligible for the award of contracts by any federal agency.[9] This same clause requires disclosure of other matters bearing on responsibility, such as convictions, civil judgments, indictments, and delinquent federal taxes. Contract solicitations also contain FAR 52.209-6, which prohibits contractors from awarding subcontracts in excess of $35,000 to any company that is debarred, suspended, or proposed for debarment, though this restriction does not apply to subcontracts purely for the supply of Commercial Off The Shelf items. A first-tier subcontractor must disclose in writing to the contractor whether, as of the date of subcontract award, it or its principals are or are not debarred or suspended by the government.

The GSA maintains a listing of all individuals and entities that are suspended, debarred, or proposed for debarment on the SAM, an online database of federal contractors. Found at www.sam.gov, SAM identifies entities that are the subject of government-wide exclusions from receiving federal contracts or certain subcontracts. Interestingly, SAM also permits users to search archived records for suspension or debarments that no longer are active, but that nonetheless may be relevant to due diligence efforts in the M&A context.

In addition to the suspension and debarment regulations in the FAR and NCR, Congress has enacted legislation that automatically excludes from both procurement and nonprocurement transactions any corporation that has been convicted of a felony within the preceding twenty-four months, unless an SDO affirmatively has determined that suspension and debarment would be unnecessary to protect the interests of the government.[10] Additionally, individuals and DOD contractors who employ them are also subject to certain conduct-related restrictions and penalties. For instance, a person who is convicted of fraud or any other felony arising out of a DOD contract is prohibited from working in a management or supervisory capacity, serving on the board of directors, or working as a consultant for a defense contractor or any first-tier subcontractor for at least five years following the conviction, and a contractor that knowingly employs such a person subject to this prohibition may face a criminal fine of up to $500,000.[11]

✓ **Best Practice Tip:** Consult the SAM website at www.sam.gov for information on any exclusion of the Target (including its subsidiaries and affiliates) from federal contracting. Confirm with the Target that it is not subject to any automatic exclusions, for example, because of a prior felony conviction in the last two years.

2. Past Performance on Competitive Procurements

The Target's past performance record is relevant to its ability to compete for future government contracts, along with offering additional insight into the Target's operational

9 FAR 52.209-5.

10 *See* Consolidated Appropriations Act of Fiscal Year 2018, Pub. L. No. 115-141, § 746 (Mar. 23, 2018).

11 10 U.S.C. § 2408.

track record. And as discussed in further detail in chapter XI, section F, the Acquirer may need to consider the effect the transaction will have on the Target's past performance references in pending bids and key pipeline opportunities, particularly where the Target is being split from a corporate parent or other affiliates.

a. Types of Past Performance Records

Past performance records can include the Target's Contract Performance Assessment Reporting System (CPARS) reports, the Target's records in the Federal Awardee Performance and Integrity Information System (FAPIIS), and other relevant records of the Target's past performance, such as show cause notices, contract deficiency reports, stop work orders, etc.

CPARS information should be available in reports received by the Target from its customers. It generally includes information about the contractor's record of conforming to contract requirements and to standards of good workmanship; forecasting and controlling costs; adhering to contract schedules, including the administrative aspects of performance; exhibiting reasonable and cooperative behavior and commitment to customer satisfaction; reporting into databases; demonstrating a record of integrity and business ethics; and showing business-like concern for the interest of the customer.[12] For each contract exceeding the simplified acquisition threshold, contracting officers are responsible for preparing an evaluation of contractor performance at the time the work under the contract is completed. In addition, interim evaluations are prepared by agencies to provide current information for source selection purposes, for contracts with a performance period, including options, exceeding one year.[13] The evaluation is generally for the entity, division, or unit that performed the contract.

FAPIIS is a searchable online database, available at www.fapiis.gov, that provides information about whether an entity has any records of administrative agreements, defective pricing, Department of Defense (DOD) determination of contractor fault, human trafficking findings, nonresponsibility determinations, determinations that the Target is not qualified, subcontractor payment issues, and terminations for cause, default, or material failure to comply with the contract.

To elicit other relevant records associated with the Target's past performance, it may be useful to include diligence requests for copies of any records related to past performance, including CPARS reports, show cause notices, contract deficiency reports, stop work orders, terminations, etc.

---

12 FAR 42.1501.

13 FAR 42.1502(a). The content and format of performance evaluations are based on procedures established by the agency, and are tailored to the size, content, and complexity of contractual requirements. These procedures also require an assessment of contractor performance against, and efforts to achieve, the goals identified in the small business subcontracting plan when the contract includes FAR 52.219-9, "Small Business Subcontracting Plan."

b. Past Performance as an Evaluation Factor and Indicator of Operational Concerns

"Past performance" is a mandatory evaluation factor in all source selections for negotiated competitive acquisitions expected to exceed the simplified acquisition threshold, except in acquisitions where the contracting officer documents the reasons that past performance is not an appropriate evaluation factor.[14]

In the context of a merger or acquisition, a Target's past performance information offers valuable insight into how government customers view the Target's performance, its adherence to cost and schedule requirements, and, generally, government customers' perceptions of the Target as a supplier of goods and services to the government.

The past performance of the Target may be a reliable indicator of future performance. At the very least, the Target's past performance information can have a significant impact on competitive standing in future competitive procurements and source selection decisions. And the information contained in a Target's CPARS reports and FAPIIS records may not be the only information government customers are considering when reviewing the Target's proposal for a contract re-compete, which is why it is important to perform diligence not only on these records but also any other records related to the Target's past performance. Review of the Target's past performance evaluations, particularly any negative or unfavorable past performance information, provides the Acquirer with a roadmap for mitigating the impact of the Target's past performance problems in future procurements.

> ✓ **Best Practice Tip:** Based on the review of the Target's past performance information during the due diligence process, identify potential areas of operational, business segment, or customer weakness (including troubled contracts) and conduct targeted diligence of those areas to assess the situation, including why the Target may be having difficulty meeting contract requirements or customer expectations.

c. Past Performance Information of Predecessors and Affiliates

It is important to review the Target's key pipeline opportunities, including pending proposals, to identify any instances where the Target has relied on the past performance of its parent or other affiliates.

The FAR provides that an agency's past performance evaluation during negotiated competitive acquisitions "should take into account past performance information regarding predecessor companies and key personnel who have relevant experience, among other items, when such information is relevant to the acquisition."[15] Therefore, the diligence of the Target's past performance should also include the past performance of any corporate predecessors.

---

14 *See* FAR 15.304(c)(3)(i) and (iii).

15 FAR 15.305(a)(2)(iii).

Parent or affiliate past performance information may be particularly significant when an Acquirer is purchasing particular assets or only part of a Target's business. Sometimes, offerors rely on past performance for the offeror's parent or an Affiliate in a proposal. An agency properly may attribute the experience or past performance of an offeror's parent or affiliated company, where the offeror's proposal demonstrates that the resources of the parent or affiliated company will affect the offeror's performance. However, where the Target will no longer belong to the same corporate family after the transaction closes, such past performance references can be at risk of being disregarded.[16] In some cases, the Target may be able to enter into a teaming arrangement, including a prime-subcontractor relationship or a joint venture, and continue to rely on the past performance records of its parent or Affiliate as a teammate. Ultimately, whether the Target may continue to rely on past performance records of its former parent or affiliate will depend on the terms of the solicitation. For a further discussion of the potential protest risks associated with a Target's reliance on past performance records of entities that will no longer be within its corporate family after the transaction closes, see chapter XI, section F.

C. Existing Arrangements for Classified Contracts

1. Assessing a Company's Existing Compliance Program

The adequacy of the Target's overall compliance program is reflected in part by its existing arrangements for classified contracts.

A cleared facility must have specific procedures in place to comply with the requirements of the Department of Defense National Industrial Security Program Operating Manual (NISPOM).[17] The NISPOM is issued by the DOD, in consultation with other affected US government agencies.[18]

To perform classified work under US government contracts, an organization must obtain a facility security clearance (FCL).[19] An FCL is an administrative determination that a facility is eligible for access to classified information or award of a classified contract involving information at or below the level of the clearance being granted.[20] Any facility that performs on contracts requiring such access or that possesses or processes classified information must have an FCL, and each separate business entity within an organization, if performing on contracts requiring access to classified information, must

---

16 *See Calibre Sys., Inc.*, B-411884, 2016 CPD ¶ 2 at 9, 2015 WL 9701026 (Nov. 16, 2015) (agency improperly attributed past performance of corporate parent to awardee where record did not establish that awardee had available to it the resources or experience of its parent).

17 DOD 5220.22-M (2006).

18 *See* Exec. Order No. 12829, 58 Fed. Reg. 3479 (Jan. 6, 1993), *as amended* (establishing the National Industrial Security Program ("NISP").

19 Department of Defense National Industrial Security Program Operating Manual (DOD 5220.22-M), 2-100 (2006), including Change 2, issued May 18, 2016. This manual and other national industrial security program reference materials, can be found on the Defense Security Service website, www.dss.mil.

20 *Id.* A rule published on May 7, 2018, by the Information Security Oversight Office (32 CFR 2004, 83 FR 19950), refers to the determination of a company's eligibility for access to classified information as an "entity eligibility determination." DOD refers to this determination as an FCL in current DOD issuances.

be cleared under a separate FCL.[21] Personnel clearances are also required for persons that the government refers to as "key management personnel" (as a minimum, these include the senior management official, board chair, and the facility security officer—FSO), and other employees who require access to classified information in order to perform on the classified contract.[22] Individuals (other than those key management personnel already referred to, who must always be cleared) may be processed for a personnel security clearance (PCL) under a classified contract if the contractor determines that their access to classified information is essential to performing tasks and services related to performance of the contract.[23] A PCL or an FCL may be granted at the Confidential, Secret, or Top Secret level, in increasing level of classifications.

a. Companies under Foreign Ownership, Control, or Influence

Companies under foreign ownership, control, or influence **(FOCI) are subject to additional rules and requirements under the NISPOM** compliance procedures.[24] Each cleared facility must designate an FSO, who must be an employee of the cleared company.[25] The FSO is responsible for overseeing the facility's compliance with the National Industrial Security Program (NISP), as discussed below. Cleared companies are also required to designate a cleared senior official to "establish and execute an insider threat program" at the company.[26] For DOD classified contracts, as well as classified contracts with some other agencies, the Defense Security Service (DSS) conducts periodic assessments to verify the cleared facility's compliance with security requirements.[27] Routine DSS security assessments of a company's NISP program take place no more than once annually, and additional follow-up assessments may be conducted if the DSS finds deficiencies. Assessments may also be conducted by the DSS based on specific concerns or security program issues as they arise. US companies applying for an FCL from the DSS, requesting a clearance upgrade, or reporting changes to basic information about a company (e.g., foreign interests, changes of name, location, senior management officials) must use the DSS-prescribed web-based system to submit the necessary information to the DSS.[28] Companies that require a facility clearance from the Department of Energy (DOE) should submit their required information

---

[21] NISPOM 2-108, 2-109.

[22] *Id.* at 2-104.

[23] *Id.* at 2-105.

[24] A company is under FOCI whenever a foreign interest has the power, directly or indirectly, whether or not exercised, and whether or not exercisable through the ownership of the US company's securities, by contractual arrangements or other means, to direct or decide matters affecting the management or operations of the company in a manner that may result in unauthorized access to classified information or that may adversely affect the performance of classified contracts. *See* NISPOM 2-300.a.

[25] *Id.* at 2-103.

[26] *Id.* at 1-202.

[27] DSS provides NISP services, including adjudication of eligibility for an FCL, for DOD components (i.e., military departments and DOD agencies) and for thirty-two non-DOD federal departments and agencies.

[28] This is the Electronic Facility Clearance ("e-FCL") system at the time of publication of this manual, whjch is slated to be replaced by the National Industrial Security System ("NISS"). Information about registering for these systems, as well as access to the systems themselves, is available from the DSS website, at www.dss.mil.

to the DOE for review by DOE staff. Because the DOD and DOE have a reciprocity agreement regarding mutual recognition of FCLs granted by each agency, facilities that have classified contracts with DOD components and with DOE will only need one facility clearance, from either DOD or DOE. Under the terms of that reciprocity agreement, the DSS and DOE will consult with each other to determine which agency will be responsible (i.e., have "security cognizance") for overseeing the company's compliance with the NISPOM. Compliance reviews not conducted by the DSS or DOE will be handled by other agencies. The DSS, DOE, and other government agencies that oversee NISP compliance are referred to in the NISPOM as "Cognizant Security Agencies" or "CSAs."[29]

2. Identification of Foreign Ownership, Control, or Influence and Security Issues Arising from the Acquisition

a. Forms and Reports

A review of mandatory forms and reports serves as a good starting point for assessing security issues and the Target's compliance with the NISPOM. First, the Acquirer should review the results of annual DSS, DOE, and other agency security assessments, inspections, and advice and assistance visits, going back several years, to determine the level of the Target's clearance and its record of compliance. Each separate facility of a company at which classified work is performed will have its own FCL and will have had separate assessments; therefore, it is necessary to review each of the separate assessment findings. In addition, each cleared company will have filed certain forms with the CSA and must have received certain forms from the government contracting agency (GCA) or the prime contractor for each contract requiring access to classified information. These forms should be reviewed to identify FOCI and other security issues.

A form DD-254, *Contract Security Classification Specification*, is issued by the GCA or the prime contractor for each contract requiring access to classified information. This form is part of the contract or subcontract and is usually unclassified. It provides security classification guidance (classification level and safeguarding requirements, access requirements, and performance requirements) to the contractor, as well as contact information for the government or prime contractor point of contact. It also specifies whether the company's classified contracts require access to "proscribed" classified information (i.e., Top Secret, Communications Security, or COMSEC, other than classified keys used for data transfer), Special Access Program, Restricted Data, or Sensitive Compartmented Information).[30] If so, this can have implications for a company under FOCI, because additional specific approvals from the GCA itself, such as a National Interest Determination (NID),[31] may be

---

29 *See* NISPOM 1-104.

30 NISPOM 2-303.c.(2) n.1.

31 An NID allows a company operating under a Special Security Agreement to perform on contracts involving proscribed classified information upon a determination by the GCA that release of proscribed information to the company shall not harm the national security interests of the United States. *See* NISPOM 2-303.c.(2); *see also* chapter III, section B. An NID is not required by the DOD for companies under FOCI that have mitigated their FOCI by operating under a Proxy Agreement or Security Control Agreement.

required to allow the company to perform on a contract requiring access to proscribed information, depending on the FOCI mitigation arrangement in place.

Additionally, each cleared company must submit to the DSS a Standard Form (SF) 328, *Certificate Pertaining to Foreign Interests*, which details any foreign ownership or foreign interest in or at the cleared company.[32] A revised SF-328 will normally have to be submitted to the CSA when a merger or acquisition of a cleared company has been completed, or when there have been significant changes to any of the Target's answers to the questions on the SF-328.[33] Cleared companies with FOCI mitigation agreements that require appointment of government-approved directors are also required to provide formal reports annually to the CSA, with details about implementation of the terms of the mitigation agreement during the prior year. These reports should also be reviewed by the Acquirer.

b. Deal Structure

In addition to reviewing forms and reports, the potential parties to the transaction should assess the implications for the Target's clearance based on the proposed structure of the deal (e.g., whether the deal is in the form of a stock purchase or an asset purchase, and whether the acquisition would result in control of the cleared company by a foreign interest).[34] A stock purchase often does not require a new facility security clearance—the Target's clearance may continue with the CSA's approval. However, obtaining this approval will require review by the CSA of information regarding the purchasing entity or entities for security issues, including FOCI issues, caused by the change in ownership. Changes in ownership could affect the company's clearance. For example, a change from US control to foreign ownership or control would invalidate or terminate the FCL, unless appropriate FOCI mitigation measures are put in place by the new owners. Also, the CSA's assessment of risk caused by a change in the country or company from which the foreign ownership originates could trigger a substantial change in any existing FOCI mitigation scheme or render it impossible for the CSA to mitigate the FOCI sufficiently to allow the company to perform classified work.

Unlike stock acquisitions, asset sales have a profound impact on the FCL, because FCLs do not transfer with assets. In the event of an asset sale, the company into which the acquired assets are placed will need an appropriate FCL to continue performance on the classified contracts. If the assets are transferred into an uncleared entity, the company will have to be sponsored for an FCL by a government contracting activity, or by a cleared company that will issue a classified subcontract to the company being sponsored. The acquiring company would then have to meet the requirements for eligibility for an FCL.

---

32 *See* NISPOM 2-302.

33 *See id.* The DSS has published, and posted at www.dss.mil, a "Change Conditions Reporting Job Aid" describing when a report of changes affecting eligibility for an FCL must be reported. This job aid describes what must be reported when a change in ownership that affects answers to a Target company's SF-328 must be reported.

34 NISPOM Appendix C, at C-3, defines a foreign interest as: "Any foreign government, agency of a foreign government, or representative of a foreign government; any form of business enterprise or legal entity organized, chartered or incorporated under the laws of any country other than the United States or its territories, and any person who is not a citizen or national of the United States.

Note that FCL determinations and contract novations are separate processes administered by separate government offices and officials.

3. Integration of the Target into a Corporate Structure

Once the Acquirer has considered the issues presented by a Target's facility clearance, it should evaluate how to integrate the cleared Target into its corporate structure, including any difficulties this may present (e.g., mitigating FOCI will often involve limitations on communications between the parent and FOCI-mitigated subsidiaries, and operating under CSA-approved written plans and procedures, such as an Affiliated Operations Plan covering shared services, an Electronic Communications Plan, and a Technology Control Plan to protect export-controlled information).

If relevant, the potential Acquirer should examine any measures that the Target already has in place to mitigate FOCI. A company under FOCI cannot hold an FCL unless FOCI is negated or mitigated to the satisfaction of the CSA.[35] Therefore, if a Target under FOCI holds an FCL, it is necessary to understand the FOCI mitigation arrangement and how well it is implemented. Although an acquisition by a US-controlled entity would normally lead to termination of the FOCI mitigation scheme already in place, an acquisition by a foreign entity or an entity with significant foreign ownership or control will trigger reevaluation by the CSA of FOCI and of any required mitigation necessitated by the new ownership or control, even if the Target has an existing FOCI mitigation program in place. Accordingly, prior to the acquisition, it is necessary to evaluate the FOCI mitigation plan that would likely be implemented following the acquisition, which may well be different than the mechanism in place prior to the time of the acquisition.

In dealing with a cleared Target, the potential Acquirer should bear in mind that the NISPOM requires cleared companies to notify the CSA, at the "commencement" of "negotiations for the proposed merger, acquisition, or takeover by a foreign interest."[36]

✓ **Best Practice Tip:** Persons who are not US citizens cannot normally hold a management position in a cleared company, if the position requires a personnel security clearance. The senior management official, board chair, and facility security officer must all have personnel clearances as a prerequisite for the FCL.[37] Permanent resident aliens are not eligible for US personnel clearances, even though they may be "US persons" under export control regulations.[38]

---

35 *See* NISPOM 2-102.d.

36 *Id.* at 2-302.b.

37 See the DSS "Change Condition Reporting Job Aid" for a description of which persons must, at a minimum, be cleared at various forms of business organizations in order for the company to be granted an FCL.

38 *See* NISPOM 2-209 (advising that "[e]very effort shall be made to ensure that non-US citizens are not employed in duties that may require access to classified information," but allowing, that "in those rare circumstances where the non-US citizen possesses unique or unusual skill or expertise that is urgently

✓ **Best Practice Tip:** If a transaction involves implementation of a new FOCI mitigation scheme, it is likely that the sale will close before the FOCI mitigation arrangement is in place. If the parties are working in good faith with the appropriate US government agency to achieve FOCI mitigation, this does not typically present a problem. One of the factors that the US government agency will consider in analyzing whether the parties are working in good faith with the government is the timeliness of the disclosure of the transaction to the government. Reporting a transaction to the CSA for the first time after, or even just shortly before, closing of the transaction, commonly results in invalidation[39] of the Target's FCL while the CSA is evaluating the details of the transaction.

For FCLs administered by the DSS, if a required formal FOCI mitigation arrangement cannot be completed immediately upon closing of the transaction, a written plan to mitigate or negate the FOCI should be submitted to the DSS in the form of a "Commitment Letter," with documentation needed for an acceptable FOCI Action Plan. The Commitment Letter must be approved by the DSS prior to closing of the transaction in order to avoid invalidation or termination of the FCL upon closing.[40] Companies should contact the DSS or other CSA as early as possible to schedule a meeting to discuss the details of their pending transaction and the company's plan to mitigate or negate the FOCI.

D. Foreign Sales

Government contractors may specialize in selling products and services that do not have commercial use or that are used in a manner that differs from commercial use. As a result, government contractors are subject to laws and regulations that apply to sales to foreign governments and export laws that apply to defense products and services.

Any due diligence of a government contractor should include a review of compliance with the Foreign Corrupt Practices Act, Anti-Boycott Act, Anti-Kickback Act, export controls, and rules regarding embargoed countries (promulgated by the Office of Foreign Assets Control or OFAC). The laws are of particular importance to a government contractor because a violation of these laws can result in debarment of the company from

---

needed to support a specific US government contract involving access to specified classified information and a cleared or clearable US citizen is not readily available," a non-US citizen may be granted a Limited Access Authorization). This exception is almost never applied and is difficult to obtain.

39 *Invalidation*" of an FCL renders the company unable to bid on or receive any additional classified contracts. As part of the invalidation, the DSS will advise the government agencies that have awarded classified contracts to the company of the invalidation. The contracting agencies will determine if the company may continue to perform on an existing classified contract while the invalidation is in effect. "*Termination*" of an FCL renders a company unable to bid on or receive any additional classified contracts, and also ineligible to continue performance of current classified contracts.

40 A template for the content of a FOCI Commitment Letter and FOCI Action Plan for submission to the DSS can be found in the Industrial Security, then Foreign Ownership, Control, and Influence sections, of the DSS website.

exporting goods and services or debarment of the company from contracting with the US government.

Many small or evolving Targets do not understand the complex and often unexpected application of these laws to their business and may not realize that these laws apply to their activities. There may be limited or no compliance procedures in place, and the Target may not be sophisticated enough to reliably identify noncompliant activities. As a result, the Acquirer must become completely familiar with the business and make its own assessment as to whether the Target operates in compliance with these laws. The lack of a compliance or training program in these regulatory areas should be viewed as a red flag requiring more due diligence.

E. Export Control Compliance

Every corporation that regularly exports commodities from the United States should have an export controls compliance program. If the company is a regular exporter of goods, services, or technology from the United States but does not have an export controls compliance program, this is a major red flag. In going forward with the transaction, it will be doubly important to scrutinize the Target's export activities and records in order to assess the potential legal exposure that any export control violations may create for the Acquirer.[41]

✓ **Best Practice Tip:** To avoid the consequences of past or ongoing export control violations, a thorough due diligence review is necessary to identify any possible export control problems prior to completing an acquisition. In some cases, voluntary disclosures or requests for government guidance may be necessary to address past or ongoing violations or to clarify the treatment of relationships or transactions under the Export Administration Regulations (EAR) or International Traffic in Arms Regulations (ITAR).[42]

A government contractor may believe that it does not have any export compliance issues, because its sole customer is the US government. However, the Target may well engage in the export of Department of State or Department of Commerce-controlled items if it has non-US subcontractors (or primes), or if it is attempting to secure business

[41] If the Target has been charged with a violation of export control laws by a US export control or law enforcement agency, then a paper trail exists and should be thoroughly researched. The Acquirer should examine not only the facts giving rise to the violation and whether the matter has been completely resolved, but also whether the Target has eliminated any underlying weaknesses or gaps in the Target's compliance program that could cause current or future problems. In some cases, the Target will have already voluntarily disclosed the violation to the enforcing agency. Documents related to such disclosures should be requested as well.

[42] Under the doctrine of successor liability, the successors of an acquired company may be held liable for that company's export violations that occurred before the acquisition. The 2002 *Sigma-Aldrich* administrative case made clear the government's ability to hold a successor liable for the export control violations of acquired companies. *See In the Matter of Sigma Aldrich Bus. Holdings, Inc., et al.*, Case Nos. 01-BXA-06, 01-BXA-07, 01-BXA-11.

in other countries. Anyone performing due diligence on a government contractor should probe further into any representation that the Target has not engaged in any activity regulated by the US export control laws by asking a few basic questions:

- Does the Target have any foreign subcontractors?
- Do employees travel outside the United States for any purpose?
- Are any materials shipped to or from locations outside the United States?
- Does the Target have a business plan that involves expansion into non-US markets?
- Has the Target (or is the Target currently) soliciting business outside the United States?

✓ **Best Practice Tip:** The existence of an export control violation may not mean the end of the transaction. Remedial programs, voluntary disclosures, and/or termination of noncompliant contracts can be included as a condition to closing. The Acquirer can also require that a compliance audit be conducted prior to closing, with all violations to be reported to the relevant security agency prior to closing.

CHAPTER 7

Other Risk Areas

OUTLINE

A. Assignment and Change of Control Provisions
   1. Prime Contracts
   2. Subcontracts, Joint Venture Agreements, and Teaming Agreements
   3. Transaction Considerations
B. Warranties and Indemnities
   1. Warranties
   2. Statutory Indemnities
   3. Contractual Indemnity for Liability to Third Persons
C. Organizational Conflicts of Interest
   1. Federal Acquisition Regulations and Defense Acquisition Regulations Coverage of Organization Conflicts of Interest
   2. How Organizational Conflicts of Interest Can Arise in Mergers and Acquisitions Transactions
   3. Mitigation of Organizational Conflicts of Interest
D. "Revolving Door" Restrictions
   1. Relationship Between the "Revolving Door" Restrictions and the Procurement Integrity Act
   2. Overview of "Revolving Door" Restrictions
   3. How "Revolving Door" Issues Can Arise
E. Political Law Considerations
   1. "Pay-to-Play" Rules
   2. PAC and Campaign Finance
   3. Lobbying and Foreign Agents Registration Act
   4. Gifts and Ethics
F. Intellectual Property under Government Contracts
   1. Technical Data and Computer Software
      a. Definitions
      b. Unlimited Rights

A. Assignment and Change of Control Provisions

Whether a transaction involves the transfer of assets or a stock purchase, the parties should assess the assignment or change of control clauses in the prime contracts and subcontracts at issue.

1. Prime Contracts

As a threshold matter, prime government contracts are subject to the anti-assignment statutes discussed in chapter XII. As discussed in more detail in that chapter, the transfer of a prime contract as an asset (i.e., through an asset sale) generally requires novation approval from the US government. The Acquirer should ensure that after closing, the contract to be transferred will sit within an entity that has adequate resources to perform, including sufficient financial resources and the assets that were used in performance of the contract prior to the transaction. Careful consideration should also be given to how to demonstrate to the government that the Acquirer can successfully perform the contract going forward.

In the context of a stock purchase, consent from the government is not typically required, but an Acquirer after closing may need to give notice of a change in ownership to the government under FAR 52.215-19 and enter a name change agreement, if the Target's name will change.

2. Subcontracts, Joint Venture Agreements, and Teaming Agreements

By contrast, subcontracts, joint venture agreements, and teaming agreements are creatures of state contract law. Many prime contractors and other counterparties prohibit assignment without consent. Additionally, counterparties may also require consent (or notice) if a subcontractor seeks to undergo a change of control through, for example, a stock sale. There are many reasons counterparties include these provisions in their contracts, not the least of which is that significant subcontracts can be subject to government approval and a sale of the subcontract could put at risk a higher-tier contractor's ongoing ability to use the subcontractor. Additionally, a higher-tier contractor may condition an assignment on consent in order to reassess the contract terms in light of the financial and performance status of the Acquirer (or simply to use the need for consent to leverage for more favorable terms).

In contrast to the novation process for prime government contracts, there is no recognized process for resolving consent issues that arise under these other types of contracts. As a result, at times, it can be difficult to predict how easily consent may be obtained and how long it may take to obtain such consent. In the end, although not common, consent may at times be withheld, even when the consent clause states that approval "will not unreasonably be withheld."

3. Transaction Considerations

Given these potential uncertainties, navigating the notice and consent requirements is a key element of a successful transaction. The inability to secure consent from a counterparty on a key revenue-generating contract can derail a deal or result in an adjustment to the purchase price.

As a result, it is important that both the Acquirer and the Target begin early to identify contracts that contain consent and notice requirements that the anticipated transaction may trigger. Once the world of necessary consents and notices has been scoped, it is important to develop a unified message to the customer. This message may highlight, for example, that the same individuals will continue to oversee contract performance, the same assets will be used to perform, and the transaction positions the Target to be a stronger contractor and offer better performance to the customer. Of course, customer communications may be complicated by the fact that, until the deal is made public, it may not be possible to discuss the transaction with the customer to determine if that party will take issue with the transaction. That said, Acquirers may push for pre-public discussions with certain key customers (to the extent permissible under the law) to gauge the customers' reactions to the potential transaction and assess whether there may be difficulty in securing consent or otherwise continuing a relationship after closing.

✓ **Best Practice Tip:** Identify all provisions that limit assignment of rights or call for approvals on change of control or ownership. Where an agreement constitutes a material portion of the Target's value or is otherwise strategically important, consider obtaining, as a condition of closing, the consent or approval of the other party to the agreement or a means of adjusting the purchase price in the event the customer refuses to approve the assignment.

B. Warranties and Indemnities

1. Warranties

Warranties may appear throughout a government contract and can be an important area for consideration when conducting diligence on a potential Target. For instance, warranties may appear within notes on contract drawings, in technical specifications, and/or in standard publications that are incorporated into or referenced in the contract. Additionally, the FAR allows, but does not require, the government to adapt and include a contractor warranty in fixed-price government contracts.[1] It provides sample warranty clauses that may be used for different types of contract work (i.e., supplies, systems and equipment, services, or construction).[2] Each such clause warrants that the work of the contractor and its subcontractors at every tier (including suppliers) conforms to the contract requirements and is free of any defect in material or workmanship.[3] With respect to commercial item

[1] *See* FAR 46.710 ("[M]any situations that may influence the warranty terms and conditions appropriate to a particular acquisition, the contracting officer may vary the terms and conditions of the clauses and alternates to the extent necessary.").

[2] *See* FAR 52.246-17–21.

[3] *Id.*

contracts, the government may also incorporate warranties of merchantability and fitness for a particular purpose.[4]

In addition to incorporating these clauses in prime contracts, the government may also require the prime contractor to obtain, for the government's benefit, those warranties that their subcontractors provide in normal commercial practice.[5]

Reviewing the warranty provisions a Target has accepted and assessing the Target's ability to comply with such provisions can be important as a contractor's obligation under certain warranties often requires it to remedy, at the contractor's expense, any failure to conform or any defect and any damages to government property as a result of the defect.[6]

✓ **Best Practice Tip:** Review all warranty provisions in the Target's current or recently completed material contracts and ask about warranty claims. Where there are unexpired warranties, identify any potential or pending warranty claims and evaluate the Target's potential liability under the warranty remedy provisions as against reserves maintained by the Target.

2. Statutory Indemnities

In addition to reviewing warranty revisions, an Acquirer would be well advised to inquire into and review any statutory indemnities in which the Target may participate. Examples of these programs include:

- Support Anti-Terrorism by Fostering Effective Technologies Act of 2002 (The SAFETY Act)[7]—The SAFETY Act can offer two basic levels of protection, Designation or Certification, to contractors that may be subject to third-party liability as a result of an act of terrorism. A Designation award caps third-party liability at the level of insurance that the Department of Homeland Security (DHS) designates that a contractor shall maintain. Additional protection may come in the form of a Certification that permits the contractor to avail itself of the Government Contractor Defense. If a Target is engaged in developing anti-terrorism technologies or otherwise may be vulnerable to a physical or cyber terrorist attack, an Acquirer should inquire into whether the Target has applied or may be eligible to apply for SAFETY Act protection. For those Targets that have secured SAFETY Act protection, an Acquirer should review the Target's SAFETY Act Designation and Certification (as applicable) and confirm the Target maintains the requisite level of liability protection as prescribed by the DHS.

---

4 *See* FAR 52.212-4(o) "The contractor warrants and implies that the items delivered hereunder are merchantable and fit for use for the particular purpose described in this contract."

5 *See, e.g.*, FAR 52.246-21(g)(1).

6 *See, e.g.*, FAR 52.246-17(c), 52.246-18(c), 52.246-19(c), 52.246-20(b), 52.246-21(c) and (d).

7 6 U.S.C. § 441.

- The Price-Anderson Nuclear Industries Indemnity Act (the Price-Anderson Act)[8]—Under the Price-Anderson Act a Target may secure indemnification for legal liabilities resulting from a nuclear incident when supporting a Department of Energy (DOE) contract. Similar to the SAFETY Act, the government may require the Target to maintain a certain level of financial protection. After this protection is exhausted, the government may indemnify the Target for up to roughly $10 billion. If a Target discloses that it has secured protection under the Price-Anderson Act, an Acquirer should review the indemnification provisions in the Target's DOE contracts and confirm that the Target maintains the requisite level of financial protection under its agreement with the DOE.
- Public Law 85-04 (PL 85-804)—PL 85-804 allows the president (and through executive order, thirteen agencies) to authorize indemnification for contractors engaged in unusually hazardous activities related to national defense. It is typically available only when "commercial insurance is unavailable, prohibitively expensive, or insufficient in coverage."[9] The FAR specifies the indemnification clauses available for incorporation into government contracts under PL 85-804.[10] It is fairly rare to secure coverage under PL 85-804 and any suggestion by a Target that such protection is available should be carefully reviewed, including by verifying that the relevant contract(s) incorporate such protection. In addition, an Acquirer should also confirm that the activities subject to the indemnification are those that would reasonably be expected to receive such protection, as the Target may be required to demonstrate it remains entitled to PL 85-804 protection during a contract re-compete or for additional contracts for similar activities.

3. Contractual Indemnity for Liability to Third Persons

Cost-reimbursement government contracts typically include a standard FAR clause providing that the government will insure for claims by third parties against its contractors.[11] The clause provides that the contractor shall be reimbursed for liabilities and expenses arising out of performance of the contract that are not covered by the insurance a contractor is otherwise required to carry under the clause. This coverage generally applies regardless of the negligence of the contractor and covers loss or damage to property, death, and bodily injury. Notably, the damages must be in the form of a judgment or government-approved settlement, do not cover liabilities resulting from willful misconduct or lack of good faith on the part of the company's management, and must be covered through appropriated funds. Contractors typically settle these liabilities at the time of contract close-out using Standard Form 1437, Settlement Proposal for Cost-Reimbursement Type Contracts.

---

[8] 42 U.S.C. § 2210.

[9] *See* Kevin P. Mullen, *Extraordinary Contractual Relief under Public Law 85-804*, Briefing Papers No. 02-13, 1, 3 (Dec. 2002).

[10] *See* FAR 50.403-3.

[11] *See* FAR 52.228-7 (Note that there is no comparable standard provision in fixed-price contracts.).

If a Target holds cost-reimbursement contracts that contain FAR 52.228-7, an Acquirer may be well advised to confirm the Target maintains the minimum level of insurance required by the clause and to confirm whether the Target has any outstanding liabilities for which it intends to seek reimbursement under this provision. Additionally, if a Target is involved in performing cost-reimbursement contracts that may be prone to giving rise to third-party liabilities, an Acquirer may seek to confirm this clause is included in the relevant contracts.

C. Organizational Conflicts of Interest

Organizational conflicts of interest (OCIs) can arise where a contractor has an actual or perceived inability to provide unbiased advice or can benefit unfairly from information in its possession. Although most contractors—particularly those with a services focus—routinely monitor internally for OCI concerns, an acquisition presents unique considerations. For example, the combining of companies or change in ownership can present renewed complications that may not have been present when the Target operated completely separate from the Acquirer. As a result, an Acquirer should carefully consider whether the acquisition of the Target will create OCIs concerning current or future contracts involving either the Acquirer or the Target. Depending on the language of an OCI clause, the analysis of potential FOCI issues may include the Acquirer's subsidiaries or parent.

1. Federal Acquisition Regulations and Defense Acquisition Regulations Coverage of Organization Conflicts of Interest

The purpose of the OCI rules is to avoid situations in which the government's interests in fair, competitive, and unbiased performance of work under a contract are compromised by a contractor's other interests or the performance of work under other related contracts. For example, an OCI may arise when "because of other activities or relationships with other persons, a person is unable or potentially unable to render impartial assistance or advice to the Government, or the person's objectivity in performing the contract work is or might be otherwise impaired, or a person has an unfair competitive advantage."[12] FAR Subpart 9.5 sets forth the general rules, responsibilities, and procedures for identifying, evaluating, and resolving OCIs. In general, OCIs fall within three categories:

- **Biased Ground Rules**—These conflicts may arise where a company is involved in preparing the specifications or statement of work for a future contract or participates in shaping the "ground rules" that will apply to a future procurement.
- **Impaired Objectivity**—These conflicts may arise where a company performing work under a contract has other interests that might bias its judgment in performing objectively. For example, impaired objectivity conflicts may arise where a contractor is providing program management or advisory services, and

12 *See* FAR 2.101.

the advice involves the contractor's own products or services or those of a competitor. In this situation, the advice may not be objective because of its business interests.

- **Unequal Access to Information**—These conflicts may arise where a company has government-provided access to non-public information in the course of performing a contract and that information might provide the company with an unfair competitive advantage in competing for another contract.

Although OCIs are not limited to any particular type of procurement, OCIs are more common in contracts involving (a) management support services, (b) consultant or other professional services, or (c) systems engineering and technical assistance.[13] Agencies are expected to identify actual or potential OCIs that may affect a procurement as early as possible in the acquisition process, and to take steps to neutralize, mitigate, or avoid all significant conflicts before contract award. FAR 9.504(a). GAO case law recognizes that an OCI may arise not only within the offeror itself, but also in relation to its affiliates or even teammates, as well as from former government employees who may provide unequal access to information of the sort contemplated by the OCI regulations.

2. How Organizational Conflicts of Interest Can Arise in Mergers and Acquisitions Transactions

Although many contractors are accustomed to monitoring internally for actual or potential OCIs in the ordinary course of business, a transaction brings a new level of complexity to this question by injecting a host of additional programs and contracts of an Acquirer (and its subsidiaries and other affiliates) into the OCI analysis. An Acquirer is well advised to consider early on in the M&A process whether significant OCIs might arise for itself or the Target as a result of the transaction or if the transaction may be contrary to a specific OCI prohibition in the Target's or Acquirer's contracts. Failure to perform this analysis can present risk to the successful execution of a transaction and might also lead an Acquirer to overestimate the value of the transaction. For example, a significant OCI may require the combined company to divest a conflicting contract or halt pursuit of a key pipeline opportunity.

✓ **Best Practice Tip:** Careful review of potential OCIs is critical in any acquisition involving a government contractor, in particular when the contractor has a significant services focus to its business. If possible, contracts personnel from the Target and the Acquirer should be involved in the due diligence process early on to assist with identification and assessment of OCI issues.

[13] *See* FAR 9.502(b).

In assessing the OCI risk presented by a proposed transaction, an Acquirer may find it helpful to rely on its OCI policies and procedures, along with the individuals with primary responsibility for maintaining and implementing those procedures. It is often helpful for this assessment to follow a defined process or methodology, including the following:

- The Acquirer should identify those sectors of the Target's and the Acquirer's own businesses where OCI issues are most likely to arise. For instance, is the Target or the Acquirer involved in preparing the specifications or statement of work for a future contract or participating in shaping the "ground rules" that will apply to a future procurement? Do any of the Target's contracts include specific prohibitions related to identified contracts? Does either party perform work under a contract where other interests could bias its judgment in performing objectively? Does either party have access to non-public information from the government in the course of performing a contract that may give it an unfair competitive advantage in competing for another contract?
- Armed with an understanding of where OCI issues are most likely to arise, the Acquirer should consider areas of potential overlap to assess the likelihood of any present or future OCIs. In this analysis, the Acquirer should carefully review the programs and types of contracts being performed for government customers by the Target, as compared to programs and contracts in which the Acquirer is involved or likely to be involved. This includes specific consideration of both current and future contracts. For example, where the Target provides advisory and assistance services to a government customer in support of government acquisitions, source selection activities, and evaluations, an actual or potential OCI can exist where the Acquirer has received, or is in line for award of, a production contract under the program for which the Target has provided acquisition support work.
- If the Acquirer's or the Target's contracts raise actual or potential OCIs, the Acquirer should consider whether the conflicts are significant and whether they can be mitigated. For example, the inquiry will focus on whether the contracts at issue might foreclose potential government business opportunities for the Acquirer or the combined entity.

3. Mitigation of Organizational Conflicts of Interest

The Acquirer should carefully consider whether any significant OCIs that are identified during diligence can be mitigated before moving forward with the transaction and plan to work with the relevant contracting officers to address OCI concerns after the announcement of the transaction. Certain types of OCIs can be mitigated more effectively than others, but ultimately it will be up to the contracting officer whether an OCI can be adequately mitigated or waived.

Prior to the transaction, the parties should determine whether the holder of the contract (or multiple contracts) raising actual or potential OCI issues is prepared to take the steps necessary to avoid or mitigate the OCI issue. Such measures may include the creation of a corporate firewall, transferring the contract (or contracts) at issue to another entity, accepting other restraints imposed by the contract, moving work to a mitigated subcontractor, or divestiture of that portion of the business raising OCI concerns.

The most common method for addressing OCIs among government contractors is creating corporate firewalls. A firewall is a mitigation method that involves walling off various activities through which potential conflicts of interest could arise by separating the personnel, technical, and cost information and lines of communication between business units. Although corporate firewalls may be effective in mitigating unequal access to non-public information OCIs, such firewalls may be insufficient to avoid, neutralize, or mitigate OCIs caused by biased ground rules or impaired objectivity.[14] These potential conflicts of interest are inherent in the relationship between a parent company and its subsidiary or affiliate.

If the acquisition of the Target results in the creation of an OCI that cannot be mitigated through a firewall, the Acquirer may need to consider transferring a government contract to a third party through an asset sale and novation or to accept a contractual provision imposing restraints, appropriate to the nature of the conflict, on the company's eligibility for future contracts.[15]

D. "Revolving Door" Restrictions

"Revolving door" restrictions refer generally to the restrictions imposed on government employees seeking employment in the private sector, as well as to the post-employment, conflict-of-interest restrictions imposed on former government employees and their employers. The primary post-employment conflict-of-interest statute, 18 U.S.C. § 207, prohibits certain activities by former employees of the executive and legislative branches. Additional restrictions are imposed on presidential appointees by executive order, on members of Congress and congressional employees by congressional rules, and on

---

14 In *LEADS Corp.*, GAO held that "while a firewall arrangement may solve an 'unfair access to information' OCI, it is virtually irrelevant to an OCI involving potentially impaired objectivity . . . Likewise, due to the ultimate relationship of one entity to another, a firewall would not resolve an organizational conflict of interest involving biased ground rules." B-292465, 2003 CPD 197 at 5 (Sept. 26, 2003). See also *ICF Inc.*, B-241372, 91-1 CPD ¶ 124 at 2 (Feb. 6, 1991) (noting that ICF's proposed firewall and attempts "to limit communications between ICF and its sister corporations . . . did not eliminate the potential conflict of interest since ICF need not communicate with its sister corporations to advance their financial interest"); *Ktech Corp.*, B-285330, 2002 CPD ¶ 77 (Aug. 17, 2000) (noting that while there is not a *per se* rule against creating firewalls to mitigate OCIs, the sufficiency of safeguards will be strictly scrutinized); *Aetna Gov't Health Plans, Inc.*, B-254397, 95-2 CPD ¶ 129 at 12 (July 27, 1995) (finding that OCIs will be viewed with a "presumption of prejudice" to competing offerors).

15 *See* FAR 9.507-1 and 9.507-2. FAR 9.507-2(b) provides in relevant part that "[t]he restraint imposed by a clause shall be limited to a fixed term of reasonable duration, sufficient to avoid the circumstance of unfair competitive advantage or potential bias." It further provides that "[t]his period varies," and offers examples of when the period might end: "It might end . . . when the first production contract using the contractor's specifications or work statement is awarded, or it might extend through the entire life of a system for which the contractor has performed systems engineering and technical direction. In every case, the restriction shall specify termination by a specific date or upon the occurrence of an identifiable event."

certain executive branch employees, including former military officials, by agency supplemental post-employment restrictions, and on state and local government employees by state and local laws and ordinances. Further, former government officials who are lawyers may be subject to conflict-of-interest bar rules. While a detailed analysis of these many restrictions is outside the scope of this manual, this section provides a brief overview of the restrictions and the consideration that should be given to issues involving any former government employees hired by the Target.

1. Relationship Between the "Revolving Door" Restrictions and the Procurement Integrity Act

Violations of the above-described "revolving door" restrictions may also trigger Procurement Integrity Act (PIA) liabilities.[16] The PIA prohibits a covered individual (described below) from disclosing or obtaining bid or proposal information or source selection information.[17] A covered individual is someone who held one of seven positions,[18] or engaged in one of seven types of procurement-related decisions.[19] More generally, the PIA provides that a person shall not knowingly obtain contractor bid or proposal information or source selection information before the award of a Federal agency procurement contract to which the information relates."[20] Notably, person is not defined in this section and has been interpreted "to apply to any contractor, other business entity, or individual who obtains information even if that person is not participating in the procurement."[21] A PIA violation may occur willfully or inadvertently through communications involving a US government employee.

The PIA's impact may extend beyond the covered individual who may face civil or criminal liability, as a federal agency may, in response to a PIA violation, cancel a procurement, rescind a contract, recover funds previously expended under the contract, or reduce a contractor's price or fee.[22] Therefore, an Acquirer would be well advised to assess whether a Target's compliance regime positions employees to avoid potential PIA violations by, for example, training employees regarding the proper conduct of government officials, instructing employees to avoid situations where PIA violations may occur, and providing a sufficient reporting mechanism that allows employees to raise potential PIA concerns internally.

---

16 41 U.S.C. § 2101.

17 *Id.*; *see also* FAR 3.104 (implementing PIA regulations).

18 The seven positions are: (1) Procuring Contracting Officer; (2) Source Selection Authority; (3) member of a Source Selection Evaluation Board; (4) chief of a financial or technical evaluation team; (5) Program Manager; (6) Deputy Program Manager; or (7) Administrative Contracting Officer.

19 The seven types of covered procurement-related decisions are (1) award a contract, (2) award a subcontract, (3) award a modification to a contract or subcontract, (4) award a task or delivery order, (5) establish overhead or other rates, (6) approve issuing a payment or payments, or (7) pay or settle a claim.

20 41 U.S.C. § 2102(b).

21 John Cibinic, Jr., James F. Nagle, & Ralph C. Nash, Jr., Administration of Government Contracts (5th ed. 2016).

22 FAR 52.203-8; FAR 52.203-10.

2. Overview of "Revolving Door" Restrictions

18 U.S.C. § 207 contains a series of overlapping criminal restrictions on the ability of former US government employees to engage in certain matters relating to the US government. Although these provisions do not bar a former US government employee's hiring by any particular private entity, they do restrict the activities in which the former government employee may engage on behalf of the new employer. These restrictions on employment may be for a one-year, two-year or lifetime period, depending on the former government employee's seniority and level of involvement in the matters while working for the federal government. Some of these restrictions prohibit "switching sides" on matters the former employee worked on or supervised during his or her government service. Others prohibit the former official from making communications with or appearances before his or her former agency (or, in some cases depending on seniority, with senior officials from across the executive branch) for a statutory cooling off period.

Broader restrictions are imposed by presidential executive order. In 2017, President Trump signed Executive Order 13770 which prohibits presidential appointees from engaging in even behind-the-scenes lobbying activities with respect to their former agency or other senior executive branch officials. Similarly, the 2018 National Defense Authorization Act prohibits former senior Department of Defense (DOD) military and civilian officials from engaging in behind-the-scenes lobbying activities with respect to the DOD.[23] Many states and localities have also adopted similar provisions.

Violations of the federal criminal restrictions are punishable by up to one year in prison (five years for a willful violation) and by imposition of monetary fines. The attorney general can also bring a civil action with a monetary penalty of up to $50,000.[24] Violations of the Trump Executive Order can result in an additional five-year bar on lobbying activities and a civil action against the former government employee.[25] Similar penalties can be assessed for violations of state and local revolving door rules. And while the rules typically impose liability directly only on the former employee, prosecutors may be able to use a conspiracy or aiding and abetting theory to pursue the former government employee's new employer.

3. How "Revolving Door" Issues Can Arise

All federal, state, and local government contractors must be vigilant in screening whom they hire for potential post-employment restrictions. US government contractors should insist that potential hires obtain an ethics opinion from the designated agency ethics official (DAEO) outlining the restrictions imposed on the individual. Moreover, because the DAEO letters are sometimes incomplete or not fully informed by the relevant facts, government contractors should also undertake an independent review of the post-employment restrictions that will apply.

23 *See* Pub. L. No. 115-91, § 1045.

24 *See* 18 U.S.C. § 216.

25 *See* Exec. Order 13770 § 5.

The Acquirer should determine whether the Target has hired or recruited, or is in the process of hiring or recruiting, any former federal, state, or local government employees, and whether such employees present any conflict-of-interest issues or other restrictions for the Target and the Acquirer. As a threshold matter, the Acquirer should also determine what procedures the Target has in place for the recruitment and hiring of former government employees, such as any screening procedures or questionnaires utilized by the Target's Human Resources Department and training provided to the relevant decision makers, in order to comply with the post-employment restrictions and the PIA.

During the due diligence review, the Acquirer should ascertain whether the Target's employment roster includes any former government employees and what revolving door or PIA restrictions, including DAEO opinions, may be applicable to such employees. The Acquirer may be well advised to undertake an independent analysis of the revolving door restrictions applicable to each former government employee hired by the Target, particularly if the employee may be involved in communications or appearances before, or behind-the-scenes work related to, the US government (for former US government employees) or their former state or local government employer (for former state or local government employees). With respect to any former government employees with these job duties, the Acquirer should:

1. Identify all agencies for whom the former government employees worked and the position(s) held by such employees during their government employment.
2. Identify all matters in which any former government employees were personally and substantially involved and that relate to the activities of the Target.
3. Identify any employment restrictions applicable to the former government employees (e.g., one-year, two-year, or lifetime ban).

In addition, in order to assess the risk of potential violations of the post-employment restrictions and the PIA, the Acquirer should ascertain the degree to which the Target has been monitoring the activities of any former government employees subject to post-employment restrictions.

Finally, identification of any post-employment restrictions applicable to former government employees hired by the Target can trigger the need for post-acquisition measures, such as "information walls" to prevent potential conflicts of interest or providing former government employees with additional guidance regarding these restrictions. Going forward, the Acquirer will need to avoid assigning former government employees to projects that could implicate post-employment restrictions. Additionally, any major changes in an employee's duties will require review to ensure continued compliance with applicable post-employment restrictions.

E. Political Law Considerations

In light of the intense scrutiny that interactions between companies and government officials receive from the press and regulators, when considering a deal involving a government contractor, the Acquirer should carefully weigh the political law risks presented. A Target's inadvertent violation of the complicated rules regulating the Target's dealings with government officials may result in negative headlines that harm the Target's brand and jeopardize required regulatory approvals. In addition to the optics and reputational risks, violations of some political laws, including "pay-to-play" statutes, can impose significant civil penalties on government contractors, including the loss of key contracts and the disgorgement of revenues. Because these complex laws are not intuitive, they present numerous traps for the unwary, making it easy to make an inadvertent violation. In addition to the revolving door issues discussed above, political law diligence should involve a review of the Target's policies, practices, and activities in the following areas.

1. "Pay-to-Play" Rules

Many states and some localities have adopted so-called "pay-to-play" laws and ordinances that restrict the ability of government contractors and individuals and Political Action Committees (PACs) affiliated with government contractors to make certain political contributions. Many of these laws effectively prohibit existing or prospective contractors from making contributions to certain candidates, political parties, political committees, and groups that contribute to candidates. Contractors who make such contributions face civil penalties, may be barred from doing business with the state or locality for a period, and may be forced to disgorge compensation received from an existing government agency customer or client for a period of years following the date of the contribution. In rare cases, the Acquirer itself may face penalties or loss of business on account of a prohibited political contribution by the Target or one of the Target's executives.

These pay-to-play laws often prohibit contributions by the contractor itself and contributions by certain individuals affiliated with the contractor, such as executives, owners, directors, staff whose compensation could be tied to the award of the contract, and even in some jurisdictions, all employees and family members of the above individuals. Some states also restrict both making the contribution and *soliciting others* to make contribution. Still other jurisdictions permit the contributions but require the contractor or prospective contractor to file regular public reports that disclose them.

While frequently overlooked in the diligence process, a single inadvertent violation of a pay-to-play rule can result in enormous business consequences. A small personal contribution by an executive at a government contractor to the campaign of a personal friend, for example, could conceivably result in the loss of the contractor's largest customer. An Acquirer should therefore include a review of the Target's pay-to-play compliance policies and procedures during the diligence process. To ensure compliance with these restrictions, government contractors should adopt a policy that requires certain covered political contributions to be preapproved by the company's legal or compliance department or that prohibits such contributions entirely. If the Target does not have such a policy or if the policy is too narrow, this may be a red flag, increasing the risk that the Target or an individual affiliated with the Target has already made a political contribution that could jeopardize one of the Target's existing or prospective government contracts. In addition to reviewing the policies themselves, the Acquirer should also request copies of the Target's records of political contributions submitted for approval to determine how regularly the policy is followed and enforced and to assess whether any contributions were approved that should not have been.

In many cases, public records permit the Acquirer to independently verify pay-to-play compliance, to a degree. The Acquirer should obtain a list of the Target's top state or local government customers and prospects and cross-check that list with a list of jurisdictions that have adopted pay-to-play laws and ordinances. The Acquirer should then conduct campaign contribution searches in the relevant state campaign finance databases to assess whether any contributions were made that might jeopardize those contracts. If a problematic contribution is identified, it may be necessary to adjust the purchase price or terms of purchase to account for the added risk assumed by the Acquirer.

2. PAC and Campaign Finance

The Federal Election Commission (FEC) and each state regulate campaign finance differently. These rules tend to be complex, and violations can present major reputational and legal risks for government contractors. In light of these risks, Acquirers of government contractors should include campaign finance within the subject areas for diligence. Acquirers should be especially sensitive to these risks when purchasing a Target that operates a PAC, has a government affairs department, retains outside lobbying firms, or whose executives are politically active.

During diligence, Acquirers should obtain a list of all PACs affiliated with the Target, identify any campaign finance compliance policies and programs adopted by the Target, review PAC bylaws, articles of incorporation, and fundraising solicitations, and seek confirmation that the company has not illegally reimbursed any employee's personal political contributions. The Acquirer should also review any PAC reports for potential red flags. If, for example, the PAC has extremely high contribution rates, those high levels of contributions might be an indication that the Target has been using high-pressure (and potentially coercive) tactics to increase the size of the PAC. Similarly, if the PAC reports indicate that the PAC is receiving contributions from lower-level employees, that might be an indication that the PAC is unlawfully soliciting those who do not fall within the class of employees to whom the Target is legally permitted to direct PAC solicitations.

If the Acquirer decides to proceed with the purchase, it should also prepare for the process of transferring the Target's PACs to the purchasing entity. This process can be cumbersome, and the Acquirer should begin to address these issues *before* closing. For example, if the Target's federal PAC will be terminated, this termination should generally be done prior to the closing; otherwise, the two PACs will need to be merged and the Target PAC's prior contributions will count against the ongoing contribution limits of the Acquirer's PAC. At the federal level, PAC mergers also require amendments to FEC reports, integration of data and contribution histories between the PACs, and establishing a process to ensure that neither PAC makes an excessive contribution going forward considering the premerger contributions of the two PACs.

3. Lobbying and Foreign Agents Registration Act

The federal government, every state, and many localities have adopted "lobbying" rules regulating the activities of those who attempt to influence government policies. Many jurisdictions define lobbying to include more than simply attempting to influence legislation, extending the term to encompass efforts to influence executive branch actions, including, in many cases, government procurements. It is not uncommon, however, for government contractors to overlook these "procurement lobbying" rules.

Federal, state, and local lobbying rules typically require that companies and/or individuals that satisfy the definition of "lobbyist" or "lobbyist principal" register and file public reports describing their activities. The failure to register, the failure to file reports, or the filing of late or inaccurate registration statements or reports can result in monetary penalties and significant business and reputational risk.

In addition to these federal, state, and local lobbying registration and reporting rules, if the Target is a foreign company or has foreign ownership or operations, the Acquirer should also consider whether the Foreign Agents Registration Act (FARA) is implicated. FARA is a broadly written, and increasingly enforced, federal criminal statute that requires, among other things, agents of foreign companies to register and report with the US DOJ if they engage in political activities in the United States.

To ensure that the Acquirer does not assume any unexpected lobbying or FARA risks, during the diligence process, the Acquirer should ask the Target to identify jurisdictions where the company, its employees, or its outside consultants are registered as lobbyists. The Acquirer should also review the Target's lobbying and FARA compliance policies, training programs, reporting processes, and any history of lobbying-related enforcement actions or penalties. It is also helpful to review any contracts with lobbying firms and vet those firms to determine whether the Target is relying on consultants with a questionable track record. Publicly filed lobbying reports should also be reviewed for red flags. Lobbying reports that simply "cut and paste" the last report's disclosures may suggest that the Target is not carefully reviewing the reports for accuracy. Missing or late reports, unresolved enforcement matters, or the failure to register altogether in states where the company has an active presence can also be a cause for concern. When FARA is potentially implicated, the Acquirer should also pay careful attention to the Target's interactions with foreign governments to assess whether the Target should have registered under FARA or whether an exemption applies.

Even before closing, the Acquirer should begin to work through the necessary steps to transition the lobbying filings from the Target to the Acquirer. In some cases, the Target will need to file termination reports in the states in which it was active, and the Acquirer will need to be prepared to register as a lobbying entity promptly after closing. In some cases, the Acquirer will simply assume the Target's reporting requirements. In either case, however, the Acquirer should establish a process to ensure that any registrations and reports are filed in a timely manner and that any deadlines are not missed in the flurry of initial post-merger activity.

4. Gifts and Ethics

Many states and localities impose limits on the amounts and types of gifts that government contractors and others may provide to state or local government employees. Indeed, some states prohibit government contractors from providing virtually anything of value to government officials, including a cup of coffee. Even if there is no "quid pro quo," gifts from certain prohibited sources can trigger criminal and civil penalties and reputational damage. For these reasons, Acquirers should be especially wary of Targets that routinely fly government officials to conferences and retreats, pay for meals, or provide gifts or other "swag." The diligence process should therefore involve a review of company policies, training programs, and reporting procedures for gifts to government officials. Prior allegations of gift rule violations or enforcement matters arising out of such gifts can be a major red flag. If the company maintains a register of gifts to government officials, that register should also be reviewed for compliance concerns.

F. Intellectual Property under Government Contracts

Intellectual property (IP) is often among a Target's most valuable assets. During the due diligence process, the Acquirer should submit information and document requests to the Target requesting that the Target identify its IP—most significantly, patents, technical data, and computer software[26]—licensed, developed, used, or delivered in performing its government contracts. The purpose is to identify potential risks and to assess the value in the Target's IP.[27] The US government has its own statutory and regulatory scheme for IP that does not follow the same rules as general commercial intellectual property law. In recent years, DOD agencies have been particularly aggressive in pursuing IP rights not only through the data rights clauses, but also through the data delivery, including the deferred delivery, provisions in their contracts. It is critical, therefore, that these provisions (and compliance therewith) be reviewed and assessed during diligence.

---

[26] The government uses the term "technical data" to cover what would be "trade secrets" in a commercial context.

[27] This section does not discuss copyrights, because copyright protection generally is not a key consideration in government contracts. FAR 27.404-3(b) gives the government a royalty-free license in the copyrighted data delivered under the contract. The scope of the license parallels the government's license in covered technical data under FAR 52.227-14. This means that for copyrighted data first produced in the performance of the contract, the government may reproduce, prepare derivative works, or distribute copies of the data to the public. FAR 27.404-3(a)(4); 52.227-14(c)(1)(iii). The same is true for computer software, except that the government may not distribute copies to the public. *Id.* For DOD contracts, DFARS 227.7203-9 likewise grants the DOD a copyright license coextensive with the other data and software rights the agency obtains under DFARS 252.227-7013 and 7014. One important consideration relating to computer software and copyright is that under the DFARS, if software is further modified—for example, if it is ported to a new platform—it could be considered a "derivative work," a wholly separate work under a different copyright, under which the government would retain rights. *See* DFARS 252.227-7014(c).

✓ **Best Practice Tip:** Initial IP diligence questions include:

- Does the Target produce and deliver products (which may include software) to customers (government and commercial)?
- Do any of the Target's products have IP protection in the form of patents, copyrights, or trade secrets?
- Were any of the Target's products generated or modified in the performance of a US government contract?
- Has any information about any of the Target's products (such as blueprints or source code) been delivered to the government?
- Has the Target taken all requisite actions to protect its IP rights vis-à-vis the government, including marking of technical data and computer software with the prescribed rights legends?
- Does the Target have the right to transfer third-party licenses required for the use of its IP?
- Does the Target use any open source software in any of its products?
- Does the government or any higher-tier contractor have ownership rights in the IP or the ability to restrict the Target's ability to use its IP?

The Acquirer should first consider the Target's industry and products. For example, if the Target is an aerospace company developing technology for the DOD or software for federal civilian agency government customers, then the Target has likely generated valuable IP in relation to its government contracts. It is therefore essential to ascertain what IP rights the Target holds, and what IP rights it may have licensed or given away purposely or inadvertently. The Acquirer should also consider the type of arrangement under which the Target has worked with the government in generating IP. These arrangements, discussed in more detail below, include research and development contracts, Cooperative Research and Development Agreements (CRADAs), and Other Transaction Authority (OTA) agreements. There can be substantial variation in the allocation of IP rights among these various arrangements.

The categories of IP rights discussed below include technical data, computer software, and patents. The distinctions in the definition of these terms and licensing rights between the FAR and the DFARS are also noted when applicable. This section also discusses treatment in the government IP rights scheme for technical data and computer software covering products that qualify as "commercial items." Finally, this section discusses "marking" requirements, which is the method by which contractors identify their assertion of certain categories of IP rights in relation to technical data and computer software that the contractor is providing to the government.

1. Technical Data and Computer Software

a. Definitions

The data rights clauses of the FAR and the DFARS set forth the rights the government receives to use "technical data" and "computer software" either generated in the performance of a government contract or delivered under a government contract. It is important to note that these clauses only apply to traditional procurement instruments and not, for example, to grants, CRADAs, or OTAs.

The rights granted under these clauses are unique to the government context, with no commercial analog. The information protected is typically a hybrid of information that would ordinarily be protected by copyright or trade secret. Generally speaking, the contractor will retain title (i.e., ownership) to technical data and computer software, with the government receiving license rights which vary in scope depending on a number of factors, including the type of procurement instrument and the extent to which government funding was used in developing the IP.

The FAR and the DFARS clauses covering technical data and computer software are similar, but not identical. For example, in the FAR, the term "technical data" is defined as "recorded information (regardless of the form or method of the recording) of a scientific or technical nature (including computer databases and computer software documentation)."[28] Notably this definition does not include computer software or certain other information developed incidentally to contract administration.[29] While the FAR treats all types of technical data and computer software in one clause, the DFARS has separate clauses for technical data and computer software.[30] And, unlike the FAR, the DFARS definition of technical data does not include computer databases.[31]

In both cases, the term "technical data" is distinct from "data deliverables" or "data requirements," which are the contractual obligations to deliver technical data (or computer software) to the government in a specified format. Specifically, "technical data" refers to the subject of the government's license rights or permitted use of data deliverables. Contracts may include a clause that allows the government to order additional data generated in the performance of a contract for three years after the government's acceptance of all data deliverables under a contract.[32] Acquirers should review a Target's contracts, even completed ones, to ascertain if the government retains rights to order additional data and acquire the applicable rights in that data.

"Computer software" is defined in the FAR to cover both a "computer program," or object code, which is the "series of instructions, rules, routines, or statements," which "allow or cause a computer to perform a specific operation or series of operations," and also, related "recorded information" comprising source code listings, design details,

---

28 FAR 52.227-14.

29 *Id.*

30 *See* FAR 52.227-14; DFARS 252.227-7013(a)(14); -7014(a)(14).

31 DFARS 252.227-7013(a).

32 FAR 52.227-16.

algorithms, processes, flow charts, formulas, and related, recorded information and material that would enable the computer program to be produced, created, or compiled.[33] Computer software is not defined to include computer databases and computer software documentation.[34] The DFARS has a different, but similar, definition of computer software: "computer programs, source code, source code listings, object code listings, design details, algorithms, processes, flow charts, formulae and related material that would enable the software to be reproduced, recreated, or recompiled. Computer software does not include computer data bases or computer software documentation."[35]

As noted previously, the contractor typically retains title to or ownership of technical data and computer software used or generated in the performance of a government contract. But, the pertinent question for Acquirers is whether the government has obtained license rights, and, if so, the extent of those rights in the data or software. The regulations provide for three general categories of rights in noncommercial technical data and computer software: Unlimited Rights, Limited/Restricted Rights, and Government Purpose Rights (GPR). There are some notable exceptions, however:

- In some cases, the contracting officer may deviate from the clauses and include customized IP clauses—"specifically negotiated license rights"—to meet specific government requirements.[36]
- If the data was generated in the performance of a Small Business Innovation Research (SBIR) contract, SBIR data rights will apply.
- If the data qualifies as "commercial," the government will receive the same rights as a commercial customer (subject to some exceptions).

✓ **Best Practice Tip:** Review government contracts for standard IP clauses, which are generally incorporated by reference in the FAR and DFARS flow-down clauses.

✓ **Best Practice Tip:** Confirm the nature of each government contract award—is it SBIR? OTA?

✓ **Best Practice Tip:** Review government contracts for customized IP clauses, which are generally located in section H of the contract.

---

33 FAR 52.227-14.

34 *Id.*

35 DFARS 252.227-7013(a)(3).

36 *See* DFARS 252.227-7013(b)(4) and 252.227-7014(b)(4) (for noncommercial data and software); FAR 27.404(c)(1) and FAR 52.227-14(g)(3) (for special tailoring of otherwise limited and restricted rights data and software).

✓ **Best Practice Tip:** Confirm whether the data qualifies as "commercial."

b. Unlimited Rights

The government obtains "unlimited rights" in technical data that has been developed with government funding; that is, the contractor developed the data while being paid for its work under a government contract.[37] Unlimited rights give the government a nearly unrestricted right to use data or software.[38] For example, the government could disclose data or software to a contractor's competitors without restriction. Those competitors could then use that data or software for any purpose they see fit, including commercial purposes or to compete on a government contract. For this reason, if a Target has granted the government unlimited rights in technical data or software, the technical data may already be in the hands of the Target's competitors (and of little value). For computer software, a notable difference between the FAR and DFARS definitions is that the FAR definition of unlimited rights prohibits the government from distributing copies of copyrighted computer software to the public.[39]

c. Limited/Restricted Rights

On the other hand, the government obtains only "limited rights" when the technical data to be delivered or licensed to the government has been developed at private (contractor) expense.[40] For computer software, limited rights are called "restricted rights." For both technical data and computer software, this is the rights category under which the government obtains less expansive rights and is the preferred rights category under which the Target has licensed its technical data or computer software to the government. Generally, the government is not permitted to use or disclose this type of data outside the government.[41] The only exception is use for maintenance or repair.[42] The government obtains unlimited rights in such "form, fit and function data" and also in data delivered "that constitutes manuals or instructional and training material for the installation, operation, or routine maintenance and repair of items. . . ."[43] Under DOD contracts, the latter is described as data "[n]ecessary for installation, operation, maintenance or training

---

37 FAR 52.227-14(b)(1); DFARS 252.227-7013(b)(1).

38 The FAR and DFARS have slightly different definitions of unlimited rights. *Compare* FAR 52.227-14(a) (The FAR definition of unlimited rights is "the rights of the Government to use, disclose, reproduce, prepare derivative works, distribute copies to the public, and perform publicly and display publicly, in any manner and for any purpose, and to have or permit others to do so") *with* DFARS 252.227-7013(a) ("Unlimited rights means rights to use, modify, reproduce, perform, display, release, or disclose technical data in whole or in part, in any manner, and for any purpose whatsoever, and to have or authorize others to do so.")

39 FAR 52.227-14(c)(1)(iii).

40 FAR 52.227-14(a); DFARS 252.227-7013(b)(3).

41 FAR 52.227-14(g) and (g)(3) (Alternate II); DFARS 252.227-7013(a)(14).

42 FAR 52.227-14(b).

43 FAR 52.227-14(b)(1).

purposes" (OMIT data), which does not include "detailed manufacturing or process data" (DMPD).[44] Even in those cases, the government is required to notify the contractor of any disclosure.[45] In sum, for technical data developed at private expense, the government is permitted to use and disclose the data within the government, including to other contractors, for purposes of maintenance and repair, but not for manufacturing purposes.[46] Likewise, under "restricted rights," the government only receives a license to disclose the computer software to support service or maintenance contractors, who are also bound by the restrictive rights limitations.[47]

d. Government Purpose Rights

For DOD contracts, the DFARS diverges from the FAR by establishing a third category of rights in technical data and computer software called Government Purpose Rights (GPR). GPR are available when the government and private funding have been used to develop data or software through "mixed funding."[48] The FAR does not have an equivalent license for data developed with mixed funding. The key difference between GPR and unlimited rights is that the government is only authorized to release the data or software to third parties, such as other contractors, for "government purposes," meaning for any activity in which the government is a party, including cooperative agreements with foreign governments or competitive reprocurements.[49] However, unlike unlimited rights, the government cannot disclose or distribute the data or software with rights that would allow recipients of the data or software to use it for commercial purposes. The data and software are also subject to an exemption under the Freedom of Information Act.[50] While limited and unlimited rights exist in perpetuity, GPR convert to unlimited rights at the end of five years, or as otherwise agreed by the parties.[51]

e. Small Business Innovation Research Rights

Certain contracts and grants administered by the Small Business Administration (SBA) may provide for another special category of data rights referred to as SBIR rights, which are available to small technology businesses conducting research and development work under SBIR and Small Business Technology Transfer (STTR) awards.[52] SBIR rights attach even if there was no private funding, where the government's rights would otherwise be

---

44 DFARS 252.227-7013(b)(1).

45 DFARS 227.7103-5(c); DFARS 252.227-7013(a)(14).

46 DFARS 252.227-7013(a)(14).

47 FAR 52.227-14(g).

48 DFARS 252.227-7013(b)(2) and 252.227-7014(b)(2).

49 DFARS 252.227-7013(a)(12); DFARS 252.227-7014(a)(12).

50 Tax Analysts v. United States Dep't of Justice, 913 F. Supp. 599 (D.D.C. 1996) (DOJ did not "control" data provided under a contract, which restricted DOJ's right to use, transfer, and dispose of such data, and, for that reason, the data did not constitute an "agency record" for FOIA purposes).

51 DFARS 252.227-7013(b)(2)(ii); DFARS 252.227-7014(b)(2)(ii).

52 FAR 52.227-20(a); DFARS 227.7104; DFARS 252.227-7018.

unlimited.[53] For privately funded data, the contractor may still assert limited or restricted rights under SBIR or STTR contracts.[54]

As with GPR, SBIR rights are maintained for a set number of years, generally four years (or five under the DFARS) from acceptance of all items delivered under the contract.[55] The rights may be extended through subsequent SBIR awards through three phases of SBIR contracts. In phase I, the contractor establishes the technical merit, feasibility, and commercial potential of the proposed research and development effort, as well as the contractor's quality of performance.[56] Phase I awards are generally fairly small, not exceeding $150,000 over six months.[57] In phase II, the contractor extends the research and development efforts initiated in phase I, to further the technical and commercial potential of the phase I project.[58] In phase III, the contractor's work "derives from, extends, or completes efforts" made under the prior phases.[59] Phase III work may be funded by other federal agencies, or even the private sector, but does not receive funds from the SBIR program.[60] As long as the subsequent awards take place during the prior phase, the SBIR data protection will continue.[61]

Under the FAR SBIR provision, the government may use the data or software within the government for any government purpose, but cannot use or disclose the data or software outside the government, except to support, maintenance, and repair contractors.[62] Under the DFARS scheme, SBIR rights essentially mirror limited/restricted rights, so the rights are more restrictive.[63] Under the FAR, once SBIR rights expire, the regulations permit unrestricted disclosure and use for any government purposes.[64] Under the DFARS, SBIR rights convert to unlimited rights.[65]

✓ **Best Practice Tip:** Review the Target's government contracts to ascertain and confirm what rights category the Target has granted the government for technical data and computer software generated and delivered under each contract. This part of diligence is especially important if the IP is significant to the value of the Target. Do not assume that data generated under an SBIR contract is covered by SBIR rights—the Target must have properly asserted its SBIR rights across each phase of the SBIR awards.

---

53 *See* FAR 52.227-20; DFARS 252.227-7018.

54 DFARS 52.227-20(f); DFARS 252.227-7018(b)(2) and (3).

55 FAR 52.227-20(d); DFARS 252.227-7018(b)(4).

56 15 U.S.C. § 638(e)(4)(A).

57 *See* https://www.sbir.gov/about/about-sbir.

58 15 U.S.C. § 638(e)(4)(B).

59 *Id.* at § (e)(4)(C).

60 *See Id.*

61 *See* https://www.sbir.gov/tutorials/data-rights/tutorial-2.

62 FAR 52.227-20(a).

63 DFARS 252.227-7018(a)(19).

64 FAR 52.227-20(d).

65 DFARS 252.227-7019(b)(1)(vi).

f. Segregability

The DFARS data and software rights scheme incorporate the concept of "segregability."[66] Segregability allows for the determination of the source of funding for a deliverable to be broken down into subparts, so that rights can be determined at the lowest practicable level. This allows the contractor to specify that technical data created with mixed funding, and ordinarily subject to GPR, is broken out into constituent limited rights and unlimited rights slices, to the extent possible. The DFARS permits the segregation of technical data down to the subitem or subcomponent level or any segregable portion of a process.[67] For computer software, segregability can be down to the level of a module or subroutine that performs a specific function.[68] Segregability can result in gaps in a data package, which may require the government to negotiate a separate license with the contractor for rights to the gap in the deliverable data or software created by the segregable subitem.

g. Commercial Items

A "commercial item" is defined as "[a]ny item . . . that is of a type customarily used by the general public . . . and . . . [h]as been sold, leased, or licensed to the general public . . . [or] [h]as been offered for sale, lease, or license to the general public."[69] Commercial computer software is that which is developed or regularly used for nongovernmental purposes. This means that the software has been sold, offered for sale, or will be available commercially, in time to satisfy the delivery requirement of a contract, or that the software satisfies any of the foregoing categories and would require only minor modification to meet the requirements of the contract.[70]

For commercial items, the government generally obtains only the technical data or computer software rights provided to commercial customers.[71] The government only acquires the rights in commercial software provided by the contractor's standard commercial licensing agreement.[72] However, even for commercial items, contractors must still grant the government the right to disclose commercial software to maintenance and repair contractors that have agreed to restrictions on further disclosure.[73]

Contracting officers are normally instructed not to challenge the presumption that commercial items and software were developed at private expense.[74] As a limited exception, the DFARS provides for five categories of commercial data for which the government acquires unlimited rights, including form, fit, and function data, and "OMIT"

---

66 DFARS 227.7103-4(b); DFARS 227.7203-4(b).

67 DFARS 227.7103-4(b).

68 DFARS 227.7203-4(b).

69 FAR 2.101.

70 DFARS 252.227-7014(a)(1); *see also* FAR 2.101 ("'commercial computer software' means any computer software that is a commercial item.")

71 FAR 12.211.

72 FAR 12.212.

73 FAR 52.227-19.

74 FAR 12.211.

data, which, as noted above, is data necessary for operation, maintenance, installation, and training activities.[75] This data does not provide an ability to produce the product, and generally would not constitute valuable IP.[76]

Finally, open source software (OSS) is also viewed as a form of commercial license and, therefore, nearly always treated as commercial software under the FAR and DFARS.[77] OSS used under a government contract would have the same deliverable requirements and licensing terms as are provided to the public. Some government contracts include express prohibitions on the use of OSS. In other cases, even in the absence of an express prohibition, the OSS may have been used by the Target under terms that would require impermissible disclosure or use by the public under the terms of the government contract.

h. Marking Requirements

Contractors must identify in their proposal the data and software the contractor intends to produce with other than unlimited rights.[78] The FAR and DFARS contain prescribed marking requirements, which are implemented through legends that must accompany all technical data and computer software for which the contractor asserts limited, restricted, or GPR delivered to the government.[79] Failing to apply the proper marking may result in the loss of the limited or restricted rights status that would otherwise have applied.[80] The DFARS encourages the government to permit contractors the opportunity to correct inadvertently omitted markings, but there is no guarantee that the government will allow the contractor to rectify a mistake or omission.[81]

Data delivered with markings that are not authorized by the FAR or DFARS are considered to be nonconforming, and risk loss of IP rights protection.[82] Contractors must follow the forms prescribed in the FAR and DFARS clauses. Further, unjustified markings that incorrectly or improperly assert limited or restricted rights may result in a government determination of entitlement to unlimited rights, which the contractor may appeal under the contract's Disputes clause.[83]

2. Patents

The principles for rights in patents under government contracts, cooperative agreements, and grants are governed by the Bayh-Dole Act, 35 U.S.C. §§ 200-212.[84] The government

---

75 DFARS 252.227-7015(b)(1).

76 *See* DFARS 252.227-7013(a)(11) and (b)(1)(v) (describing such data as useful in maintaining an item or integrating it with other products and systems, but not valuable for use in *manufacturing* an item).

77 FAR 21.212; see DFARS 252.227-7014(a)(14).

78 FAR 52.227-15; DFARS 252.227-7017.

79 FAR 52.227-15; DFARS 252.227-7013.

80 DFARS 227.7103-10(c) and DFARS 227.7203-10(c).

81 *Id.*

82 FAR 52.227-14(e); DFARS 252.227-7013(e) and -7014(e).

83 FAR 52.227-14(e); DFARS 252.227-7013(e) and -7014(e).

84 As discussed in section 4, CRADAs are covered by the Stevenson-Wydler Technology Innovation Act of 1980, 15 U.S.C. 3710.

holds an unrestricted license to use, and allow contractors to use under a government contract, all patents first conceived or reduced to practice during the performance of a government contract.[85] It is essential, therefore, for the Acquirer to identify all patents held by a contractor that were conceived or reduced to practice during performance of a government contract.

28 U.S.C. § 1498, which is the statutory basis for bringing a patent claim against the government, is applicable to all patents regardless of their funding. While the government cannot be enjoined from infringing a patent, it can be forced to pay a reasonable royalty, if infringement is found.[86]

Similar to technical data and computer software, a contractor may elect to retain title to a subject invention developed under a government contract.[87] Bayh-Dole, however, gives the government a fully paid-up, nonexclusive license to practice or have practiced inventions for or on behalf of the US government throughout the world.[88]

Contractors can lose title to a subject invention if it fails to take adequate steps to commercialize a patent.[89] In that situation, the government can exercise what are referred to as "march-in" rights, which allow the government to grant additional licenses to the patent. A contractor's failure to commercialize a subject invention is something to keep in mind during the diligence process, particularly if the subject matter of a patent covers an item that may have critical importance for public health or national security purposes. More significantly, a contractor may lose title to an invention developed in connection with a government contract, if the contractor fails to report that invention to the government within two months after the inventor discloses it in writing to the contractor personnel responsible for patent matters.[90] Among its responsibilities under Bayh-Dole, a contractor must ensure that it can properly convey title or licensing rights as required under its government contract.[91] Previously, simply having "personnel identified as responsible for the administration of patent matters" at the contractor was largely sufficient to meet this requirement.[92] New regulations, however, additionally require contractors to obtain from their employees written assignments, assigning all of the employees' rights and titles to subject inventions to their contractor employers.[93] Bayh-Dole also contains monitoring and reporting requirements that must be followed to ensure the government has the proper rights in the subject invention.

Last, the patent rights clauses contain a requirement for substantial US manufacturing. Specifically, before a subject invention can be exclusively licensed, the contractor must get the licensee to agree to manufacture the subject invention substantially

---

85 FAR 52.227-13.

86 28 U.S.C. § 1498.

87 FAR 52.227-11; DFARS 252.227-7038.

88 35 U.S.C. § 202(c)(4).

89 35 U.S.C. § 203.

90 FAR 52.227-11(c) and (d).

91 Stanford v. Roche, 131 S. Ct. 2188, 2199 (2011), *aff'g* 583 F.3d 832 (Fed. Cir. 2009).

92 *See* FAR 52.227-11(e)(2); DFARS 252.227-7038(e)(2).

93 37 C.F.R. § 401.14(f)(2).

in the United States.[94] "Substantially" has not been clearly defined in this context. If a contractor breaches this clause, the government has grounds to exercise march-in rights, although it is not required to do so.[95]

> ✓ **Best Practice Tip:** For patented inventions developed under government contracts, ensure that the Target adhered to the duties and obligations under the Bayh-Dole framework. If the Target missed a step, the patent may be unenforceable, or title may have been forfeited to the government.

3. Other Transaction Authority Agreements

OTAs are agreements other than contracts, grants, or cooperative agreements that are authorized by statute for DOD, NASA, Department of Energy (DOE), Health and Human Services, Department of Homeland Security, and Department of Transportation, as well as specific agencies within these departments.[96] OTA agreements are designed to provide a streamlined method for pursuing prototype projects and training into follow-on production, although, in practice, their use is expanding. Among other characteristics, these agreements permit flexibility with regard to IP rights. Neither Bayh-Dole, the FAR, nor the DFARS applies to OTAs, and there are no other specific statutory limitations.[97] The idea behind OTAs is to offer commercial contractors an opportunity to enter into a flexible arrangement for research and development and prototyping with authorized agencies, without the constraints imposed by the generally applicable federal procurement IP framework.

Given the flexibility afforded under OTAs, these agreements require particularly close diligence when reviewed by the Acquirer. OTAs may include customized IP provisions covering technical data, computer software, and patents that may or may not resemble the general FAR and DFARs requirements.[98]

4. Cooperative Research and Development Agreements

CRADAs are research and development vehicles that allow contractors and the government to work together on independent research and development projects, share technical know-how, and increase the commercialization of federally developed technology.[99] CRADAs are a contract for a specific type of independent research and development project, allowing the contractor access to government facilities and technology. The

---

94 FAR 52.227-11(i); FAR 52.227-12(i); DFARS 252.227-7038(g).

95 *See* FAR 52.227-11(j)(4); 52.227-12(j)(4); DFARS 252.227-7038(h).

96 10 U.S.C. § 2371; 51 U.S.C. § 20113; 42 U.S.C. § 7256; 42 U.S.C. § 247d-7e; 6 U.S.C. § 391; 49 U.S.C. § 5312.

97 10 U.S.C. §§ 2320 and 2321.

98 For additional information regarding OTAs, see the Department of Defense OTA Guide 2018, available at: https://aaf.dau.mil/ot-guide/.

99 *See* 15 U.S.C. § 3710a.

government does not provide funding to contractors through CRADAs.[100] Instead, the government allows the contractor to utilize government facilities and personnel in a nonprocurement context to further its development projects.

Patent rights under CRADAs, as governed by the Stevenson-Wydler Act, are fairly similar to those under Bayh-Dole, granting title in any subject invention to the contractor in exchange for a government-purpose license.[101] The Stevenson-Wydler Act contains the word "normally" to describe this rights scheme, granting some flexibility for negotiation between the contractor and the government.[102]

On the copyright and trade secret front, the government is prohibited from disclosing any trade secrets or commercial information it receives from its contractor collaborator under a CRADA.[103] As with all data rights protections, the contractor should take appropriate steps to mark copyright and trade secret information when it shares this information with the government in the course of the collaboration.

G. Small Business Issues

1. Overview of Small Business Requirements in Federal Procurement

When the Target is a small business, a number of issues affecting its continued eligibility to receive awards of small business set-aside contracts must be considered during the due diligence process. These issues include potential loss of business and revenues associated with such contracts following an acquisition, as well as the diminished attractiveness of the Target to both government agencies and prime contractors. While contractors generally can continue performance of small business set-aside contracts after exceeding their size limit, if the Target is no longer small post-closing, government agencies would no longer receive small business "credit" for contracts awarded to the Target, and prime contractors would no longer be able to use those subcontracts to meet their obligations under their small business subcontracting plans.

A "set-aside for small business" is the reservation of an acquisition exclusively for participation by small business concerns.[104] A small business set-aside may be open to all small businesses, and a small business set-aside of a single acquisition or a class of acquisitions may be total or partial.[105] Under the Small Business Act[106] and implementing regulations, it is the policy of the government to provide maximum practicable opportunities in its acquisitions to small business; veteran-owned small business; service-disabled

---

[100] *Id.* at § 3710a(b)(3)(A), (d)(1).

[101] *Id.* at § 3710a(b)(2).

[102] *Id.*

[103] *Id.* at § 3710a(c)(7)(A).

[104] *See* FAR 19.501(a).

[105] *Id.*

[106] 15 U.S.C. § 631.

veteran-owned small business (SDVOSB); historically underutilized business zones (HUBZone) small business; small disadvantaged business, including participants in the SBA 8(a) Business Development ("8(a)") Program; and women-owned small business (WOSB) concerns.[107] Such concerns must also have the maximum practicable opportunity to participate as subcontractors in the contracts awarded by any executive agency, consistent with efficient contract performance.[108]

Regulations issued by the SBA impose size and status recertification requirements on certain types of long-term contracts that are greater than five years in duration. The SBA rules also require recertification when a small business concern becomes other than small or ineligible for its small business program due to an acquisition or merger, such as when the small business concern is acquired by a large business, or when an approved contract novation has taken place. This recertification requirement applies to any type of contract and at any time that a small business's size or status changes because it is merged with, acquired by, or acquires other businesses. The SBA recertification requirements are discussed in section F.2.c.

2. Impact of Acquisition on Small Business Status and Contracts

a. Small Business Size Status

Small business size status is based on criteria, commonly referred to as "size standards," established by the SBA on an industry-by-industry basis. Small business size standards are applied by (a) classifying the product or service in an industry that, based on the North American Industry Classifications System (NAICS),[109] best describes the principal nature of the product or service at issue; (b) identifying the size standard established by the SBA for that industry; and (c) specifying the size standard in the solicitation, so that offerors can appropriately represent themselves as "small" or "large" businesses for that procurement.[110] The NAICS industry codes are based either on average annual revenues or number of employees. Under the SBA's size regulations, the calculation of a concern's size includes the receipts, employees, or other measure of size of all of a firm's domestic and foreign affiliates.[111]

When a small business has an affiliate, the size of the affiliate may negatively impact the small business' size status. Under the SBA's affiliation rules, in general, concerns are affiliates of each other "when one concern controls or has the power to control the other, or a third party or parties controls or has the power to control both[,]" whether exercised

---

[107] The US Department of Veterans Affairs ("VA") also has authority to set aside procurements for veteran-owned small businesses and SDVOSBs under the Veterans Benefits, Health Care, and Information Technology Act of 2006. *See* 38 U.S.C. §§ 8127–28.

[108] *See* FAR 19.201(a).

[109] *Id.* at 107.

[110] *See* FAR 19.102(b); *see also* the SBA's regulations in 13 C.F.R. Part 121.

[111] *See* 13 C.F.R. § 121.103(a)(6).

or not.[112] Power to control includes both affirmative control, such as exercising management control over a concern, as well as negative control, such as one concern having a presence on the board of directors equal to that of other concerns or having the right to approve or block certain business decisions.

In determining whether affiliation with another business concern exists under this standard, SBA considers factors such as common ownership, common management, contractual relationships, and previous relationships with or ties to another concern. The business concerns need not be in the same line of business to be considered affiliates. Power to control exists when a party or parties have 50 percent or more ownership of a business, but it may also exist with considerably less than 50 percent ownership through contractual arrangement, or when one or more parties own a large share as compared to other parties. In determining whether affiliation exists, the SBA will consider the totality of the circumstances, and it may find affiliation even though no single factor is sufficient to constitute affiliation.[113]

There are limited exceptions to affiliation coverage, such as small business investment companies and venture capital or other investment firms meeting certain SBA-specified requirements.[114] However, even if an investment in a small business concern is made by a venture capital operating company or investment company, the SBA's affiliation rules will still apply based on the types of control exercised by the investing entity.

1. The Present Effect Rule

Under the SBA's Present Effect Rule, in determining affiliation, the SBA considers stock options, convertible securities, and agreements to merge (including agreements in principle to merge) to have a "present effect" for purposes of determining whether a person or concern controls another concern. The SBA treats such options, convertible securities, and agreements as though the rights granted have been exercised.[115] The SBA does not give present effect to agreements to open or continue negotiations toward a possible merger or sale of stock at some later date, nor does it consider such agreements to be "agreements in principle."[116] The SBA's regulations further provide that "[o]ptions, convertible securities, and agreements that are subject to conditions precedent which are incapable of fulfillment, speculative, conjectural, or unenforceable under state or Federal law, or where the probability of the transaction (or exercise of the rights) occurring is

---

112 13 C.F.R. § 121.103(a). Some types of affiliation do not require an explicit finding of control because the SBA applies a rebuttable presumption of affiliation in certain circumstances. See 13 C.F.R. § 121.103(f) (affiliation based on identity of interest), (g) (affiliation based on the newly organized concern rule).

113 *See* 13 C.F.R. § 121.103(a)(5).

114 *See* 13 C.F.R. § 121.103(b).

115 *See* 13 C.F.R. § 121.103(d)(1).

116 *See* 13 C.F.R. § 121.103(d)(2); *see also* WRS Infrastructure & Env't, Inc. v. United States, 85 Fed. Cl. 442, 445 (2009) (citing *Size Appeal of PCCI, Inc.*, SBA No. SIZ-4531 (Jan. 17, 2003)); *cf. Size Appeal of Nuclear Fuel Services, Inc.*, SBA No. SIZ-5324 (Feb. 2, 2012) (reversing SBA area office's finding of an agreement in principle where there was a tentative proposal to acquire appellant, no indication of acceptance of the proposal, the proposal stated it was nonbinding and subject to numerous conditions, and negotiations continued for eight months after the proposal was sent).

shown to be extremely remote, are not given present effect."[117] This means that once an agreement in principle is executed by the parties, the corporate transaction (i.e., merger or acquisition) contemplated by the agreement will be deemed to have occurred for purposes of determining the Target's size status.

Decisions issued by the SBA Office of Hearings and Appeals (OHA) have raised a note of caution with respect to the use of letters of intent (LOIs) in transactions involving small businesses. An LOI is typically prepared as an acknowledgment that a merger or acquisition between companies is under consideration. Companies involved in transactions involving a small business should be aware of the risk that detailed LOIs, even where explicitly made nonbinding, may be deemed to create affiliation between a Target small business and a potential Acquirer.[118] The OHA has stated that whether a document between the parties is an LOI, or is actually an agreement in principle, is to be determined not by the caption on the document, but by the substance of the entire document. Even where an LOI is styled as a "nonbinding" agreement, there is a risk that it will be accorded "present effect" if the LOI has been signed by both parties, the parties have conducted substantial negotiations, the Acquirer has performed substantial due diligence, the LOI includes many specific terms that may be part of the final agreement, and the Acquirer has stated its intention to purchase the Target.[119]

✓ **Best Practice Tip:** A document captioned as an LOI may, by its terms, be considered sufficiently binding to be given present effect as an agreement in principle and to create an affiliation between the Acquirer and the Target. An LOI may be interpreted as binding on the parties if it too closely resembles a formal contract. A finding of affiliation can result in premature loss of the Target's small business status and its ability to compete for set-aside contracts, and it could adversely affect the Acquirer's ability to transfer small business contracts and subcontracts.

2. The Former Affiliate Rule

When a small business has a "former affiliate," an entity with which it used to be affiliated, the annual receipts of a former affiliate are not included if affiliation ceased before the date used for measuring size.[120] The exclusion of annual receipts of a former affiliate applies during the entire period of measurement, not just the period after which

117 *See* 13 C.F.R. 121.103(d)(3).

118 *See Size Appeal of WRS Infrastructure and Env't, Inc.*, SBA No. SIZ-5007 (Oct. 1, 2008) (SBA area office reasonably concluded that LOI was not speculative, was intended to succeed, included salient terms, like price, and resulted in holding company's purchase of small business). *See also WRS Infrastructure & Env't, Inc.*, 85 Fed. Cl. 442 (affirming OHA's finding that company's LOI to purchase another business was agreement in principle); *Kadix Sys., LLC*, SBA No. SIZ-5016 (Dec. 16, 2008) (document captioned as LOI may, by its terms, be sufficiently binding to be given present effect as an agreement in principle).

119 *WRS Infrastructure & Env't, Inc.*, 85 Fed. Cl. at 445.

120 *See* 13 C.F.R. § 121.104(d)(4).

affiliation ceased.[121] A dissolved or liquidated firm, which has ceased to exist as an entity, is a former affiliate.[122] This means that even if two firms were affiliated for a portion of the period used for measuring size, as long as the affiliation ceases during that period, the size of the former affiliate will not factor into the size of the concern in any way.

> ✓ **Best Practice Tip:** Consider whether a sale or acquisition could cease affiliation and reduce the size of a business that is close to or exceeding its size standard.

b. Status Under Other Small Business Programs

Acquisition of a small business also can impact its eligibility for small business programs. As noted above, procurements can be set aside for veteran-owned small business, SDVOSBs, HUBZone small business, small disadvantaged business, and WOSBs, and each small business program has distinct eligibility requirements.[123] Participation in all of these small business programs is contingent upon the small business being owned or controlled by qualifying individuals (i.e., a woman, a service-disabled veteran, a socially and economically disadvantaged individual, a US citizen), and acquisition by another firm would change the ownership and control of the small business.[124] All of these programs require the firm to be directly owned by a person, and so acquisition by a company would directly impact the small business' eligibility for the small business programs.

Even if a participant in a small business program is acquired by an individual who would also be eligible for participation in the same small business program, the acquiring person should not assume that the company's participation in the program will automatically continue after the acquisition. In the 8(a) Program, if the individual upon whom eligibility for the 8(a) Program was based relinquishes ownership or control of the company, any 8(a) contracts or orders awarded to the company must be terminated for convenience unless the SBA administrator waives this requirement.[125] The waiver of this requirement must be requested in writing prior to the change of ownership or control unless the change is due to death or incapacity of the owner.[126] A concern performing an 8(a) contract must notify the SBA in writing immediately upon entering into an agreement or agreement in principle to transfer all or part of its stock or ownership interest or assets to another party.[127] Similarly, a participant in the HUBZone program

---

121 *Id.*

122 *See Size Appeal of Hallmark-Phoenix 8, LLC*, SBA No. SIZ-5046 (June 22, 2009).

123 *See* 13 C.F.R. Part 124 (small disadvantaged businesses, including participants in the 8(a) Program); 13 C.F.R. Part 125 (SDVOSBs); 13 C.F.R. Part 126 (HUBZone small businesses); 13 C.F.R. Part 127 (WOSBs); 38 C.F.R. Part 74 (veteran-owned small businesses and SDVOSBs under VA procurements).

124 13 C.F.R. § 124.101; 13 C.F.R. § 124.1002; 13 C.F.R. § 125.11(g); 13 C.F.R. § 126.200; 13 C.F.R. § 127.200; 38 C.F.R. § 74.2.

125 13 C.F.R. § 124.515(a), (b).

126 13 C.F.R. § 124.515(c).

127 13 C.F.R. § 124.515(g).

or VA veteran-owned small business program must notify the SBA or VA, respectively, of a material change that could affect its eligibility for the program, such as a change in ownership.[128]

If the Target is a participant in these small business programs, be mindful that its value and ability to obtain new contracts will change if it is no longer eligible for the small business program of which it is a participant. Even if it can retain a set-aside contract after acquisition (see below), an acquiring company should not assume it is buying the Target's small business size or status.

c. SBA Rules on Size and Status Recertification for Long-Term Contracts and Where an Acquisition, Merger, or Novation Takes Place

Generally, a firm that was awarded a contract set-aside for small businesses or participants in small business programs is considered a small business (or a participant in small business programs) throughout the life of that contract.[129] The contracting officer also has the authority to request holders of multiple-award contracts to recertify their size or status in connection with a specific order.[130] Additionally, for all types of set-asides except for 8(a) set-asides, SBA regulations require recertification of size or status under certain types of long-term contracts that are greater than five years in duration (including options), including Government-Wide Acquisition Contracts (GWACs), General Services Administration MAS contracts, and multiagency contracts. Under the SBA regulations, for these types of long-term contracts, a contracting officer must request that a business recertify its small business size or status no more than 120 days prior to the end of the fifth year of the contract, and no more than 120 days prior to exercising any option thereafter.[131]

Thus, for long-term contracts, companies will be required to recertify their small business size or status prior to the sixth year of performance and every time an option is exercised thereafter. If the contractor certifies that it is other than small or no longer eligible for the small business program, the agency can no longer count the options or orders issued under the contract toward its small business prime contracting goals.[132] The agency and the contractor must immediately revise all applicable contract databases, such as the SAM, to reflect the new size or status.[133] However, the SBA rules specifically provide that size or status recertification does not change the terms and conditions of the contract, and any limitations on subcontracting, nonmanufacturer, and subcontracting plan requirements remain in effect throughout the life of the contract.[134] This means that recertifying as other than small or ineligible as an SDVOSB, HUBZone small business,

---

128 *See* 13 C.F.R. § 126.501; 38 C.F.R. § 74.15(a).

129 *See* 13 C.F.R. § 121.404(g); 13 C.F.R. § 124.503(h)(1)(iii); 13 C.F.R. § 125.18(e)(1); 13 C.F.R. § 126.601(h)(1); 13 C.F.R. § 127.503(h)(1).

130 *Id.*

131 *See* 13 C.F.R. § 121.404(g)(3); 13 C.F.R. § 125.18(e)(2); 13 C.F.R. § 126.601(h)(1); 13 C.F.R. § 127.503(h)(1).

132 *Id.*

133 13 C.F.R. § 121.404(g)(3).

134 *See* 13 C.F.R. § 121.404(g)(3); 13 C.F.R. § 125.18(e)(2); 13 C.F.R. § 126.601(h)(1); 13 C.F.R. § 127.503(h)(1).

or WOSB will not cause a business to lose a long-term contract as a result of growing its size or changing its status. However, the SBA has expressed its intent that a firm that grows to be other than small or fails to meet the small business program requirements when recertifying its size or status is not eligible to compete for those set-aside orders after recertification.[135]

For set-aside contracts other than 8(a) set-asides, if the contract is novated, the acquiring contractor must recertify its small business size or status or inform the agency that it is other than small or no longer eligible for the small business program.[136] If the new contractor no longer has the size or status of the original contractor, the agency can no longer count the options or orders issued pursuant to the contract toward its small business goals.[137]

If a contractor has been awarded a set-aside contract and it acquires, is acquired by, or merges with another concern and novation is not required, the contractor must recertify its small business size or status or inform the agency it is other than small or no longer eligible for the small business program within thirty days of closing the acquisition.[138] If the contractor no longer has the size or status it had when awarded the contract, the agency can no longer count the options or orders issued pursuant to the contract toward its small business goals. The agency and contractor must also revise all applicable federal contract databases to reflect its new size and status.[139]

The SBA's rules also require size recertification in additional circumstances. If there is a merger, sale, or acquisition, recertification is required: (a) for all affiliates of the acquired or acquiring concern who are no longer small; (b) for both the acquiring concern and the acquired concern if each has been awarded a small business contract; (c) for a joint venture when an acquired concern, acquiring concern, or merger concern is a participant in a joint venture that has been awarded a contract or order as a small business; and (d) if the merger, sale, or acquisition occurs after a proposal is submitted but prior to award, the offeror must recertify its size to the contracting officer prior to award.[140]

> ✓ **Best Practice Tip:** If a company is acquiring any amount of stock of a small business or merging with a small business, confirm whether recertification is required before completing the transaction. Recertification, if required, must be done within thirty days of the transaction becoming final.

---

135 *See* Conforming Statutory Amendments and Technical Corrections to Small Business Government Contracting Regulations, 83 Fed. Rg. 12,849, 12,850 (March 26, 2018) (to be codified at 13 C.F.R. § 121.404(g), 13 C.F.R. § 125.18(e)(1), 13 C.F.R. § 126.601(h)(1), 13 C.F.R. § 127.503(h)(1)).

136 *See* 13 C.F.R. § 121.404(g)(1); 13 C.F.R. § 125.18(e)(1)(i); 13 C.F.R. § 126.601(h)(1)(i); 13 C.F.R. § 127.503(h)(1)(i).

137 *Id.*

138 13 C.F.R. § 121.404(g)(2)(i); 13 C.F.R. § 125.18(e)(1)(ii); 13 C.F.R. § 126.601(h)(1)(ii); 13 C.F.R. § 127.503(h)(1)(ii).

139 *Id.*

140 13 C.F.R. § 121.404(g)(2)(ii).

H. Terminations

1. Convenience—Fixed-Price Contract

The termination for convenience clause (T4C) is a required clause in every government contract.[141] Under this clause, the government has the right to terminate the contract whenever such termination is in the best interest of the government. This permits the government to end performance of a contract without being liable for breach damages.

Certain government programs may require the government to terminate a contract for convenience upon certain events. For example, the SBA requires the termination of an 8(a) contract when the contractor enters into a transaction by which it is no longer an eligible 8(a), or if the contract is novated to another contractor, unless a waiver is obtained.[142]

Major government contractors include a statement in their financial disclosures (e.g. 10Ks, annual reports) that their government contracts are subject to termination for convenience. Upon a termination for convenience the contractor is entitled to recovery of its costs of performance to date and of implementing the termination (settlement expenses), including the cost of preparing its settlement proposal and negotiating with its subcontractors.

2. Default—Fixed-Price Contract

A termination for default (T4D) is the government contracts' equivalent of a termination for cause in a commercial contract. The government has the right to terminate a contractor for default if the contractor fails to: (a) deliver the specified work on schedule, (b) make progress so as to endanger timely performance of the contract, or (c) perform any of the contract provisions.[143] The government is to provide the contractor with a show cause or cure notice and an opportunity to remedy the cause underlying the termination prior to defaulting a contractor for failure to deliver the specified work on schedule or failure to perform.

If the government's termination for default is sustained, the contractor is potentially liable for several forms of damages. First, the contractor has an obligation to return to the government progress payments that have been received but which were not liquidated by delivery and acceptance of work. Second, the government can recover its excess costs in obtaining completion of the work from a reprocurement vendor. This is the corollary to the acquirer's recovery of "cover" in commercial contracts.[144] Third, the contractor is liable for the government's incidental costs, such as the costs incurred in securing a replacement vendor.

The standard default clause also allows the government to obtain other remedies provided by law. While some decisions have hinted at contractor liability for consequential

---

[141] *See, e.g.*, FAR 52.249-6 (fixed-price contracts).

[142] 13 C.F.R. § 124.515.

[143] FAR 52.249-8 (Fixed Price Supply and Service).

[144] *Cf.* UCC 2.712.

damages, such damages are almost never sought by the government in a termination for default.

If it is determined that the contractor was not in default, or if the termination for default is overturned for any reason, the default is converted to a termination for convenience. In that instance, the contractor's rights are determined as though the original action had been a T4C. Accordingly, the contractor is not entitled to recover anticipatory profits or consequential damages.

3. Cost-Reimbursement Contracts

The termination clause for cost-reimbursement contracts covers both terminations for convenience and for default.[145] The primary differences between the two remedies are that in a default (a) the contractor's fee might be less than in a termination for convenience, and (b) the contractor will not be entitled to recovery of settlement expenses. In addition, the default may have consequences for past performance evaluations in future competitive procurements, as discussed in chapter VI, section B.2. But, even in a default, the contractor still obtains recovery for its incurred costs for accepted work up to the amount that has been funded on the contract. The funding limit applies to performance and termination costs. However, the contractor is not required to continue with termination work in the absence of adequate funding.

An additional risk to be assessed is that a contractor may have incurred substantial facilities and equipment costs that it intended to amortize over the life of a long-term contract. Recovery of unamortized costs is difficult, particularly in the absence of adequate funding to cover such costs.

> ✓ **Best Practice Tip:** Identify major contracts or programs where: (a) the Target has any unresolved show cause notices or cure notices; (b) timely performance may be at risk, including where the Target has failed to meet milestone schedules; (c) the Target has material unamortized facility or equipment costs that it intends to amortize over a contract or program that might be terminated; and (d) the Target has booked unexercised options.

I. Defense Federal Acquisition Regulation Supplement (DFARS) Business Systems

1. Overview of DFARS Business System Clauses and Applicability

a. Rule background

On February 24, 2012, the DOD issued a final rule mandating withholding of a percentage of payments when a contractor's business system has one or more significant deficiencies.

[145] *See* FAR 52.249-6.

A significant deficiency is defined as "a shortcoming in the system that materially affects the ability of officials of the Department of Defense to rely upon information produced by the system that is needed for management purposes."[146] In addition to the cash flow implications of withholds, disapproved business systems may also affect a Target's ability to be awarded contracts and may tie up Target resources in remediating significant deficiencies.

b. Clauses

In order to be subject to a withhold, a contract must have both the Contractor Business System Clause[147] and the applicable system clause for the system containing the deficiency. The system clauses are:

- DFARS 252.215-7002, Cost Estimating System Requirements
- DFARS 252.234-7002, Earned Value Management System
- DFARS 252.242-7004, Material Management and Accounting System
- DFARS 252.242-7006, Accounting System Administration
- DFARS 252.244-7001, Purchasing System Administration
- DFARS 252.245-7003, Property Management System

c. Applicability

As noted, a contractor may not have business system withholds applied unless DFARS 252.242-7005, Contractor Business Systems, and the applicable system clause(s) have been included in the contract. Specific contract criteria must be met for the system clauses to be included in a Target's contract.

For DFARS 252.242-7005, Contractor Business Systems, to be included the contract must be subject to CAS.[148] For DFARS 252.215-7002, Cost Estimating System Requirements, to be included one of the following criteria must be met:

- Recipient is a large business who in the preceding fiscal year received DOD prime contracts and subcontracts greater than $50 million for which cost and pricing date were required, or
- Recipient has awards greater than $10 million where the procuring contracting officer and administrative contracting officer determine an audit to be in the government's best interest (e.g., significant estimating problems believed to exist).

DFARS 252.234-7002, Earned Value Management System (EVMS), applies to cost or incentive contracts and subcontracts valued at $100 million or greater.[149] Cost and

146 DFARS 252.242-7005, Contractor Business Systems.

147 *Id.*

148 48 C.F.R. 9903.201-1.

149 Prior to September 28, 2015, DFARS 252.234-7002, Earned Value Management System (May 2011) was included in all contracts valued at $20 million or more. The May 2011 EVMS clause required cost or incentive contracts and subcontracts valued at $50 million or greater to have an earned value management system that had been determined by the cognizant federal agency to be in compliance with ANSI 748. DFARS Deviation No. 2015-O0017 raised the threshold from $50 million to $100 million.

incentive contracts and subcontracts valued at $20 million or greater must comply with American National Standards Institute/Electronic Industries Alliance Standard (ANSI/EIA) 748; however, the Defense Contract Management Agency is not required to complete EVMS compliance surveillance activities on these contracts. For cost or incentive contracts or subcontracts under $20 million, application of earned value management is a risk-based decision.

DFARS 252.242-7004, Material Management and Accounting System, is included in awards when the recipient has had $40 million or more in DOD cost reimbursement prime or subcontracts or DOD fixed-price contracts that provided for progress payments over the simplified acquisition threshold during the contractor's preceding fiscal year and where the Administrative Contracting Officer and auditor determine that material management and accounting system review is needed.

DFARS 252.242-7006, Accounting System Administration, is included in cost-reimbursement, incentive-type, time-and-materials, or labor-hour contracts, or fixed-price contracts with progress payments made on the basis of costs incurred by the contractor or on a percentage or stage of completion.

DFARS 252.244-7001, Purchasing System Administration, is included in awards expected to exceed $25 million over the next twelve-month period, including those represented by prime contracts, subcontracts, and modifications.

DFARS 252.245-7003, Property Management System, is included in all contracts with government-furnished property or contractor-acquired property.

✓ **Best Practice Tip:** Determine how the Target identifies contracts with business system clauses and verifies that the clauses were correctly included in their contracts.

2. Criteria by System

Each of the six system clauses identifies or references the criteria contractors must comply with in order to have an acceptable business system. Generally, all systems have requirements for management reviews, internal controls, documented policies and procedures, and training. Accounting system criteria address internal control environment, accounting framework, organizational structure, cost accounting compliance, general ledger and subsidiary ledger control, adjusting entries, timekeeping, labor distribution, unallowable costs, identification of costs by contract line item, preproduction costs, indirect rates, and billing. The following are requirements specific to each clause:

- The EVMS clause requires compliance with the 32 EVMS guidelines in ANSI/EIA 748. The ANSI/EIA guidelines address the following earned value concept areas: organization, planning and budgeting accounting, analysis, and revisions.
- The cost estimating clause requirements address system description, use of estimating data, estimate reviews and approvals, roles and responsibilities, estimating methods, budgeting techniques, errors and omissions, negotiations, and subcontractor estimates.

- The property management clause references criteria found in FAR 52.245-1, Government Property. As part of an acceptable property management system, contractors are expected to maintain records to identify government property, track maintenance, secure and maintain the property, obtain approval to use the property on other contracts or for other uses, report discrepancies, perform and disclose periodic inventory counts, and comply with property closeout requirements.
- Material management criteria address requirements for a system description, material costing and allocation, bill of material and schedule accuracy, control weakness identification and resolution, record maintenance and accuracy, transfer of parts, and comingled inventories.
- Purchasing system criteria address requirements for a system description, flow-down clauses, organization plans and structure, requisition authority, transaction history, make-or-buy, competition, suspension and debarment, vendor evaluation and oversight, cost or price analysis, sole and single source awards, negotiations, discounts, contract selection, subcontract changes, government notification of subcontract award, kickbacks, conflict of interest, counterfeit electronic parts, and percent of subcontracted effort.

> ✓ **Best Practice Tip:** Determine how the Target conducts internal or third-party assessments against business system criteria. Request examples of recent audit workplans and results to determine the depth of the assessment(s).

3. Government Audit, System Determination, and Withhold Practices

The DCMA and DCAA conduct audits of business systems based on results of the last system audit/system adequacy status, known contractor risks and issues, and the amount of time passed from the last audit of the system. The contracting officer will make an initial system adequacy determination based on the audit results. Contractors have an opportunity to respond to audit findings and initial determinations, after which the contracting officer will make a final determination. If the final determination is to disapprove the system, the contracting officer is required to direct the contractor by notice to withhold 5 percent of performance-based payments, progress payments, and cost-reimbursement, labor-hour, and time-and-materials payments on contracts containing DFARS 252.242-7005. If more than one system is determined inadequate, a maximum of 10 percent billed under each of the identified covered contracts may be withheld.

The contracting officer will reduce withholds to 2 percent upon receipt of an acceptable corrective action plan from the contractor within forty-five days of the contracting officer's notice. Once the contractor has corrected all significant deficiencies the contracting officer shall discontinue the withhold(s) and release any payments previously withheld. Targets should have established policies and controls for applying and releasing withholds.

✓ **Best Practice Tip:** Request that the Target provide a status of all business system audits, adequacy determinations, and planned DCMA/DCAA audits. If a business system has not been audited in the prior three years determine if the Target has conducted a recent internal or third-party compliance assessment.

4. Subcontracting Considerations

As identified in the purchasing system criteria, Targets are required to flow down business system clauses to applicable subcontracts. Additionally, Targets should be aware of a subcontractor's accounting system adequacy status if a cost-reimbursable contract is being contemplated. Prime Targets are also required to have oversight of government property under subcontractor control.

J. Cybersecurity

1. Overview and Applicability

The protection of government data and information on non-federal IT systems has become a significant and public focus of federal agencies. On November 18, 2013, the DOD issued a final rule mandating protection requirements around unclassified controlled technical information (UCTI) for all DOD contractors and subcontractors. DFARS clause 252.204-7012 became effective immediately, and to be compliant contractors had to establish reporting and accountability requirements and flow UCTI requirements to subcontractors. Additionally, contractors had to continually monitor all systems that stored, manipulated, or transmitted UCTI for cyber events. Compliance with the fifty-one required security controls developed by the National Institute of Standards and Technology (NIST) and issued in SP 800-53 was necessary to be compliant with the DFARS requirements.

In 2015, interim rules were published which modified DFARS 252.204–7012, Safeguarding Covered Defense Information and Cyber Incident Reporting, and introduced requirements for compliance with NIST SP 800-171, which is specifically focused on contractors. The information focus moved from UCTI to covered defense information (CDI) and the clause also revised cyber incident reporting requirements. The rule was finalized in October 2016.

Additionally, effective June 15, 2016, FAR 52.204-21, Basic Safeguarding of Covered Contractor Information Systems, provides fifteen basic safeguarding requirements that contractors must implement. The objectives of this rule are to improve information security for federal contract information stored on or transmitted over contractor systems as well as in a cloud environment.

FAR 52.204-21 and DFARS 252.204–7012 apply to all contracts, including acquisitions of commercial items other than commercially available off-the-shelf items, when a contractor's information system may contain covered federal contract information.

2. Safeguarding Information

DFARS 252.204–7012 defines CDI as information that must be controlled. Technical information or other information (as described in the Controlled Unclassified Information (CUI) Registry) that requires safeguarding or dissemination controls and is:

1. Marked or otherwise identified in the contract, task order, or delivery order and provided to the contractor by, or on behalf of, DOD in connection with the performance of the contract; or
2. Collected, developed, received, transmitted, used or stored by, or on behalf of, the contractor in support of the performance of the contract.

"Information system" is defined in the same clause as a discrete set of information resources organized for the collection, processing, maintenance, use, sharing, dissemination, or disposition of information. "Covered contractor information system" is an unclassified information system that is owned, or operated by or for, a contractor and that processes, stores, or transmits covered defense information.

These definitions set the stage for the safeguarding provisions of DFARS 252.204–7012, which requires the following primary activities for covered contractor information systems that are not part of an IT service or system operated on behalf of the government:[150]

- Provide adequate security on all covered contractor information systems.
- Comply with the security requirements of NIST 800-171.
- Notify the DOD chief information officer (CIO) within thirty days of NIST 800-171 security requirements not implemented at the time of award.
- Submit requests to the DOD CIO for security variations from NIST SP 800-171.
- Verify cloud providers that store, process, or transmit CDI in performance of the contract meet security requirements equivalent to the Federal Risk and Authorization Management Program (FedRAMP) and that the provider complies with DFARS 252.204–7012 cyber incident reporting requirements.

As part of compliance with NIST 800-171 contractors are required to develop, document, and periodically update system security plans (SSPs) for covered contractor information systems. SSPs, along with plans of actions and milestones (POAMs) describe the contractor's current control framework, how it aligns with the security requirements of NIST 800-171, where gaps exist, and the contractor's detailed plan to remediate gaps. SSPs and POAMs may be requested by contracting officers to be included in a solicitation response.

Agencies are not required, but are permitted, to use a contractor's compliance with NIST 800-171 security requirements as an evaluation criterion in contract award. Therefore, it's important to understand where a Target stands in their compliance evaluation and gap remediation.

---

[150] DFARS 252.204–7012(b)(1) defines distinct requirements for covered contractor information systems that are part of an IT service or system operated on behalf of the government.

3. Cyber Incident Reporting

In addition to security controls and safeguarding requirements, contractors are required to report all cyber incidents. DFARS 252.204–7012 defines a cyber incident and requires the following:

- Report cyber incidents to DOD within seventy-two hours.
- If malicious software is involved, submit the software to the DOD Cyber Crime Center.
- Conduct a review for evidence of compromised CDI.
- Obtain a DOD-approved medium assurance certificate to report cyber incidents.
- Preserve and protect images of affected information systems for at least ninety days from the cyber incident report submission.
- Provide DOD access to equipment necessary to conduct a forensic analysis.
- Provide DOD with damage assessment information gathered in the contractor's review for evidence of compromised CDI.

4. Subcontracting Considerations

Contractors are responsible for determining if information flowed to subcontractors meets the definition of CDI and are required to flow down DFARS 252.204–7012 and FAR 52.204-21 to applicable subcontracts. Subcontractors are required to notify prime contractors when they request a security variation from the DOD CIO. To meet subcontractor oversight requirements, many contractors require subcontractors to complete a form describing their compliance with DFARS 252.204–7012 and/or will include DFARS 252.204–7012 compliance as part of their subcontractor certification and representation form.

✓ **Best Practice Tip:** When evaluating a Target's cybersecurity risk requirements do not focus solely on their compliance with NIST 800-171 security requirements. Other considerations include processes, policies, and controls for:

- Identifying systems considered to be in-scope.
- Overseeing and monitoring of subcontractor compliance.
- Identifying cyber incidents and meeting incident reporting deadlines.

5. Cybersecurity Maturity Model Certification Program

In 2020, the DOD began rolling out the Cybersecurity Maturity Model Certification Program (CMMC). The DOD has developed a new set of cybersecurity controls and, over a five-year period, DOD procurements will be assigned a protection level from one to five, with level five embodying the most stringent protections. In order to be awarded a contract, a contractor will need to have a third-party certification that its cyber protections meet the level assigned to the contract.

✓ **Best Practice Tip:** While the CMMC program will continue to evolve, Acquirers should request information concerning a Target's plans to meet the CMMC program requirements.

CHAPTER 8

Acquisition Documents and Pre-Closing Activities

OUTLINE

A. Nature of the Acquisition
   1. Structure of the Acquisition
   2. Nature of the Target (Public vs. Private)
   3. Economics of the Transaction (Deal Consideration)
   4. Ancillary Agreements
B. Representations and Warranties
C. Disclosure Schedules
D. Covenants Between Signing and Closing
E. Conditions to Closing
F. Classified Business

This chapter of the manual describes the basic building blocks of the definitive agreements typically used to acquire a government contractor. The structure of the acquisition, the nature of the Target, and the interests of the Acquirer will necessarily drive the deal team to emphasize or consider different issues when structuring the transaction and preparing and negotiating the definitive agreements. Within this important context, the basic framework tends to be the same across transactions and can be broken down as follows: structure of the acquisition, economics of the transaction and related deal considerations, the representations and warranties of the parties, interim conduct covenants, conditions to closing, and termination provisions. It is important to note when structuring an acquisition that there are also important tax considerations, which are generally beyond the scope of this manual.

A. Nature of the Acquisition

1. Structure of the Acquisition

One of the first decisions the deal team will have to make is whether to acquire the entire entity or just certain assets owned by the Target. There are specific advantages and disadvantages to each approach. By acquiring the entire entity, the Acquirer can more easily keep the operating assets together and, subject to required third-party consents, will generally have a better sense of the business it is acquiring and how all the pieces fit together. Also, by acquiring the entire entity, the Acquirer will assume all of the liabilities of the Target, whether known or unknown. This potential for unknown liabilities puts a premium on the due diligence process and, where available, post-closing indemnification remedies.

In contrast, an asset sale provides the Acquirer with the opportunity to identify only those assets it wants to buy and assume only those liabilities it specifically agrees to assume. However, an asset sale can be more complex and introduce added execution risk because the nature of the transaction requires the parties to detail with some specificity each asset being acquired from or retained by the Target. Also, the requirement to obtain third-party consents is typically much more burdensome, especially where novation of government contracts is required. Furthermore, while courts will typically respect the form of the transaction, potential successor liability claims could be raised by creditors of the Target in the case of an acquisition of all or substantially all of the assets of a Target. From the Target's perspective, an asset sale may also be less desirable because, in addition to the execution risk, it can be difficult for the Target to dispose of the liabilities that are not assumed by the Acquirer, and there may also be adverse tax consequences for the Target's stakeholders.

In acquiring the Target, the basic structural forms the Acquirer has at its disposal are a merger or share purchase. The two most prevalent forms of merger are the forward merger, where the Target merges directly into the Acquirer, and the reverse triangular merger, where the Target merges with a wholly owned subsidiary of the Acquirer and, as a result, itself becomes a subsidiary of the Acquirer. Alternatively, the Acquirer can contract with each of the stockholders of the Target to acquire their shares directly. In the context of either a merger or share purchase, the business being acquired generally stays intact. In the case of a reverse triangular merger and a share purchase, the corporate form of the Target entity actually does not change. Rather, the prior stockholders of the Target are replaced by the Acquirer. Because the corporate form does not change, third parties that are under contract with the Target prior to the acquisition are still under contract with the same legal entity following the acquisition. As a result, the number of third-party consents required in the context of a reverse triangular merger or share purchase tends to be much lower, which reduces the execution risk for both the Acquirer and the Target. However, a careful reading of change of control assignment language is still warranted during the due diligence process, as contracts frequently include third-party consent language even in the context of a share purchase or reverse triangular merger.

Depending on the size of the Target stockholder base, a merger is often easier to execute than a share purchase. Mergers typically require majority consent of the Target stockholders, subject to state law, appraisal or dissenter's rights and the provisions of the Target's charter documents, which, in privately held companies, often include class and super-majority voting provisions for certain events such as a change of control. A share purchase, by contrast, requires unanimous consent of the stockholders in order for the Acquirer to obtain complete control. Consequently, share purchases are typically most relevant in the context of a closely held company.

2. Nature of the Target (Public vs. Private)

A second key consideration that will drive much of the decision making in the acquisition is whether the shares of the Target's stock are publicly or privately held. Acquisitions of publicly traded companies subject to the reporting requirements of the Securities and Exchange Commission (SEC) tend to have larger valuations and more complex securities law and regulatory issues than acquisitions of privately held companies, but they can often be simpler from a due diligence and negotiation point of view. In theory, publicly traded companies are required to disclose all material information about the company to the public. Assuming properly functioning markets and adequate disclosure, the value of a business and its potential risks are then priced in the company's share price. As a result, publicly held targets generally tend to push for less detailed representations and warranties in the acquisition documents; minimal, if any, post-closing remedies for breach of representations and warranties; and more limited closing conditions that require an Acquirer to close the acquisition absent a material adverse change in the Target's business. At the same time, Targets will preserve their ability to terminate the transaction consistent with the fiduciary duties of their boards of directors.

Conversely, Acquirers generally require privately held Targets to give more detailed representations and warranties that survive the closing of the transaction, to indemnify the Acquirer for breaches of representations and warranties and other specified risks, to place a portion of the deal consideration in escrow to support the indemnity obligation, and to satisfy more detailed and onerous conditions to closing. In addition, the materiality threshold for privately held companies tends to be lower given the trend for smaller valuations.

3. Economics of the Transaction (Deal Consideration)

The purchase price for an acquisition and the form of the payment can either be very simple or surprisingly complex. Of course, the simplest form of deal consideration is cash, but the amount of cash—particularly in connection with a privately held target—can be subject to a number of considerations. For example, parties will often negotiate earn-outs to bridge a valuation gap between what a Target thinks it is worth and what an Acquirer is willing to pay. Acquirers can also issue stock as the currency in the transaction, which can introduce complexity relating to how to value the stock and whether the stock will be issued as restricted securities or registered securities under applicable SEC rules and regulations. An Acquirer can also pay with debt, intended to be paid off using the Target's future revenue streams, but the risks to the Target in this approach are obvious.

4. Ancillary Agreements

Depending upon the nature of the business being sold, in addition to a transaction agreement, ancillary agreements that address issues other than the core purchase of assets or equity consideration and the payment of considerations may be necessary. These include:

- Transition Services Agreements—This type of agreement provides for the Target to continue to provide intra-company services after the sale is closed, for some period of time. This type of agreement facilitates the acquisition of a division or subsidiary of a larger company, where most infrastructure services are centrally provided or provided by employees not being acquired. Services could include payroll services, benefits processing, tax services, accounting systems, and services such as accounts receivable, accounts payable, labor charging, warehousing, email, personnel and staffing, sourcing, communications, etc. If the Acquirer is acquiring the infrastructure and related personnel, the Acquirer may be asked to provide transition services back to the Target.
- Supply Agreements/Purchase Agreements—If the Target is a division or subsidiary of a larger entity, the Target may have purchased or sold services to other businesses within the selling entity through intra-company work arrangements. Sometimes it makes sense for that intra-company arrangement to continue after the closing of the sale. However, intra-company arrangements generally do not contain all the types of terms one would expect to see in a third-party arrangement, such as indemnification clauses, late charges, confidentiality, and choice of law. A supply or purchase agreement can be used to set out the additional terms for intra-company arrangements.
- Subcontract Pending Novation Agreements—This type of agreement describes the parties' obligations during the period between closing and the government's execution of a novation agreement. Until the novation agreement is executed, the responsible and performing party to the government contract(s) remains the Target, which also continues to receive payment under the contract(s). This agreement may also be necessary for purposes of complying with contract clauses that require consent to subcontract, such as FAR 52.244-2.
- Real Estate Agreements—Many transactions involve some sort of real estate documentation, and the parties may need to enter into ancillary agreements to address specific issues relating to leases, subleases, entry/usage licenses, deeds, and the like.
- Intellectual Property Agreements—A transaction may raise a number of IP-related issues, including IP licenses.
- Employment Agreements—Employee-related agreements can include employment agreements, retention agreements, stay bonus agreements, new employee proprietary information agreements, disclosures about benefit plans and new benefit plans.

B. Representations and Warranties

The Acquirer will most likely insist that the Target make extensive representations and warranties about its ability to enter into and consummate the proposed transaction and about the state of the Target's business. If the acquisition is considered a merger of equals, or if the Acquirer is issuing securities as the deal consideration (illiquid securities in particular), the Acquirer will often give reciprocal representations and warranties. The representations and warranties generally cover extensive topics related to the state of the business, from the accuracy and completeness of the financial statements of the company to detailed lists identifying material contracts and the substantive components of the contracts, to the adequacy and status of the Target's intellectual property, to employment and environmental risks—and everything in between. In deals involving the acquisition of a government contractor, a representation and warranty covering specific government contracts risks and potential liabilities may be negotiated. The extent of the government contracts representation and warranty may vary between private and public company deals, among other factors. The representations and warranties serve several functions.

First, the representations and warranties serve an important due diligence function to complement and confirm the more extensive due diligence performed by the broader deal team pre-signing. Second, in the event that the representations and warranties are breached, and the Acquirer discovers the breach prior to closing, the breach may provide the Acquirer with the ability to terminate the transaction prior to closing. Third, in the context of a private transaction, the representations and warranties can serve an important indemnification function. If the Target has breached its representations and warranties, and the Acquirer incurs a loss related to the breach, the Acquirer will, in most private transactions, have the right to seek indemnity from the Target's stakeholders and/or a third-party insurer in cases where representations and warranties insurance is used. Finally, the representations and warranties can also serve an important integration function. Often, representations and warranties will call for specific information to be disclosed in a schedule attached to the agreement, which is used by the Acquirer to assist in the integration process post-closing.

Over the past several years, the use of representations and warranties insurance in acquisition transactions has become much more commonplace. The rationale is that having a large, creditworthy financial institution bearing the bulk of the risk associated with inaccurate seller representations in lieu of the seller reduces the friction inherent in the negotiation of the representations. The use of representations and warranties insurance reduces (or eliminates) the seller's post-closing economic exposure arising out of the representations, thus reducing its incentive to scale back the representations substantially from what the buyer requests. A buyer can therefore expect a more fulsome set of representations than it might otherwise get. However, interjecting a third-party insurer does introduce other complexities. The insurer will naturally expect to underwrite and conduct due diligence on the representations and the buyer's due diligence of the target to ensure the parties are not shifting all risk to the insurer. The insurer will expect the buyer to have completed thorough due diligence on the target, and to provide copies of its diligence reports, and to certify at the time the policy is placed that the buyer is not actually aware of any inaccuracy of the target representations. In the case of a target company engaged in federal contracting, an insurer will often indicate government contract regulatory compliance as an area of heightened diligence scrutiny in its underwriting, signaling that if it is not satisfied with the regulatory diligence and compliance, such matters may be excluded from the policy. Therefore, a buyer is well advised to undertake a thorough diligence review of the target company and to tailor the representations to its business accordingly. Appendix 5 contains a sample of representations and warranties that are specific to government contracts.

✓ **Best Practice Tip:** The crafting of the representations and warranties should always be carefully tailored to the Target in order to preserve the value of the acquisition to the Acquirer. The goals and intent of the Acquirer in the acquisition and the potential risks should be carefully considered; specific representations and warranties may or may not be appropriate in the context of a given acquisition. Notwithstanding the existence of extensive or "tight" representations and warranties, nothing a practitioner can insert in the agreement can truly replace an effective due diligence process pre-signing. For a variety of reasons, it is very difficult to terminate an agreement once it is signed, even in the face of a material breach. Typical indemnification provisions or purchase price adjustments are rarely adequate to compensate an Acquirer for liabilities incurred that might have been prevented with an effective due diligence process.

C. Disclosure Schedules

As mentioned briefly above, the representations and warranties in the definitive agreement typically call for the Target to prepare (often) extensive disclosure schedules supporting the representations and warranties. Acquirers should view the disclosure schedules as providing an opportunity to confirm meaningful due diligence by requiring the Target to list specific information for the Acquirer. For example, the representations and warranties typically call for the Target to list each of its material contracts and to denote any restrictions on the Target's ability to compete in certain markets. From the Target's perspective, the disclosure schedules are an opportunity to qualify the representations and warranties made in the definitive agreement—to, in effect, tell the Acquirer all the things that are not consistent with the representations and warranties. Targets will take the position that, by qualifying the representations and warranties in the disclosure schedule, the risk of loss related to the events described in the disclosure schedule shifts to the Acquirer. Accordingly, the negotiating teams typically spend quite a bit of energy on the interplay between the representations and warranties and the disclosure schedule and the impact of any disclosure on the Acquirer's contractual remedies.

✓ **Best Practice Tip:** The disclosure schedules may very well be the most important part of the acquisition documents but, too often, they get the least amount of attention. It is critical for each of the legal specialists supporting the deal team and for each of the business owners responsible for the transaction to have a thorough understanding of the disclosure schedules and each agreement or matter listed or described on the disclosure schedules prior to signing. Because of the nature of the deal dynamics, Targets often delay delivery of the schedules until the eve of signing, whether as a matter of strategic choice or otherwise. Effective deal managers will arrange for disclosure schedules to be delivered early enough in the process to ensure sufficient review time and will advise the client of the risks in failing to provide adequate review.

D. Covenants Between Signing and Closing

While acquisitions can sometimes be structured with a simultaneous signing and closing, more often than not there is a significant period of time between signing the definitive agreements and closing the transaction. During this interim period, third-party, regulatory, and stakeholder consent is obtained, and integration planning begins. The parties will typically devote considerable attention to negotiating covenants that control the conduct and obligations of the parties between signing and closing, as well as the conditions to the parties' obligations to close the transaction.

The covenants governing the parties' conduct between signing and closing are typically quite extensive. The Acquirer, or both parties in a merger of equals or transaction where the Acquirer's stock is the deal consideration, will expect the other side to agree to extensive restrictions on its ability to conduct business outside the ordinary course. The conduct covenants are designed to protect the value of the business between signing and closing. Of course, from the Target's perspective, the Target will do everything it can to loosen the restrictions so that it can operate in the ordinary course without the risk of giving the Acquirer the opportunity to terminate the transaction for breach. In addition to specific restrictions on the conduct of business, the covenants between signing and closing typically contain detailed obligations of the parties to support the transaction. These obligations include covenants to obtain regulatory and stockholder consent, maintain confidentiality, terminate employee benefits plans, and refrain from soliciting alternative offers to acquire the Target, a so-called "no-shop" provision.

E. Conditions to Closing

Conditions to closing, together with the termination provisions of the agreement, are another area of the acquisition agreement that can be difficult to negotiate. Both sides want a "tight deal" that provides certainty to the process. Acquirers, however, may want flexibility to get out of the deal in the event that the business they thought they were buying turns out not to be worth what they thought it was at the time of signing. In a public deal, the conditions are typically limited to stockholder consent, regulatory consents, bring down of the representations and warranties, and the absence of a material adverse change in the business. In a private deal, Acquirers are often more aggressive and push for conditions to closing that allocate more risk to the Target, such as obtaining third-party customer consents, acceptance of employee offer letters, and limited due diligence clean up. In the end, however, both deal dynamics and relevant case law make it very difficult for an Acquirer to get out of a deal absent a material adverse change in the business and, even then, courts interpreting the agreement provisions tend to set the bar fairly high for termination due to a material adverse change.

A Target, of course, will want to do everything it can to force the Acquirer to close and keep from terminating the transaction. At the same time, the board of directors of a Target has a fiduciary duty to act in the best interests of the company's stockholders. In the acquisition context, the fiduciary duty generally requires the Target to preserve its ability to terminate the transaction in order to take a superior offer and, increasingly, simply to the extent the board of directors believes its fiduciary duty requires it to terminate the agreement. Acquirers can manage this risk more effectively in private transactions, but in public deals, often the best an Acquirer can do is to make it difficult for a competing bidder to make a better offer, preserve and enhance its ability to outbid an interloper, and impose a break-up fee in the event a Target's board of directors exercises a fiduciary out. The parameters of what is required in the transaction agreement to preserve the Target board's legitimate interest in meeting its fiduciary duty, and what restrictions an Acquirer may permissibly impose, are subject to constantly evolving case law and, accordingly, intense negotiations ensue.

F. Classified Business

In some transactions, it will not be possible to complete due diligence on sensitive topics, such as classified business, or to gather personnel information. If that is the case, then the Acquirer should include in the transaction agreement a covenant that the Target facilitate due diligence in those areas between signing and closing. In addition, the Acquirer should include, as a condition to closing, that the Acquirer be satisfied with the due diligence in terms of scope and outcome.

> ✓ **Best Practice Tip:** Due diligence of a classified business will require the consent of the classified customer. To facilitate agreement by the customer, the Acquirer should identify a person with the appropriate level of security clearance and acceptable to the customer as the individual who will conduct the due diligence into the classified matters.

CHAPTER 9

Antitrust Requirements

OUTLINE

A. Overview
B. Contemplating Potential Merger or Acquisition—Antitrust Due Diligence
C. Negotiating the Merger Agreement—Antitrust Risk Provisions
D. Determining Merger Filing Requirements
    1. US and Rest of the World Reportability Requirements
    2. Merger Review Outside the United States
E. HSR Filing and Review Process
    1. Managing the Creation and Flow of Deal Documents
    2. Filing Preparation and Coordination—Failure to File
    3. Merger Review Process and Timing
        a. Initial Waiting Period
        b. Pull and Refile
        c. Second Request
F. Substantive Antitrust Review of Mergers and Acquisitions
    1. Horizontal Mergers
        a. US Department of Justice and the Federal Trade Commission Horizontal Merger Guidelines
        b. Industry Specific Concerns
    2. Vertical Mergers
        a. Agency Guidance
        b. Industry Specific Concerns
G. Coordination of Multiple Government Investigations
H. Consent Decrees and Litigation
    1. Consent Decrees
    2. District Court Litigation
I. Pre-Closing Activities and Integration Efforts—"Gun Jumping"

A. Overview

This chapter provides an overview of the antitrust review process at the Federal Trade Commission (FTC) and the US DOJ Antitrust Division, with respect to defense industry transactions. While this discussion focuses on mergers, the subjects and issues addressed below are similar for mergers, acquisitions, or other forms of business combinations. This chapter is intended to provide corporate counsel an understanding of the issues and considerations at every stage of the US merger review process.

Section 7 of the Clayton Act prohibits mergers, acquisitions, and certain joint ventures that have the effect of substantially lessening competition in any line of commerce or activity in any part of the United States. Both the FTC and the DOJ have the jurisdiction to review, investigate, and challenge M&A. Pursuant to the Hart-Scott-Rodino Act (HSR Act), parties to a transaction that meet certain statutory reporting requirements must make an HSR filing with both the FTC and DOJ, at which point the merger review process begins. The Premerger Notification Office (PNO), which exists within the FTC, is initially responsible for managing HSR filings and assigns the transaction to both regulatory agencies for an initial review. The FTC or DOJ must then request authority to open an investigation by notifying the PNO. Only one agency will receive clearance to assess the transaction to determine whether the transaction raises any substantive competition concerns.

Ultimately, the reviewing agency must determine whether the transaction at issue will be allowed to proceed as submitted, or whether the agency will seek to block or modify the transaction in order to address a perceived harm to competition. The sections below describe the efforts that can be made to help ensure that the transaction receives clearance during the merger review process, including undertaking a thorough initial analysis of the antitrust risks posed by the potential transaction and negotiating an appropriate merger or acquisition agreement.

B. Contemplating Potential Merger or Acquisition—Antitrust Due Diligence

A company's top priority should be to perform necessary antitrust due diligence before deciding to proceed with a merger or acquisition. Antitrust counsel can assist in accurately evaluating the risks and value of a proposed transaction. A thorough due diligence process can help counsel to avoid or minimize potential challenges during the merger review process.

Typically, due diligence involves the preparation of a preliminary antitrust risk analysis based on the review of publicly available information, internal documents, documents created to analyze the transaction, and financial and sales data. The preliminary risk analysis first examines whether premerger application filings are required in the United States and in foreign jurisdictions as significant fines can be assessed for failure to file.[1] Antitrust counsel can assist in developing a reasonable expectation as to the

[1] In the United States, parties who fail to make mandatory HSR filings premerger may be subject to a myriad of penalties, including agency enforcement action, civil penalties for each day of violation, and required corrective filings that could extend the merger review period.

timing of the completion of the agency review and the closing of the transaction. Certain transactions posing greater antitrust risk may require careful staging of US and foreign filings and/or engaging in agency advocacy efforts prior to filing. The preliminary risk analysis also involves a review of the potential competitive issues that the agencies will be interested in and evaluates strategies for minimizing antitrust risks.

In addition, there are significant antitrust risks that may arise during the due diligence process itself. Documents created to analyze the proposed transaction are likely to be required as part of the HSR filing. In a transaction that will undergo agency review, it is important to refrain from creating documents that could independently contribute to agency concerns. Business executives, investment bankers, and other consultants communicating about a proposed transaction should follow the guidance of antitrust counsel as to types of statements that might prove unhelpful when the documents contemplating a transaction are created, which is discussed in greater detail in section E.1 later in the chapter.

The due diligence process may also raise concerns that the parties to the proposed transaction could be improperly sharing competitively sensitive information. If the parties to a transaction are competitors even in broad terms, there must be precautions taken to protect the flow of competitively sensitive information, which includes non-public information and documents relating to future plans, current and projected prices, costs, and profits. For further guidance on protocols for exchanging information prior to the closing of the transaction, refer to section I of this chapter.

C. Negotiating the Merger Agreement—Antitrust Risk Provisions

When negotiating a merger or acquisition agreement, both the seller and buyer may be uncertain about the course of potential investigation, litigation, or remedies that could be demanded by the agencies during the merger review process. Typically, the seller is interested in ensuring that the deal closes quickly once the transaction agreement is signed, because any delays in closing could decrease the value of the company. The seller may also be concerned about whether the buyer will be committed to obtaining agency clearance of the transaction or whether the seller will be compensated in the event that the transaction is blocked or the buyer decides to abandon the transaction. Conversely, the buyer may be concerned about whether the potential remedies or divestitures that an agency may require will impact the efficacy of the transaction and whether it can abandon the transaction if regulatory approval is delayed or denied.

To mitigate these types of risks, parties to a transaction often negotiate monetary measures to allocate antitrust risk or other similarly focused terms that specify a required level of commitment to take certain actions, limit specific actions, or stipulate conditions under which the parties could terminate the agreement. Monetary measures could include a ticking fee, which is a payment that the buyer agrees to pay the seller if the closing is delayed or if the deal is terminated for any stipulated reason, including failure to obtain required approvals from antitrust agencies (either in the United States or abroad). A buyer may require the seller to pay a breakup fee to offset the risks of the transaction not closing. These breakup fees are typically intended to compensate the buyer for the costs of pursuing the transaction and to incentivize the seller to move forward with the transaction. A seller can also negotiate a reverse breakup fee, which is a termination fee paid by the buyer to the seller if it is unable to close the transaction due to its failure to obtain the required antitrust clearance. Reverse breakup fees are a means for compensating the seller for costs associated with a lengthy merger review. In addition, a high fee can incentivize the buyer to cooperate in obtaining speedy approval and create a guaranteed option that allows the buyer to walk away prior to the termination date as long as it pays the fee.

Parties can also allocate antitrust risk through provisions that specify the level of such commitment or cooperation, such as "efforts" clauses and material adverse effect (MAE) clauses. Efforts clauses typically require parties to the transaction to use "commercially reasonable efforts," "reasonable best efforts," or "best efforts" to obtain the required antitrust clearance and allows the parties to terminate the transaction agreement if the other party does not meet its commitments. MAE clauses allow parties to terminate the transaction agreement if there is a significant change in circumstances during the pendency of a deal. Definitions in the MAE clause may include changes related to the specific deal, such as loss of customers or employees, damaged supplier relationships, or disruption of business. Both "best efforts" and MAE clauses can be used in conjunction with other antitrust risk-shifting provisions.

Finally, the parties could use termination clauses that define the circumstances under which the parties may terminate the agreement. These clauses typically include an "outside" or "drop dead" date beyond which either party may terminate the agreement if the transaction has not closed. Such clauses could also specify different types of events that would allow the parties to terminate the agreement, such as an action by the agency extending the merger review process.

Counsel needs to carefully consider the implications of each type of provision discussed above. Insisting on extreme risk allocation terms could seriously impede the negotiation process. More important, counsel must also evaluate the likelihood of prolonged regulatory investigation and how these risk allocation terms can complement each other. For example, when a buyer is not willing to meet the agency's divestiture obligations, the seller may want to negotiate a higher reverse breakup fee to protect against the buyer walking away from the transaction. Engaging experienced antitrust counsel early in the transaction planning process will help the parties better evaluate antitrust risk and negotiate agreement terms that best protect the parties' interests.

D. Determining Merger Filing Requirements

1. US and Rest of the World Reportability Requirements

The Premerger Notification Program was established pursuant to the HSR Act to provide the US antitrust enforcement agencies with the opportunity to review and possibly to enjoin transactions of a certain size before consummation. The program requires both the buyer and the seller to complete and submit separate HSR Notification and Report Forms, with the aim of avoiding costly remedial measures to restore competition after a transaction has been consummated. Note, however, that the FTC or DOJ may still investigate and challenge transactions that do not meet the reporting thresholds under the HSR Act or that have already been consummated.

Under the HSR Act, parties to acquisitions of assets, voting securities, or noncorporate interests[2] (which, as defined, includes the formation of new entities and joint venture entities) meeting certain thresholds must report the transaction to the FTC and DOJ and observe a statutory waiting period. The HSR Act employs two threshold tests for determining whether a transaction is subject to its reporting requirements: (a) the size-of-transaction test, and (b) the size-of-person test. Each acquisition of assets, voting securities, or noncorporate interests is analyzed to determine if there is a reportable event.[3]

The jurisdictional thresholds for the HSR Act are adjusted annually, based on the gross national product. Also, the PNO publishes formal and informal interpretations of various premerger notification requirements. For example, the PNO interpretations provide guidance on what types of assets and items should be included in calculating whether the entity filing the HSR form (Ultimate Parent Entity or UPE) meets the size-of-the-person test.

Any company that fails to comply with the HSR Act, including failing to file the premerger notification for a reportable transaction, may be subject to a civil penalty for each day the company is in violation of the Act. Because the rules are not only complex, but they also change continuously, it is very important to consult experienced antitrust counsel when contemplating any transaction that may be subject to HSR notification requirements.

2. Merger Review Outside the United States

Merger enforcement is increasingly global, with more than one hundred jurisdictions around the world having active merger control regimes. Jurisdictions differ both procedurally and substantively in areas such as thresholds for notification, the review period allowed for consideration of the transaction, and whether the notifications are compulsory.

Broadly speaking, there are two types of premerger notification regimes: mandatory and voluntary. Mandatory premerger notification regimes typically have a "suspensory clause," that forbids the parties from closing transactions that exceed statutory thresholds until the transaction has been cleared by the relevant governmental authority. In contrast, mandatory post-merger notification regimes require that all mergers that meet the criteria file an "application" within a certain period of time after closing. Under voluntary merger notification regimes, the parties are not obliged to submit the merger for review unless the transaction is likely to pose anticompetitive risk, and can close the deal without having to

---

[2] The HSR Rules define "non-corporate interest" as "an interest in any unincorporated entity which gives the holder the right to any profits of the entity or in the event of dissolution of that entity the right to any of its assets after payment of its debts. These unincorporated entities include, but are not limited to, general partnerships, limited partnerships, limited liability partnerships, limited liability companies . . ." 16 C.F.R. § 801.1(f)(1)(ii).

[3] The thresholds for reportable transactions are adjusted annually. The 2021 thresholds are found at 86 FR 7870 (Feb. 2, 2021).

apply for or receive a merger clearance first. While mandatory post-merger notification and voluntary merger notification regimes pose the most amount of risk for post-close merger investigations, note that it is possible for US antitrust agencies and other mandatory filing jurisdictions to open investigations after the transaction has closed.

With the surge in merger control regimes around the world and a shift toward mandatory premerger notification, even relatively small jurisdictions have an opportunity to significantly impact a proposed transaction. In addition, the extent of international cooperation between competition enforcement agencies is steadily growing. Consequently, coordinating the timing and substance of filings submitted to various jurisdictions is imperative for companies operating internationally.

Besides the technicality of if and when a merger filing is required, there are also substantive differences in the filings required by regulators. For example, in the European Union (EU), parties are required to provide a detailed analysis of the affected product markets and the competitive dynamics in addition to what is typically required by merger filings, including corporate financials and structures, and competitor and customer lists.[4] When parties to a transaction have operations or significant revenues outside of the United States, it is important to prepare in advance the types of information that will be required in each jurisdiction in order to timely respond to iterative agency requests for information.

Merger review timelines vary for every merger control regime, requiring antitrust counsel to carefully coordinate filings and advocacy strategies such that parties can receive antitrust clearance prior to the transaction's closing date.

✓ **Best Practice Tip:** As early as possible, conduct a preliminary analysis to identify potential jurisdictions in which merger control filings may be required. Also, if you foresee any potential competition concerns in a particular jurisdiction, it is a good idea to develop possible responses or remedies that may address those concerns in the early stage of the contemplated transaction.

E. HSR Filing and Review Process

1. Managing the Creation and Flow of Deal Documents

The HSR Act requires that both the buyer and seller complete and submit separate HSR Notification and Report Forms. In addition to requiring basic information about the filing party and the transaction, Item 4(c) of the HSR Form requires submission of

---

4 However, the European Commission (EC) launched its "Merger Simplification Project" at the end of 2013, intended to simplify the notification process and reduce administrative burden. As a part of this effort, the Commission adopted recent amendments to the notice on simplified procedure and extended the categories of merger cases that can be notified through a Short Form CO found at Annex II to the Implementing Regulation. See Commission Notice, 2013 O.J. C 366/04.

> . . . all studies, surveys, analyses and reports which were prepared by or for any officer(s) or director(s) (or, in the case of unincorporated entities, individuals exercising similar functions) for the purpose of evaluating or analyzing the acquisition with respect to market shares, competition, competitors, markets, potential for sales growth or expansion into product or geographic markets.[5]

The FTC interprets "4(c) documents" broadly to include, for example, offering memoranda; management presentations; internal reports, studies, or memoranda; and emails and handwritten notes.[6] Item 4(d) of the HSR Form requires submissions of certain documents prepared by or for officers or directors that relate to the acquisition, including confidential information memoranda, documents prepared by third-party advisors, and documents evaluating or analyzing synergies.

The filing party should conduct a thorough search for potential 4(c) and 4(d) documents; if the agency later discovers 4(c) and 4(d) documents not submitted with the HSR notification, it may restart the HSR statutory waiting period. Moreover, in a few cases, the agency has assessed civil penalties against companies for failure to submit such documents.[7]

Documents produced in response to Items 4(c) and 4(d) can have an outsized impact on the course of an agency's review. On the positive side, early access to these documents can provide the reviewing agency with useful insights as to the parties' intent and the transaction's likely effects on competition. On the negative side, unhelpful 4(c) and 4(d) documents are more easily found by an agency and generally will not be forgotten. It is therefore important to be thoughtful about what is written in existing documents and avoid creating new, unhelpful 4(c) and 4(d) documents. For example, carefully drafted 4(c) and 4(d) documents highlighting the existence of dynamic competition or the procompetitive justifications for a transaction may expedite agency review. Conversely, 4(c) and 4(d) documents that understate competitive alternatives by discussing only select few competitors, or how the transaction may allow the acquiring person to raise prices, reduce output or innovation, or foreclose additional competition, may prolong agency review or possibly lead to a request for significant additional information (commonly referred to as a Second Request).

Business executives, investment bankers, and other consultants communicating about a proposed transaction should follow the guidance of antitrust counsel as to types of statements that might prove unhelpful when the documents contemplating a transaction are created. And, to the extent these cautions cannot be adhered to, antitrust preplanning will alert counsel to the necessity and context of such statements such that counsel can properly frame the arguments it will make to the reviewing agency.

---

5 See Antitrust Improvements Act Notification and Report Form for Certain Mergers and Acquisitions—Instructions, available at the FTC's website at http://ftc.gov/bc/hsr/hsrform.shtm.

6 "Locating and Identifying Item 4(c) Documents" is a helpful article by Marian R. Bruno, Brian C. Mohr, and Bruce J. Prager regarding identification of 4(c) documents. See Marian R. Bruno, Brian C. Mohr, and Bruce J. Prager, Locating and Identifying Item 4(c) Documents, ANTITRUST, Spring 2002, at 46.

7 For example, in October 2007, the DOJ fined Iconix Brand Group $550,000 for failure to provide existing 4(c) documents with its HSR Notification and Report Form in connection with its acquisition of Rocawear. See http://www.usdoj.gov/atr/cases/iconix.htm.

✓ **Best Practice Tip:** Counsel clients to carefully draft potential 4(c) and 4(d) documents, as well as all documents discussing the proposed transaction, to avoid language or concepts that might invite increased antitrust scrutiny. Even if a document is not responsive to Items 4(c) and 4(d) of the HSR form, it may be discovered by the agency during a Second Request. Counsel should work with clients to review draft 4(c) and 4(d) documents.

2. Filing Preparation and Coordination—Failure to File

Should parties consummate an HSR-reportable transaction without submitting an HSR notification form, they should immediately notify the PNO and prepare a filing as soon as possible.[8] Post-consummation filings contain substantially the same information as would have been submitted had the parties filed the HSR notice prior to closing.

Parties who fail to file may be liable for civil penalties up to $40,000 (an amount that is adjusted annually) for each day they are in violation of the HSR Act. However, the FTC has discretion in assessing penalties for failure to file. As such, the parties must also provide a detailed written explanation signed by a company official as to why the failure to file occurred.

3. Merger Review Process and Timing

Once the HSR notification has been filed, the PNO assigns the files to the FTC and DOJ for an initial review. After that, one or both of the agencies will request "clearance" or authority to open an investigation into the merger. Through this clearance process, the agencies then determine which one will investigate the proposed transaction. Only one agency—the FTC or DOJ—will obtain clearance to investigate a transaction.

Generally, clearance depends on which agency has expertise in the relevant industry. However, there are some industries for which both agencies have expertise, and both may seek clearance to open an investigation. As both the FTC and DOJ have defense industry experience, the agencies frequently negotiate clearance for each transaction that arises.

a. Initial Waiting Period

The HSR Act imposes an initial waiting period of thirty calendar days for the agency to review the transaction, with the exceptions of cash tender offers or bankruptcy.[9] During the initial waiting period the parties may not close the transaction. However, either party may request early termination of the initial waiting period. If the agency finds that the transaction does not raise competitive concerns, it can grant early termination at any

8 For further guidance, please consult the FTC's website at http://www.ftc.gov/bc/hsr/postconsumfilings.shtm.

9 See 16 C.F.R. § 803.10. In the case of cash tender offers or an acquisition made in connection with Section 363(b) of the Bankruptcy Code, the waiting period is only fifteen calendar days. See 11 U.S.C. § 363(b).

time during the initial waiting period, which allows the parties immediately to close the transaction.[10]

The appointed agency will use the initial waiting period to evaluate potential competitive issues and decide whether to investigate the transaction. If the agency elects to open an investigation, it typically requests information from the parties to aid its investigation, in the form of a voluntary request letter. The voluntary request letter will ask both the seller and the buyer for baseline materials about their companies, including a description of areas where the companies compete with each other and otherwise potentially relevant products ("relevant products"); business plans, market studies, strategic plans, surveys, information on market shares and competitor positioning; a list of top customers, competitors, and suppliers; and sales and pricing data for the relevant products.

The antitrust agency uses this information to assess the competitive issues more effectively, determine whether an extended merger review is necessary, and narrow the scope of the extended review to the critical antitrust issues.

Antitrust counsel will typically prepare and make presentations to the reviewing agency early during the initial review period, to provide context or otherwise ease agency concerns about the transaction. It is in the interest of the parties to take advantage of agencies' desire to avoid devoting substantial resources to investigations that do not produce an enforcement action. A proactive customer outreach strategy can also have significant impact in this regard. The opinions and concerns of customers are critical factors in the agency's decision to challenge a transaction and complaints can dramatically extend an investigation.[11] Antitrust counsel will implement a customer outreach strategy to assess customer views on the competitive dynamics of the relevant product markets and whether or not those customers believe that the transaction should be blocked.

The FTC or DOJ may decide that the transaction does not raise substantive competition concerns and grant clearance during the initial waiting period. Note that grants of early termination of the HSR waiting period are made public in the Federal Register and on the FTC's website. If the parties are sensitive to any public disclosure of the existence of a proposed transaction, they should consider not requesting early termination. The parties should also allow enough time for the HSR review period so as not to be dependent on receiving early termination to consummate a deal within their desired timeframe.

> ✓ **Best Practice Tip:** Working with knowledgeable antitrust counsel early in the evaluative process can advance the substantive review of a proposed transaction. Experienced counsel are familiar with the enforcement agencies and the types of materials they typically seek early in the review process. Counsel can best prepare the parties for any initial meeting with the agencies and offer helpful information and materials quickly.

---

10 16 C.F.R. § 803.11(c).

11 Complaints by competitors, while considered, are generally given less weight than customer complaints. Such complaints are often motivated by a desire to prevent the parties to the transaction from becoming stronger competitors.

b. Pull and Refile

If the FTC or DOJ has not completed its investigation or still has open questions concerning the competitive effects of the transaction at the end of the initial waiting period, the buyer may opt to withdraw and refile its HSR notification form in order to give the agency another thirty days to review the transaction.

Typically, this will occur when, based on discussions with the enforcement agency, the parties believe that they can resolve remaining substantive concerns within a second thirty-day period. The goal from the parties' perspective is to avoid a significantly more in-depth request for additional information, commonly referred to as a Second Request. Parties can only pull and refile once without incurring an additional filing fee, and the buyer must refile the HSR notification within two business days of the expiration of the initial waiting period. The seller does not need to refile.

c. Second Request

If, after the initial waiting period, the reviewing agency decides that it needs to continue its investigation in more depth, the agency will issue a request for additional information and documents to each party, known commonly as a Second Request. A Second Request is effectively a request for all documents or data associated with the parties' provision of relevant products, going back three years or more. Compliance with a Second Request involves several months of collecting, reviewing, and producing potentially hundreds of thousands of the parties' internal documents, as well as compiling extensive financial and market data. The expense involved in complying with a Second Request also is very substantial and may amount to several million dollars. The parties' counsel engage in extensive negotiations with the FTC or DOJ to attempt to narrow the document and information requirements, but even with modifications, the compliance process remains very burdensome and costly. Parties can submit materials responsive to the Second Request on a rolling basis, and the reviewing agency will often request that the parties do so, with certain types of documents produced on a priority basis. Rolling documents and information into the enforcement agency, instead of overwhelming the agency with one large submission, may result in quicker resolution of the agency's investigation.

The issuance of a Second Request stops the antitrust merger review clock. The clock only begins to run again once both parties have certified "substantial compliance" with the Second Request. At that point, except in rare circumstances, a new thirty-day waiting period begins.[12] Because of the volume of information and documents that the agency must review, antitrust counsel generally negotiate a timing agreement, which includes a commitment by the parties not to close the transaction for a period of time after substantial compliance. This final waiting period allows the enforcement agency time to review the information gathered and to decide whether to challenge the proposed transaction. If the agency opts to challenge the transaction, it must seek to enjoin the transaction before the end of this extended waiting period.

---

[12] In the case of cash tender offers or acquisitions in bankruptcy, the extended waiting period is only ten days. See 16 C.F.R. § 803.10(b)(i).

During this period, the DOJ or FTC may take the depositions of key management of the parties and may also take the depositions of third parties, including the parties' customers, competitors, and suppliers. The DOJ and FTC also often serve document subpoenas on relevant third parties. Key customers are often required to submit their internal documents and information about their commercial relationships with the parties.

While complying with the Second Request, antitrust counsel will continue to discuss with the reviewing agency its substantive evaluation of the transaction, including critical or potentially dispositive issues. Parties may voluntarily submit white papers and other advocacy pieces that address the agency's concerns that the transaction will harm competition.

F. Substantive Antitrust Review of Mergers and Acquisitions

1. Horizontal Mergers

A merger of two firms that compete or could compete against each other to sell the same product or service is called a horizontal merger. A horizontal merger raises substantive antitrust concerns when there are few suppliers or potential suppliers in the relevant product market. While the clearance of any transaction will depend on its particular facts, agencies are less likely to challenge transactions when there are more than three competitors in the relevant product market.

a. US Department of Justice and the Federal Trade Commission Horizontal Merger Guidelines

Section 7 of the Clayton Act prohibits transactions where "the effect of such acquisition may be substantially to lessen competition, or to tend to create a monopoly." Section 4 of the Clayton Act grants the DOJ and the FTC the authority to challenge mergers, as well as a private right of action. Section 7 applies to various types of transactions, including acquisitions (of stock, assets, partnership interests), partial asset acquisitions (patents, trademarks, trade secrets, licenses, or leases), and formations of joint ventures. Section 7 does not require that a merger-to-monopoly be threatened or take place before the agencies can take enforcement action. Instead, under Section 7 mergers could be forbidden where "the trend to a lessening of competition in a line of commerce was still in its incipiency."[13]

The FTC and DOJ rely on the Horizontal Merger Guidelines to assist their analysis of M&As.[14] The Horizontal Merger Guidelines were originally drafted in 1968 and last updated in 2010. The Defense Science Board Task Force on Antitrust Aspects of Defense Industry Consolidation (DOD Task Force) issued a report in 1994 stating that the Horizontal Merger Guidelines are flexible enough to consider the unique issues that

---

13 Brown Shoe Co. v. United States, 370 U.S. 294, 316 (1962).

14 Horizontal Merger Guidelines of the DOJ and the Federal Trade Commission, August 19, 2010.

arise in defense transactions. Thus, the antitrust agencies use the same guidelines for defense transactions as they would for any other commercial transaction.

The Horizontal Merger Guidelines are intended to help antitrust agencies and parties assess whether a transaction is likely to harm consumers by substantially lessening competition. A transaction is considered to be potentially harmful to consumers if it would cause prices to increase, product quality to decline, or innovation to wane.

b. Industry Specific Concerns

The consolidation of the defense industry has increased the DOJ and FTC's interest in preserving competition. In April 2016, the FTC and DOJ issued a Joint Statement affirming their commitment to preserving competition in the defense industry given the increasing consolidation in the industry.[15] The agencies noted that "[m]any sectors of the defense industry are already highly concentrated."[16] The FTC and DOJ work in cooperation with the DOD to address "concerns that reductions in current or future competitors can adversely affect competition in the defense industry and thus, national security."[17] The agencies' goal in enforcing the antitrust laws is to maintain competition for the products and services purchased by the DOD. In other words, the antitrust inquiry typically focuses on whether the proposed transactions will result in an unacceptably low number of bidders, or combine the best-positioned bidders, for upcoming procurements. Also, the agencies have expressed the view that they would supplement the analysis of current market indices with that of a forward-looking analysis of whether the proposed defense merger will adversely affect short- and long-term innovation and research and development efforts in a particular area.[18]

An unusual aspect of horizontal analysis in the defense industry is that the DOD often provides financial or other assistance to facilitate entry of new suppliers. At other times, the DOD enters into the supply of defense-related products or services on its own. Thus, the DOD may be uniquely positioned to provide information about entry conditions and potential participants,[19] a fact that the antitrust agencies take into account when reviewing a transaction. However, new entry may be unrealistic in this segment, because it is expensive, difficult, and time consuming. Entry requires significant capital expenditures, large sunk costs, specialized knowledge or technology, and/or various levels of security clearance.

On the other hand, the DOD is often the only potential purchaser of certain types of products, meaning that they may be able to offset some of the expected effects of reduced

---

[15] Joint Statement of the DOJ and the Federal Trade Commission on Preserving Competition in the Defense Industry, April 12, 2016.

[16] *Id.*

[17] *Id.*

[18] *Id.*; Robert Pitofsky, The Subcommittee on Acquisition and Technology of the United States Senate Armed Services Committee, Mergers and Acquisitions in the Defense Industry, Federal Trade Commission. April 15, 1997.

[19] Robert Pitofsky, The Subcommittee on Acquisition and Technology of the United States Senate Armed Services Committee, Mergers and Acquisitions in the Defense Industry, Federal Trade Commission. April 15, 1997.

competition through sheer bargaining power. Thus, the DOJ and FTC have stated that they "rely on DoD's expertise, often as the only purchaser, to evaluate the potential competitive impact of mergers, teaming agreements, and other joint business arrangements between firms in the defense industry."[20]

Teaming agreements may also present unique antitrust issues in the defense industry. Defense contractors often enter into teaming agreements, similar to joint ventures, to pursue procurement and typically require the subcontractor to commit not to bid independently or with another partner. Such agreements not to compete could raise antitrust concerns. In general, teaming agreements are viewed as a pro-competitive integration of complementary resources. However, if there is no efficiency-enhancing integration and instead just an agreement not to compete or allocate bids, it could result in a criminal antitrust violation.

2. Vertical Mergers

When a component supplier merges with a prime contractor, it would be considered a vertical merger. Vertical merging parties typically are in a supplier-customer relationship instead of directly competing.

a. Agency Guidance

In general, the FTC and DOJ are less likely to challenge vertical mergers than horizontal mergers.[21] In June 2020, the FTC and DOJ released the Vertical Merger Guidelines, outlining the agencies' principal analytical techniques, practices, and enforcement policies with respect to vertical mergers.[22] A vertically integrated firm benefits from efficiencies, resulting in lower costs and improved quality. In addition, vertical mergers can eliminate the problem of "double marginalization," which occurs when two firms, each with market power over a complementary product, set prices independently. When two firms with complementary products merge they can set prices jointly, thus lowering prices for each component.

The FTC and DOJ may challenge vertical mergers alleging different theories of vertical harm.[23] First, the FTC and DOJ may investigate vertical mergers that are likely to foreclose rivals from access to critical inputs or raise rivals' costs. Vertical mergers where the downstream firm refuses to buy from competitors of the supplier firm post-close are also likely to raise concerns. Second, the agencies may investigate vertical mergers where the merger could increase barriers to entry by, for example, requiring new entrants to simultaneously enter at two levels. Finally, the agencies have expressed concern that a

---

20 Joint Statement of the DOJ and the Federal Trade Commission on Preserving Competition in the Defense Industry, April 12.

21 Remarks by Bruce Hoffman, Acting Director, Bureau of Competition, "Vertical Merger Enforcement at the FTC" (January 10, 2018), available at https://www.ftc.gov/system/files/documents/public_statements/1304213/hoffman_vertical_merger_speech_final.pdf

22 Vertical Merger Guidelines of the DOJ and the Federal Trade Commission, June 30, 2020.

23 See *Id.*; Federal Trade Commission and DOJ, Horizontal Merger Guidelines (1984).

vertical merger could facilitate collusion between competitors by making it easier to monitor downstream retail prices. The vertically integrated firm could also theoretically use competitively sensitive business information of an upstream or downstream rival to gain an unfair competitive advantage. All of these situations could harm competition by forcing competitors out of the relevant product market.

b. Industry Specific Concerns

The nature of subcontracting and teaming relationships in the defense industry presents more vertical antitrust issues than in most other industries. However, in practice, few vertical mergers have been prohibited (in the defense sector or otherwise).

In 1997, the Defense Science Board Task Force issued a report to address issues with vertical mergers in the defense industry. While no major problems were identified, the Task Force advised careful monitoring of future vertical mergers because of the anticompetitive issues they pose. Specifically, vertical mergers could diminish competition by (a) foreclosing the supply of inputs and creating barriers to entry; (b) incentivizing prime contractors to select the products of captive suppliers, even if inferior; and (c) enabling anticompetitive exchanges of information between competitors.

Input foreclosure, or foreclosing rivals from access to critical components or subsystems, may occur when one company has a very strong position in a component required by a prime contractor. Prior to a merger, the supplier acts as a "merchant supplier," dealing the component to all relevant prime contractors. After a vertical merger, the newly integrated prime contractor/component supplier can withhold the component from competing prime contractors who also need the component. In the alternative, the newly merged entity could also supply the component on a discriminatory basis (i.e., offer less favorable prices, a lower quality product, or less advantageous contractual terms).

A prime contractor may also have the ability to select components used on a particular program. If the prime contractor merges with a company that manufacturers the particular component, the prime contractor has an economic incentive to select the in-house component, even if it is inferior to other available components. The DOD discourages contractors from favoring captive suppliers, because it can result in inferior defense products and services or force a potentially competing supplier to exit the relevant market.

Finally, vertical transactions sometimes create organizational conflicts of interest (OCIs). An OCI can exist when a firm has a contract, such as a systems engineering and technical assistance contract (SETA), under which it assists the government in procuring products or managing programs. If a proposed transaction results in a combination of a SETA contractor with a company that is active on a hardware program that the SETA contractor oversees, the transaction can raise competitive concerns. For example, the prime contractor in such a situation can learn sensitive information about its competitors. Access to competitor's business plans, costs, pricing data, and other internal competitively sensitive information can reduce incentives to compete vigorously. In some cases, establishing firewalls to safeguard information may be an effective way for antitrust agencies to prevent inappropriate disclosures or exchanges; however, the agencies increasingly view these types of conduct remedies as a short-term solution to a temporary problem, and not a tool for protecting competition long term.

G. Coordination of Multiple Government Investigations

For transactions that potentially implicate DOD programs, the DOD, in addition to the FTC or DOJ, will actively participate in the antitrust regulatory review.[24] Because the nature of competition in the defense industry has a number of unique aspects, the antitrust agencies generally will not allow a defense-related merger to close if DOD has competitive concerns.

When the antitrust investigation of a transaction commences, the DOD will typically participate in all substantive calls or meetings. The DOD general counsel will explore whether any of the military departments have concerns with the potential transaction. This is because the lower levels of the military departments and their procurement officers frequently are the best source of market information.

The DOD also conducts its own investigation of industry-related transactions concurrently with the assigned antitrust agency. The DOD strives to maintain a competitive supplier base for all current and future DOD programs. For instance, the DOD issued a statement to reiterate its unfavorable view of consolidation among "top tier" prime contractors following the DOJ's 2015 decision to clear Lockheed's acquisition of Sikorsky.[25] In its statement, the DOD alleged that the barriers to entry at the prime contract level were very high in practice and announced their intent to request legislative authority to review defense mergers.[26] Shortly after the issuance of the statement by the DOD, the DOJ and the FTC released the Joint Statement on preserving competition in the defense industry.[27] The Joint Statement reiterated the existing merger policy, wherein the DOD can participate in the process as a critical customer and manage the affordability of its programs. In addition, the joint statement signaled that the antitrust agencies will take into consideration the DOD's expressed concerns and assessment of particular transactions.[28]

When examining a transaction in the defense industry, the DOD is primarily focused on: (a) maintenance of cost effectiveness, (b) preservation of a base of skilled personnel, (c) preservation of research and development capacity and surge capacity, (d) assurance of efficiency and quality, and (e) protection of national security. The DOD assesses the potential loss of competition for DOD contracts and subcontracts, the estimated cost savings or increases, and whether industrial or technological capabilities may be compromised.

---

24 Department of Defense, Directive No. 5000.62, October 21, 1996.

25 Getting Defense Acquisition Right, Department of Defense, The Honorable Frank Kendall, January 2017.

26 *Id.*

27 Joint Statement of the DOJ and the Federal Trade Commission on Preserving Competition in the Defense Industry, April 12, 2016.

28 *Id.*

✓ **Best Practice Tip:** Antitrust counsel should be prepared to engage with the DOD in concert with its efforts before the antitrust agencies. Parties should contact the DOD prior to the HSR review process to inform the DOD of the anticipated transaction and send the DOD a courtesy copy of the HSR filing. Given the importance of customer perspectives, the DOD's support for the transaction increases the likelihood that it will gain approval from the agencies. The parties should explain the benefits of the proposed transaction to the DOD prior to the HSR filing to alleviate the concerns of the DOD customer.

H. Consent Decrees and Litigation

1. Consent Decrees

If a proposed transaction is likely to be issued or has received a Second Request, the parties may negotiate a consent decree in order to prevent the agency from challenging the transaction in federal district court or in administrative court.

Consent decrees memorialize the parties' agreement to cure the agency's competitive concerns, which permits the transaction to close. For transactions reviewed by the DOJ, consent decrees are enforceable court orders filed in federal district court. For transactions reviewed by the FTC, consent decrees are enforceable commission orders. Consent decrees entered into with either agency are subject to public comment before they are finalized, but the parties are allowed to close their transaction during the comment period.

Consent decrees may include different types of structural remedies, depending on the nature of the enforcement agency's concerns. For example, where the parties have overlapping lines of business, the agency may require the parties to eliminate the overlaps through divestitures. In such cases, the parties would agree to hold the to-be-divested assets separate while they work to identify a target buyer, thus allowing the parties to consummate the rest of the transaction in the interim.

In some cases, the agencies will accept conduct remedies rather than structural relief, although conduct remedies are generally disfavored. For example, a consent decree may require the combined business to establish information firewalls to prevent the improper disclosure or use of competitively sensitive information. Alternatively, a consent decree may require commitments from the combined business to deal with nonaffiliated contractors on a nondiscriminatory basis.

2. District Court Litigation

If structural or conduct remedies cannot cure the reviewing agency's competitive concerns, it may seek to enjoin the transaction. As previously noted, the DOJ must seek its preliminary injunction in federal district court. The preliminary injunction hearing often resembles a trial on the merits. The hearings generally include live testimony, and preparation involves discovery, depositions, and submission of expert reports. In order for a preliminary injunction to be granted, DOJ must show: (a) significant threat of irreparable harm; (b) a reasonable probability that it will ultimately prevail on the merits, or it must raise serious questions of law and fact; (c) favorable balance of harms; and (d) that an injunction is in the public interest.

Unlike the DOJ, the FTC has the option of beginning parallel administrative proceedings even as it seeks an injunction in federal district court. When the FTC files an administrative complaint, it also normally seeks a preliminary injunction from a federal court pursuant to Section 13(b) of the FTC Act.[29] Courts have interpreted Section 13(b) as requiring the district court to preserve the status quo while the FTC challenges the merger via its administrative process, provided that "[u]pon a proper showing that, weighing the equities and considering the Commission's likelihood of ultimate success, such action would be in the public interest."[30] Practically speaking, it is more difficult for the DOJ than the FTC to prevail on a motion for preliminary injunction.

I. Pre-Closing Activities and Integration Efforts—"Gun Jumping"

Parties to a pending transaction must be careful to maintain independent operations prior to closing. Failure to do so may result in violations of the HSR Act and/or Sherman Act Section 1.[31]

The HSR Act prohibits parties to a reportable transaction from integrating their business activities prior to the expiration or early termination of the statutory waiting period, commonly known as "gun jumping." This includes activities where the parties have effectively transferred control or beneficial ownership, for example, through close coordination of pricing, selling and marketing, or production activities prior to the close of the transaction. Note that for liability to attach under the HSR Act, the parties involved need not be competitors, nor must there be an identifiable anticompetitive effect. Violations of the HSR Act can result in civil penalties of (currently) $40,000 or more per day calculated from the onset of the violation.

Even where the statutory waiting period under the HSR Act has expired, or where the transaction is not subject to the notification requirements of the HSR Act, parties must still refrain from integrating their business operations prior to the consummation of the transaction. While premature integration would not be a violation of the HSR Act, it could still violate Section 1 of the Sherman Act. Specifically, pretransaction coordination of business activities among competitors may constitute a contract or conspiracy in restraint of trade.[32] The sharing of pricing and other non-public information between

[29] 15 U.S.C. § 53(b).

[30] 15 U.S.C. § 53(b). See Transcript of Hearing at 12, FTC v. Inova Health Sys. Found., No. 1:08-cv-460 (E.D. Va. May 30, 2008); FTC v. Whole Foods Mkt., Inc., 533 F.3d 869, 877 (D.C. Cir. 2008); FTC v. Food Town Stores, Inc., 539 F.2d 1339, 1342 (4th Cir. 1976).

[31] 15 U.S.C. § 1. Also, the FTC has brought enforcement actions under Section 5 of the FTC Act (15 U.S.C. § 45), where the premerger coordination allegedly violated Section 1 of the Sherman Act.

[32] 15 U.S.C. § 1.

competitors (even those contemplating a legitimate transaction) increases their ability to collude or coordinate in a way that lessens competition between them. If a reviewing agency becomes concerned that there has been improper information flowing between parties to a transaction, it could result in a separate government investigation and possibly civil or criminal penalties.

Notwithstanding the above, certain exchanges of information and integration planning between the parties are necessary for negotiating and planning a transaction. While counsel can advise regarding the legality of specific planned exchanges, there are a few general rules to follow. First, while planning for the post-transaction integration of the companies is permissible, it is important not to implement those integration plans prior to closing. The companies must remain separate entities (both in word and deed) as long as the transaction is still pending.

Second, competitively sensitive information should not be exchanged among company personnel (for either party) who have any role in day-to-day competitive decision making. Competitively sensitive information includes customer-specific information that reveals the prices of specific products or services; costs of production of specific products or services; pricing or marketing plans; analyses or formulas for determining costs or prices of specific products or services; or detailed information regarding research and development activities in products and service areas, including new product introductions. To the extent the exchange of competitively sensitive information is necessary for due diligence, it must happen under highly controlled circumstances that prevent disclosure to personnel responsible for competitive decision making. For instance, information can be shared with outside counsel and other third parties assisting in the evaluation of the transaction to appropriately screen businesspeople from coming into contact with each other's competitively sensitive information. Further, certain types of competitively sensitive information (for example, relating to costs and prices) may be shared on an aggregated basis and, if the information is historic in nature, on a disaggregated basis. In some instances, the parties may choose to establish a clean team consisting of a small number of individuals within the organization to evaluate the information shared. A clean team agreement can include a "cooling off" period mandating the passage of some amount of time before a clean team member is able to engage in financial and strategic decisions for the individual parties. Therefore, it is important not to appoint individuals who serve critical financial and strategic functions as clean team members. Regardless of how information is shared, it should be used only for the purpose of analyzing the potential transaction and kept within a small group of necessary individuals.

> ✓ **Best Practice Tip:** Counsel can advise as to what types of integration activities may or may not be permissible under the HSR Act and Sherman Act. Coordinate early with counsel for the other party to establish integration planning guidelines and make sure they are adhered to strictly.

CHAPTER 10

The Committee on Foreign Investment in the United States Approval for Foreign Ownership and Investment

OUTLINE

A. The Exon-Florio Amendment, as Amended

The Exon-Florio Amendment to the Defense Production Act of 1950, as amended,[1] gives the president broad authority to (a) review certain investment and real estate transactions[2] and (b) suspend or prohibit any such transaction that threatens to impair the

---

[1] Defense Production Act of 1950 § 721, 50 U.S.C. § 4565.

[2] 50 U.S.C. § 4565(a)(4).

national security of the United States.[3] The Exon-Florio Amendment was overhauled by the Foreign Investment and National Security Act of 2007 (FINSA),[4] and was substantially amended by the Foreign Investment Risk Review Modernization Act of 2018 (FIRRMA),[5] which was enacted on August 13, 2018, and made key changes such as for the first time ever expanding the jurisdiction of the Committee on Foreign Investment in the United States (CFIUS) and making certain transactions subject to mandatory notification requirements.[6] The final implementing regulations of FIRRMA went into effect on February 13, 2020.

The statute is administered by the CFIUS, which conducts national security reviews of transactions subject to CFIUS's jurisdiction.[7] CFIUS is a multiagency committee that includes the Secretaries of Treasury, Homeland Security, Commerce, Defense, State and Energy; the US Attorney General; the US Trade Representative; the Director of the Office of Science and Technology Policy; and the head of any other executive department, agency, or office, as determined appropriate by the president or the Secretary of the Treasury on a case-by-case basis. The Secretary of the Treasury chairs CFIUS.[8]

Other CFIUS members include the Secretary of Labor and the Director of National Intelligence, who serve as *ex officio*, nonvoting members. Additionally, the Director of the Office of Management and Budget, the Chairman of the Council of Economic Advisers, and the Assistants to the President for National Security Affairs, Economic Policy, and Homeland Security and Counterterrorism serve as nonvoting observers.[9]

B. CFIUS's Risk Analysis

In reviewing a transaction, CFIUS conducts a risk-based analysis that assesses the "threat" posed by the foreign investor, the "vulnerability" exposed by the Target, and the national security consequences of combining that threat and vulnerability.[10] Each transaction is reviewed on a case-by-case basis to determine its specific risk profile.

C. CFIUS Jurisdiction and Voluntary vs. Mandatory Filings

Prior to FIRRMA, CFIUS had jurisdiction to review any transaction that could result in control of a US business by a foreign person.[11] FIRRMA retains CFIUS's jurisdiction over such transactions (referred to as "covered control transactions").[12] However, one of the

---

3 *Id.* § 4565(d)(1).

4 Pub. L. 110-49, 121 Stat. 246 (2007).

5 FIRRMA was incorporated into and subsequently passed as part of the John S. McCain National Defense Authorization Act for Fiscal Year 2019 (NDAA).

6 Pub. L. 115-232.

7 50 U.S.C. § 4565(k)(1).

8 50 U.S.C. § 4565(k); Exec. Order No. 13,456, 73 Fed. Reg. 4677 (Jan. 25, 2008).

9 *Id.*

10 31 C.F.R. § 800.102.

11 31 C.F.R. § 800.207.

12 31 C.F.R. § 800.210.

most notable changes resulting from FIRRMA is the expansion of CFIUS's jurisdiction to include additional types of transactions, specifically:

1. Certain real estate transactions (regardless of an investment in a US business), including purchases or leases in the United States where the property is in close proximity to a military installation or US government facility that is sensitive for reasons relating to national security.
2. Certain nonpassive, noncontrolling investments in US businesses involved in critical technology, critical infrastructure or maintenance, or collection of sensitive data of US citizens that may be exploited in a manner that threatens national security (such businesses are referred to as "TID US businesses" for **t**echnology, **i**nfrastructure, and **d**ata).
3. Changes in rights that result in control of a US business or a qualifying nonpassive, noncontrolling interest in a TID US business.
4. Transactions or arrangements designed to avoid CFIUS review.[13]

1. Investment Jurisdiction

Based on its long-standing authority and expanded reach pursuant to FIRRMA, CFIUS has broad jurisdiction over foreign investment into the United States. FIRRMA largely coupled its expansion of jurisdiction with bright-line tests about what transactions qualified for its new authorities. Nothing changed, however, with respect to its broader, long-term jurisdiction over "controlling" investment transactions, which was already substantial. Indeed, CFIUS both defines and interprets "control"[14] and "US business"[15] expansively, meaning that even many minority investment transactions were subject to CFIUS review prior to FIRRMA. Notably, CFIUS's jurisdiction can include transactions between foreign entities when the foreign Target has US operations,[16] as well as joint ventures with a foreign or foreign-owned party into which US assets are contributed.[17]

✓ **Best Practice Tip:** When considering potential CFIUS issues relating to a contemplated transaction, parties must consider both whether the transaction would be subject to CFIUS's jurisdiction and, if so, whether notification of the transaction to CFIUS would be mandatory or voluntary.

As mandatory filing requirements and CFIUS's expanded jurisdiction over nonpassive, noncontrolling investments only apply with respect to investments in TID US businesses, a key initial step is to determine whether the Target is a TID US business.

13 50 U.S.C. § 4565(a)(4).

14 31 C.F.R. § 800.208.

15 *Id.* § 800.252.

16 *See* 31 C.F.R. § 800.224.

17 31 C.F.R. § 800.301(d).

The first category of TID US business pertains to critical technology. Specifically, a US business that produces, designs, tests, manufactures, fabricates, or develops one or more "critical technologies"[18]—certain items and technology subject to US export controls—would be considered a TID US business.[19] For critical infrastructure, the second category of TID US business, FIRRMA instructs CFIUS to limit its jurisdiction over covered investments to a subset of critical infrastructure (referred to in the regulations as "covered investment critical infrastructure") that is likely to be of particular importance to US national security. The regulations define this subset in a detailed appendix that identifies twenty-eight enumerated categories of infrastructure and related activities.[20] For the final category of TID US business, there are two classes of sensitive personal data.[21] First, sensitive personal data includes the results of an individual's genetic tests, including

---

[18] Critical technologies are defined, consistent with FIRRMA, as (a) defense articles or defense services included on the United States Munitions List set forth in the International Traffic in Arms Regulations (ITAR) (22 CFR parts 120-130); (b) items included on the Commerce Control List set forth in Supplement No. 1 to part 774 of the Export Administration Regulations (EAR) (15 CFR parts 730–774) and controlled: (1) pursuant to multilateral regimes, including for reasons relating to national security, chemical and biological weapons proliferation, nuclear nonproliferation, or missile technology; or (2) for reasons relating to regional stability or surreptitious listening; (c) specially designed and prepared nuclear equipment, parts and components, materials, software, and technology covered by 10 CFR part 810 (relating to assistance to foreign atomic energy activities); (d) nuclear facilities, equipment, and material covered by 10 CFR part 110 (relating to export and import of nuclear equipment and material); (e) select agents and toxins covered by 7 CFR part 331, 9 CFR part 121, or 42 CFR part 73; and (f) emerging and foundational technologies controlled pursuant to section 1758 of the Export Control Reform Act of 2018. 31 C.F.R. § 800.214. As of this writing, the Commerce Department has issued several emerging technology controls and export controls on additional emerging as well as foundational technologies are expected.

[19] 31 C.F.R. § 800.248.

[20] The categories of covered investment critical infrastructure include (a) telecoms (certain Internet protocol networks, telecommunications and information services, Internet exchange points, submarine cable systems and related facilities (including certain data centers)); (b) power (certain systems for the generation, transmission, distribution, or storage of electric energy comprising the bulk-power system, industrial control systems utilized therefor, and certain electric storage resources physically connected to the bulk-power system); (c) oil and gas (certain refineries, crude oil storage facilities, liquid natural gas (LNG) import or export terminals, natural gas underground storage facilities or LNG peak-shaving facilities, interstate oil and natural gas pipelines, and industrial control systems therefor); (d) water (certain public water systems and treatment works, and industrial control systems therefor); (e) finance (certain systemically important financial market utilities, securities and options exchanges, and core processing services providers); (f) defense industrial base (fiber optic cables that directly serve certain military installations; facilities that provide electric power generation, transmission, distribution, or storage directly to or located on certain military installations and industrial control systems therefor; public water systems or treatment works directly serving certain military installations and industrial control systems therefor; interstate oil pipelines that directly serve the strategic petroleum reserve; rail lines and associated connector lines designated as part of the DOD's Strategic Rail Corridor Network; satellites or satellite systems providing services directly to the DOD and its components; facilities in the United States that manufacture certain specialty metals, covered materials, chemical weapons antidotes, and carbon, alloy, and armor steel plate; and—other than commercially available off-the-shelf items—certain industrial resources manufactured or operated for a Major Defense Acquisition Program, Major System, or "DX" priority-rated contract or order, or funded by the Title III program, Industrial Base Fund, Rapid Innovation Fund, Manufacturing Technology Program, Defense Logistics Agency (DLA) Warstopper Program, or a DLA Surge and Sustainment contract); and (g) ports (airports and maritime ports that are subject to CFIUS's real estate jurisdiction). *See* 31 C.F.R. Appendix A to Part 800.

[21] 31 C.F.R. § 800.241.

any related genetic sequencing data, whenever such results constitute "identifiable data" (i.e., data that can be used to distinguish or trace an individual's identity)—regardless of the amount of such data or the population on which it is collected.[22] Second, sensitive personal data includes "identifiable data," but only if certain category[23] and collection requirements[24] are satisfied.

If the Target is a TID US business, CFIUS would have jurisdiction to review an investment that constitutes a control transaction (referred to as a "covered control transaction") or that is noncontrolling but affords the investor one or more of the following:

1. Access to any material non-public technical information in the possession of the Target.[25]
2. Membership or observer rights on the board of directors (or equivalent) of the Target or the right to nominate an individual to a position thereto.
3. Any involvement, other than through voting of shares, in substantive decision making of the Target regarding critical technology, covered investment critical infrastructure, or sensitive personal data[26] (referred to as a "covered investment"; covered investments and covered control transactions are referred to collectively as "covered transactions"[27]).

---

[22] *Id.* § 800.241(a)(2).

[23] The category requirement is satisfied if the identifiable data falls within one of ten identified categories, which are: (a) financial data that could be used to determine an individual's financial distress or hardship; (b) data in a consumer report (with certain exceptions); (c) data included in health or other types of insurance applications; (d) data relating to the physical, mental, or psychological health of an individual; (e) non-public electronic communications (email, text, chat, etc.) between users of the US business's products or services if facilitating third-party user communications is a primary purpose of such products or services; (f) geolocation data; (g) biometric enrollment data; (h) data stored and processed to generate a state or federal government ID card; (i) data concerning US government personnel security clearance status, or (j) data contained in the application for a US government personnel security clearance or for employment in a position of public trust. 31 C.F.R. § 800.241(a)(1)(ii).

[24] The collection requirement is met if the US business that maintains or collects the identifiable data (a) targets or tailors products or services to any US executive branch agency or military department with intelligence, national security, or homeland security responsibilities, or to personnel and contractors thereof; (b) had such data on more than one million individuals at any point over the twelve months preceding the earliest of the completion date of the transaction, execution of a binding transaction agreement, the submission of a CFIUS notice or declaration, or certain other transaction-related actions (unless it can demonstrate no ability to collect or maintain any such data as of the completion date); or (c) has a demonstrated business objective to maintain or collect such data on more than one million individuals and such data is an integrated part of the US business's products or services. 31 C.F.R. § 800.241(a)(1)(i).

[25] Material non-public technical information is information that (a) provides knowledge, know-how, or understanding, in each case not available in the public domain, of the design, location, or operation of covered investment critical infrastructure, including vulnerability information such as that related to physical security or cybersecurity; or (b) is not available in the public domain, and is necessary to design, fabricate, develop, test, produce, or manufacture a critical technology, including processes, techniques, or methods. Material non-public technical information does not include financial information regarding the performance of an entity. 31 C.F.R. § 800.232.

[26] 31 C.F.R. § 800.211.

[27] *Id.* § 800.213.

2. Mandatory Filing Requirements

Historically, CFIUS review has ostensibly been a voluntary process, though CFIUS could request parties to notify transactions of interest or initiate filings directly. Under FIRRMA, CFIUS is still predominantly a voluntary process, though certain transactions involving TID US businesses are subject to mandatory notification requirements.

Two types of investment in TID US businesses would, absent an applicable exemption, trigger mandatory filing requirements, in which case a declaration (i.e., a short-form filing) or a full notice would need to be submitted to CFIUS at least thirty days prior to the completion date of the transaction.[28] The first category of transactions triggering mandatory filing requirements involves investment in a TID US business by an entity with substantial foreign government ownership.[29] Specifically, the acquisition of a voting interest, direct or indirect, of 25 percent or more in a TID US business by an entity in which the national or subnational governments of a single foreign state have a voting interest, direct or indirect, of 49 percent or more.[30] The second category mandates filing for any covered transaction in a TID US business that produces, designs, tests, manufactures, fabricates, or develops one or more critical technologies if a "US regulatory authorization" would be required for the export, re-export, transfer (in-country), or retransfer of such critical technologies to either (a) the person making the investment subject to CFIUS's jurisdiction, or (b) a person that individually, or as part of a group of foreign persons, holds a voting interest, direct or indirect, of 25 percent or more in a person described in (a). US regulatory authorizations include licenses, approvals, and other authorizations under the International Traffic in Arms Regulation (ITAR), the Export Administration Regulations (EAR), or regulations governing certain nuclear energy–related activities, as applicable.[31] Notably, with the exception of cases in which the parties are eligible to use any of three enumerated license exceptions under the EAR,[32] a mandatory filing is required regardless of whether any license exceptions or exemptions would apply for exports of the US business's critical technology to the given foreign person. The regulations include certain exemptions both from the expanded jurisdiction over covered investments involving TID US businesses and mandatory filing requirements, including with respect to certain

---

[28] *Id.* § 800.401. *See* 31 C.F.R. § 800.206 for the definition of "completion date."

[29] 31 C.F.R. § 800.401(b).

[30] 31 C.F.R. § 800.401; 31 C.F.R. § 800.244. The regulations do not permit dilution in the ownership chain and deem 100 percent ownership for each parent for purposes of calculating whether a foreign government indirectly owns 49 percent or more of the investing entity. Additionally, for entities with general partners, managing members, or the equivalent, the 49 percent test only applies with respect to interests in the general partner, managing member, or equivalent. *Id.*

[31] 31 C.F.R. § 800.401(c). Prior to October 15, 2020, the critical technology-specific mandatory filing criteria considered whether the TID US business's critical technologies were (a) utilized in connection with the TID US business's activity in one or more of twenty-seven identified industries, or (b) designed by the TID US business specifically for use in one or more of those industries.

[32] These license exceptions are technology and software—unrestricted (TSU) (15 C.F.R. § 740.13); encryption commodities, software, and technology (ENC) (15 C.F.R. § 740.17(b)); and strategic trade authorization (STA) (15 C.F.R. § 740.20(c)(1)). 31 C.F.R. § 800.401(e)(6).

investments from what are known as "excepted investors," which include companies that meet specified criteria associated with certain identified "excepted foreign states."[33]

✓ **Best Practice Tip:** Determine early in the deal process whether the Target is a TID US business as this is a trigger for expanded CFIUS authorities, including mandatory filings in certain cases, and an indicator that the transaction may be of heightened interest to CFIUS.

3. Real Estate Jurisdiction

FIRRMA also provided CFIUS with jurisdiction to review the purchase or lease by, or concession to, a "non-excepted" foreign person of certain real estate (a) involving certain air or maritime ports ("covered ports"),[34] or (b) that is in close proximity to, or that provides the foreign person the ability to collect intelligence on or surveil national security activities at US military installations or other sensitive US government facilities or property. The regulations implemented this new basis for jurisdiction through the concept of a "covered real estate transaction."[35] Specifically, unless one of eight exceptions[36] applies, CFIUS would have the authority to review any purchase or lease by, or concession to, a foreign person of "covered real estate,"[37] either directly or indirectly, that affords

---

33 *See* 31 C.F.R. §§ 800.401(d), (e). *See also* 31 C.F.R. § 800.219 for the definition of "excepted investor." Though subject to change in the future, the initial designated excepted foreign states are Australia, Canada, and the United Kingdom of Great Britain and Northern Ireland. *See* 85 Fed. Reg. 3116 (Jan. 17, 2020).

34 31 C.F.R. § 802.210.

35 *Id.* § 802.212.

36 The exceptions are as follows: (1) foreign persons who fall within the "excepted real estate investors" category (which is the same as excepted investors under the investment regulations); (2) covered transactions subject to CFIUS's investment-related jurisdiction; (3) certain real estate within an "urbanized area" or "urban cluster"; (4) single housing units; (5) leases and concessions of covered real estate to a foreign air carrier for which the Transportation Security Administration (TSA) has accepted a security program under 49 CFR § 1546.105; (6) leases and concessions of covered real estate at covered ports that may be used *only* for the purpose of engaging in the retail sale of consumer goods or services to the public; (7) commercial space in a multi-unit building that is covered real estate if, upon closing, the foreign person and its affiliates (i) do not, in the aggregate, hold, lease or have concession to commercial space that exceeds 10 percent of the total square footage of the commercial space in the building and (ii) do not, with each counted separately, represent more than 10 percent of the total number of tenants based on the number of ownership, lease, and concession arrangements for commercial space in the building; and (8) certain lands owned by certain Alaska Native entities or held in trust by the United States for American Indians, Indian tribes, Alaska Natives, and Alaska Native entities. *See* 31 C.F.R. § 802.216.

37 There are five types of "covered real estate": (1) real estate that is, is located within, or will function as part of, certain air or maritime ports (referred to in the regulations as "covered ports"); (2) real estate that is within "close proximity" (defined as one mile) of any military installation listed on part 1 (131 such sites) or part 2 (32 such sites) of Appendix A to the real estate regulations; (3) real estate that is within the "extended range" (defined as up to 100 miles but where applicable not exceeding the outer limit of the US territorial sea) of any military installation listed on part 2 of Appendix A; (4) real estate located within the 48 counties or other geographic areas listed on part 3 of Appendix A, which are associated with missile fields; and (5) real estate located within the 23 offshore military operating areas listed on part 4 of Appendix A, but

the foreign person at least three of four "property rights": the right to (a) physically access the real estate, (b) exclude others from physical access to the real estate, (3) improve or develop the real estate, or (4) attach fixed or immovable structures or objects to the real estate.[38] Real estate transactions are not subject to mandatory filing requirements, though CFIUS may request or initiate a filing at its discretion.[39]

Note that although CFIUS's real estate jurisdiction is addressed here for completeness, given the focus of this manual on government contractors, the primary focus of this section is on CFIUS's authority with respect to investment transactions.

D. Whether to File

Although FIRRMA introduced mandatory filing requirements for the first time ever, CFIUS remains primarily a voluntary review process. CFIUS conducts national security reviews of foreign direct investment into the United States (and certain foreign real estate transactions), but "national security" is not defined in either the CFIUS statute or regulations. Indeed, this has been deliberately left as a broad concept open to interpretation. CFIUS has reviewed transactions covering a wide range of industries, including defense, aerospace, technology, cyber security, telecommunications, financial services, healthcare, infrastructure, semiconductors, transportation, mining, identity authentication, food, and energy, among others. Companies providing products or services to the US government (directly or indirectly) or that have electronic connections or other access to US government sites may be viewed with interest by CFIUS and a filing should be carefully considered in such cases. Similarly, companies that qualify as TID US businesses are likely to be of heightened interest to CFIUS. Parties should assess the advisability of notifying CFIUS at the outset of any investment transaction subject to CFIUS's jurisdiction where the Target has a potential nexus to US national security.

> ✓ **Best Practice Tip:** Given the breadth of industries and issues that may be viewed as relevant to US national security, it is critical to conduct thorough CFIUS-related due diligence early in the transaction process to assess the Target's potential nexus to national security and possible CFIUS-related risks relative to the transaction.

Even though CFIUS is largely still a voluntary review process, CFIUS actively searches for non-notified transactions and will reach out to request that parties notify identified transactions of interest. Indeed, under FIRRMA CFIUS has increased resources and is more actively pursuing non-notified transactions. CFIUS can also initiate its own review

only to the extent located within the limits of the US territorial sea (i.e., generally 12 nautical miles from the coastline). *See* 31 C.F.R. § 802.211.

38 *See* 31 C.F.R. § 802.233.

39 *See* 31 C.F.R. § 802.402.

of a transaction if the parties do not file voluntarily.[40] In transactions involving parallel national security processes—such as in cases involving cleared facilities, export-controlled defense articles, or certain Federal Communications Commission licenses—CFIUS review may be expected and encouraged by the relevant regulatory agencies. Thus, while filing may technically be voluntary, a CFIUS filing should be strongly considered in such cases.

✓ **Best Practice Tip:** The need for CFIUS approval can disadvantage foreign bidders in an auction process, so a plan for successful CFIUS review should be part of a foreign bidder's pitch. Allocation of CFIUS-related risks is a key issue in negotiating CFIUS provisions of the purchase agreement, so a buyer's willingness to accept more mitigation risk can help bolster its bid in an auction.

E. Two Ways to File with CFIUS

There are two ways in which parties can notify transactions to CFIUS: via a joint voluntary notice (Notice), which undergoes a full CFIUS review and potentially an investigation, or a declaration, which is a short-form filing that CFIUS has thirty days to assess.

1. CFIUS Notices

a. Pre-filing Process

Should the parties initiate a CFIUS review, the first step is to prepare and file a draft Notice regarding the proposed transaction, which is known as a "pre-filing."[41] The Notice must include information required under the regulations, found at 31 C.F.R. Part 800. CFIUS will provide comments and questions on the pre-filing, which generally must be addressed before CFIUS will accept the formal Notice and begin the review. The pre-filing process has been taking substantially more time in recent years, but FIRRMA established ten-business-day time limits on CFIUS to provide comments on a pre-filing and to accept a Notice after parties formally file if the Notice stipulates that the notified transaction is a covered transaction.[42]

✓ **Best Practice Tip:** Before filing, the parties should—to the extent possible—meet with the US business's government stakeholders to brief them on the proposed transaction, introduce them to the Acquirer, and identify any foreign ownership concerns they may have. To the extent these meetings identify significant problems or concerns, it may be advisable to consider ways to address these problems as part of the overall CFIUS strategy.

---

40 31 C.F.R. § 800.501(c).

41 31 C.F.R. § 800.501(g).

42 *Id.* § 800.501(i).

✓ **Best Practice Tip:** In certain cases, a pre-filing call or meeting with CFIUS may be advisable.

b. Acquirer's Information Required in Notice of Proposed Transaction

The regulations require the Notice to include information about the transaction generally, as well as specific information about the foreign buyer or investor (the Acquirer) and the US business being acquired (the Target).[43] The information the Acquirer must provide for a Notice includes the following:[44]

- The name, address, and place of incorporation for the Acquirer and its parent companies, and the name and address of its ultimate parent's owners (for public companies, the information is required for shareholders that hold 5 percent or more of the shares of the ultimate parent)
- A description of the business of the Acquirer and its ultimate parent, as well as their Commercial and Government Entity (CAGE) Codes, Dun & Bradstreet ("DUNS") numbers, and NAICS codes (as applicable)
- A description of the Acquirer's plans for the US business with respect to reducing, eliminating, or selling research and development facilities; changing product quality; shutting down or moving US facilities outside of the United States; consolidating or selling product lines or technology; modifying or terminating US government contracts; and eliminating domestic supply by selling only to nondomestic markets
- Information regarding any foreign government ownership or control over the Acquirer
- A description of any formal or informal relationships among foreign persons holding an ownership interest in the Acquirer or between such foreign persons and other foreign persons to act in concert on matters affecting the Target
- Curriculum vitae or similar professional synopsis and personal identifier information (including social security numbers, passport and visa information, date of birth, place of birth, national identity number information, and foreign government and military service information) for all members of the boards of directors and officers of the Acquirer and all of its parent companies, as well as any individuals that own 5 percent or more of the Acquirer or its ultimate parent
- The most recent annual report for the immediate Acquirer and its parent companies (if the relevant information is captured in the consolidated financials of the ultimate parent, individual company information does not have to be provided)
- An organizational chart, both pre- and post-transaction, showing the ownership chain from the immediate Acquirer to its ultimate parent
- Copies of any partnership agreements, integration agreements, or other side agreements relating to the transaction

43 *See* 31 C.F.R. § 800.502.

44 *Id.*

c. Target's Information Required in Notice of Proposed Transaction

The information the Target must provide for a Notice includes the following:[45]

- The name, address, and place of incorporation, as well as CAGE Codes, DUNS numbers, and NAICS codes for the Target
- A description of the Target's business, including an estimate of US market share for its product and service categories, the methodology used to determine market share, and a list of its direct competitors
- Information about classified (going back five years) and unclassified (going back three years) US government contracts, though information about unclassified contracts need be provided only where the government agency has national defense, homeland security, or other national security responsibilities, including law enforcement duties related to national defense and security
- A description of products or services supplied directly or indirectly to the US government, information on whether the Target is a sole or single-qualified source of any products or services to those agencies, as well as a list of other suppliers in the market that can be so qualified or provide comparable products or services
- A description of any products or services of the Target that are rebranded or incorporated into products sold by other entities
- A list of contracts/orders received and placed within the past three years that are subject to the Defense Priorities and Allocations System (DPAS) regulations (the Acquirer's plan for ensuring continued compliance with the DPAS regulations postacquisition must also be described)
- A description of products and services the Target produces or trades in that are subject to the ITAR and EAR and their ITAR/EAR classifications
- A listing of products or technology subject to export authorization under the Department of Energy or Nuclear Regulatory Commission, as well as Select Agents and Toxins the Target produces or trades in
- A list of licenses, permits, or other authorizations issued by any other US government agency
- A listing of all technology with military applications and a description of such military applications
- The most recent annual report or financials
- Details regarding whether the Target meets the requirements of a TID US business

Some companies may have concerns about disclosing the information reflected above due to its sensitivity. CFIUS filings, however, are confidential and exempt from Freedom of Information Act, with some narrow exceptions.[46]

---

45 *Id.*

46 *See* 31 C.F.R. § 800.802(a) and 50 U.S.C. § 4565(c)(2). The exceptions are (a) information relevant to any administrative or judicial action or proceeding; (b) information to Congress or any duly authorized committee or subcommittee of Congress; (c) information important to the national security analysis or actions of CFIUS to any domestic governmental entity, or to any foreign governmental entity of a US ally

✓ **Best Practice Tip:** Although the CFIUS Notice is typically a joint filing and information is usually submitted jointly, in cases where certain information is deemed sensitive or confidential (e.g., detailed information pertaining to ownership and governance in the context of a private equity investor), such information may be submitted to CFIUS on a one-sided basis.

d. CFIUS Review Process & Timing

Upon accepting a formal filing, CFIUS conducts a forty-five-calendar-day review to determine the effects of the transaction on US national security.[47] If CFIUS clears the transaction, the process ends with written notice to the parties stating that CFIUS has concluded its review and has determined that there are no unresolved national security concerns with respect to the transaction.[48]

If CFIUS decides that the acquisition presents national security concerns, if factors are present that trigger mandatory investigation,[49] or if CFIUS simply needs more time to complete its process, a forty-five-day investigation follows the initial forty-five-day review.[50] Currently, about half of cases go to investigation.[51] FIRRMA also provides for extending an investigation from forty-five to sixty days in "extraordinary circumstances."[52] If CFIUS needs additional time to complete its process, it may encourage parties to withdraw and resubmit their Notice, which restarts the initial forty-five-day review period.

When each CFIUS review begins, the Secretary of the Treasury (as the Chair of CFIUS) must designate one or more lead agencies.[53] The lead agency takes an active role in the review, including negotiating and monitoring mitigation agreements as well as any conditions attached to approval. Throughout the course of the review and, if applicable, investigation, CFIUS typically asks additional questions of the parties. Parties have three business days to respond to such requests unless CFIUS grants an extension.

---

or partner, under certain limited circumstances and restrictive conditions; and (d) information that the parties have consented to be disclosed to third parties.

47 50 U.S.C. § 4565(b)(1)(F). FIRRMA increased the time period for the initial review from thirty calendar days to forty-five calendar days upon acceptance of written notification of any covered transaction.

48 31 C.F.R. § 800.506.

49 By statute, certain transactions require a forty-five-day investigation, including foreign government-controlled transactions and some transactions involving critical infrastructure, unless the Chairperson of the Committee (or the Deputy Secretary of the Treasury) and the head of the lead agency (or his or her delegee at the deputy level or equivalent) jointly determine that the transaction will not impair US national security. 31 C.F.R. § 800.505(b).

50 50 U.S.C. § 4565(b)(2)(C).

51 *See* https://home.treasury.gov/system/files/206/CFIUS-Summary-Data-2015-2019.pdf

52 50 U.S.C. § 4565(b)(2)(C)(ii); 31 C.F.R. § 800.508(e). "Extraordinary circumstances" means circumstances for which extending an investigation is necessary and the appropriate course of action due to a force majeure event or to protect the national security of the United States. *See* 31 C.F.R. § 800.508(f).

53 50 U.S.C. § 4565(k)(5).

If CFIUS has national security concerns with the transaction, it can address them via mitigation measures or, if it believes such concerns are unresolvable, recommend that the president of the United States block the transaction.[54] Mitigation is decided on a case-by-case basis and can range from relatively mild assurances to broad governance and access restrictions on the Acquirer. In cases where CFIUS recommends that the president stop the transaction, fails to reach a decision, or affirmatively requests a presidential decision, the president has fifteen calendar days to decide whether to allow the transaction to proceed.[55] Presidential decisions are relatively rare.[56] Typically, in cases where CFIUS opposes a transaction, the parties voluntarily abandon it rather than risk a presidential block, which is publicly announced. Most transactions are approved by CFIUS without mitigation measures.

CFIUS imposes filing fees for Notices based on the value of the transaction.[57] Filing fees do not apply to declarations, though they apply for Notices submitted following CFIUS's assessment of a declaration. Fees are assessed on a tiered approach based on transaction value. The lowest fee is $750 for transactions valued between $500,000 and $5 million (transactions under $500,000 are not subject to fees), and the highest-tier fee is $300,000 for transactions valued at $750 million or more.[58]

2. Declarations

In addition to the typical review process described above, FIRRMA established a new "declaration" process, which allows for quicker disposition of certain transactions based on abbreviated filings.[59] With a declaration, parties submit a short-form filing to CFIUS. Declarations, like Notices, require certain information about the investor and its owners, the US business that is the subject of the transaction, and the transaction itself.[60] A declaration generally requires more limited information than a Notice—for example, answering a "yes" or "no" to certain questions rather than providing detailed information.

Within thirty days of accepting a declaration (whether it was voluntary or mandatory), CFIUS must take one of four actions: it may (a) request that the parties file a Notice, (b) advise the parties that it cannot complete action based on the declaration and that they may submit a written Notice in order for CFIUS to complete action (commonly referred to as the "shrug"), (c) initiate a unilateral review of the transaction, or (d) notify the parties in writing that CFIUS has completed all action with respect to the

54 Presidential referrals would typically happen at the end of an investigation, but CFIUS may at any time during the review or investigation of a covered transaction complete the action of the committee and refer the transaction to the president, at which point the president would have fifteen days to make a decision. 50 U.S.C. § 4565(d)(2).

55 31 C.F.R. § 800.508(b); 50 U.S.C. § 4565(d)(2).

56 As of this writing, seven transactions have been blocked by the president. Six of the blocks have happened since 2012.

57 31 C.F.R. § 800.1101.

58 *Id.*

59 *See* 50 U.S.C. § 4565(b)(1)(C)(v). The final regulations cover this process in 31 C.F.R. §§ 800.401–407.

60 *See* 31 C.F.R. § 800.404.

transaction (i.e., cleared the transaction).[61] Particularly for straightforward transactions that are unlikely to present national security concerns, declarations can be a useful tool for parties to complete the CFIUS process faster, especially if they are comfortable with a "shrug" outcome being sufficient.

✓ **Best Practice Tip:** Parties should determine whether to notify CFIUS via a Notice or declaration, including based on the complexity and potential sensitivity of the given transaction. In negotiating the transaction agreement, parties considering filing a declaration should also decide whether the "shrug" outcome is sufficient for closing.

---

61 *See* 31 C.F.R. § 800.405 regarding timing for declarations, and 31 C.F.R. § 800.407 regarding actions CFIUS can take upon accepting a declaration. *See also* 50 U.S.C. § 4565(b)(1)(C)(v)(III)(aa).

CHAPTER 11

Existing Contracts—Dealing with the Anti-Assignment Statutes

OUTLINE

A. Applicable Law

In commercial contracting, assignment of a party's rights under a contract is permissible, subject to contract terms and state assignment laws. In federal contracting, the assignment of any contract with the government is prohibited. The Assignment of Contracts Act, which originated with Civil War-era legislation, provides in subsection (a):

> The party to whom the Federal Government gives a contract or order may not transfer the contract or order, or any interest in the contract or order, to another party. A purported transfer in violation of this subsection annuls the contract or order so far as the Federal Government is concerned, except that all rights of action for breach of contract are reserved to the Federal Government.

The Act, as presently codified at 41 U.S.C. § 6305(a), operates to annul a government contract purportedly assigned by a contractor to a third party. This statute is to be distinguished from related authority known as the Assignment of Claims Act, 31

U.S.C. § 3727(a)-(b). The latter statute governs the assignment of claims and/or monies due under federal contracts, permitting such assignment under certain conditions. Regulatory coverage of the Assignment of Claims Act is found at FAR Subpart 32.8. The two federal laws are at times given the same vernacular nomenclature, such as the "anti-assignment statutes" or the "Anti-Assignment Act."

The purpose of the Anti-Assignment Act is to ensure that the party who is awarded a government contract is the same party who performs it. However, if the government determines an assignment is in its interest, it may waive the Act and permit the assignment—that is, transfer of a contract to a third party—under certain conditions discussed below.

B. Case Law

There is an extensive body of case law interpreting the Anti-Assignment Act and its application to government contracts. The courts and boards of contract appeals have addressed the statute in a variety of contexts, although not with uniformity.

One line of cases has held that the Act does not bar the assignment of a federal contract when such assignment is by "operation of law." Originating with the Supreme Court's decision in *Seaboard Air Line Railway v. United States*, 256 U.S. 655 (1921), a "judicial exception" to the Act has evolved, enunciating that where a contract assignment is valid under state corporation law or some other regulatory scheme, it does not violate the Act. Many courts and boards have recognized this exception.[1] The FAR, however, does not contain an operation of law exception.

Another line of cases holds that even where the Anti-Assignment Act would otherwise apply, it may be waived by the government in certain scenarios. With an express waiver, the government consents to a proposed transfer of a contract, and the FAR novation process is employed. There can also be imputed or implied waiver of the Act where, by its course of conduct, the government recognizes a third party as the successor in interest to the contractor.[2] The government's dealing with a third party under these circumstances can constitute a "de facto" novation of a contract.

Agency contracting officers follow the regulatory requirements of FAR Subpart 42.12 on contract novations.[3] If they determine that a contract assignment is not in the interest of the government, they may invoke FAR 42.1204(c) and hold the original contractor to its obligation to perform. Reasons for such a determination could include that the

---

1 *See* L-3 Commc'ns Integrated Sys., L.P. v. United States, 84 Fed. Cl. 768 (2008); Westinghouse Elec. Co. v. United States, 56 Fed. Cl. 564 (2003); *Pettibone Corp.*, ASBCA No. 41703, 91-2 BCA ¶ 23,952.

2 Tuftco Corp. v. United States, 222 Ct. Cl. 277, 614 F.2d. 740 (1980) (finding clear assent where the contracting officer acknowledged the assignment in writing and made payment to the successor); *Healy Tibbits Builders, Inc.*, ASBCA No. 45269, 94-1 BCA ¶ 26,409.

3 The prohibition against assignment of government contracts is not limited to procurement contracts governed by the FAR. Other government contract regimes have their own novation process, such as the FAA's Acquisition Management System 3.10.1-8 (Novations and Change-of-Name Agreements) and the USPS's Supplying Principles and Practices 5-8.15 (Novation Agreements), or no specified process at all (e.g., Other Transaction Agreements).

proposed assignee is not responsible under FAR Part 9 or is not in a position to fully perform all contract requirements, as well as other factors indicating that contract performance could be jeopardized if a successor were recognized. Essentially, the government seeks assurance that the proposed assignee has the financial and technical capability to perform the contract.

Participation in the contract novation process is voluntary for both contracting parties. The government is under no obligation to sign a novation agreement with a contractor.[4] Similarly, a company is under no obligation to agree to novation of its contracts to another company.[5]

Issues may arise after the execution of a novation agreement. One of the terms in the standard FAR agreement, paragraph (b)(1), provides that the contract transferor waives any claims it may have against the government relating to the transferred contracts. In a test of this provision by a transferor, the Armed Services Board of Contract Appeals upheld the waiver, finding that it barred the original contractor's claim for certain costs arising out of pre-novation events.[6] Pre-novation claims are not waived, however, as to the contract transferee. Paragraph (b)(6) of the standard FAR agreement grants the transferee all rights, titles, and interests of the transferor under the transferred contract, as if the transferee were the original party to it. In *Vought Aircraft Co.*, ASBCA No. 47357, 95-1 ¶ BCA 27,421, the Board relied on this provision to permit a transferee, as the new contractor, to bring a claim against the government for events arising prior to the novation agreement's execution.

C. Regulations

As noted above, policies and procedures with respect to the Anti-Assignment Act are contained in FAR Subpart 42.12. Here, the government reaffirms the prohibition on contract assignments but also provides for consent to such assignments under certain circumstances. FAR 42.1204(a) states in part:

> 41 U.S.C. 6305 prohibits transfer of Government contracts from the contractor to a third party. The Government may, when in its interest, recognize a third party as the successor in interest to a Government contract when the third party's interest in the contract arises out of the transfer of—
> (1) All of the contractor's assets; or
> (2) The entire portion of the assets involved in performing the contract.

The recognition of a successor to a contract is conditioned on a transfer of assets from the incumbent contractor to the third party. Examples of qualifying transactions such as

[4] *See Tri-Delta Corp.*, ASBCA No. 17456, 75-1 BCA ¶ 11,160; Ordnance Devices, Inc. v. United States, 50 F.3d 22 (Fed. Cir. 1995).

[5] *See Biomass One Operating Co.*, ASBCA No. 41972, 94-3 BCA ¶ 27,051.

[6] *R.W. Elec. Corp.*, ASBCA No. 39486, 91-3 BCA ¶ 24,220.

asset sales, mergers, and consolidations are listed therein. The government reserves the right whether or not to recognize a successor to a contract:

> When it is in the Government's interest not to concur in the transfer of a contract from one company to another company, the original contractor remains under contractual obligation to the Government, and the contract may be terminated for reasons of default, should the original contractor not perform.[7]

A company that wishes to transfer one or more of its contracts to another party does so by written request to the "responsible contracting officer." The contracting officer's determination of whether to approve a contract transfer may be based on a number of factors, including the proposed successor's responsibility under FAR Part 9, comments received from the offices that initially awarded the contracts, and the potential for organizational conflicts of interest.[8]

D. Contract Novations

1. Federal Acquisition Regulations

The vehicle for the government's consent to the assignment of a contract is the "novation agreement." This is a three-party agreement among the government, the contract assignor (transferor), and assignee (transferee). The standard novation agreement, which effectuates the "novation" of government contracts, is set forth at FAR 42.1204(i).[9] The party requesting a contract novation submits to the contracting officer the proposed novation agreement, using the standard FAR language, and a copy of specified supporting documents. Some of these documents include the instrument describing the transaction (e.g., an asset purchase agreement or merger agreement). One key submission is a list of the contracts intended to be transferred from one company to the other. When a novation agreement is executed, this list is attached to the agreement as Exhibit A.

FAR 42.1204(g) contemplates the contracting officer's participation in a pretransaction review (usually during the period between signing and closing), through which the government may streamline the documents required by FAR 42.1204(e) by allowing alternatives to some documents, provided that government interests are protected. For example, SEC filings that contain relevant information may be substituted for original documents. After the review and approval of the documentation of the parties' transaction, the novation agreement is executed, effective as of the transaction's closing. A modification to the contract(s) is then issued by the agency, which recognizes the transferee as the contractor of record.

The novation agreement as set forth in the FAR contains a number of provisions pertaining to rights and responsibilities of the three signatories. As stated in FAR 42.1204(h), the agreement should:

---

7 FAR 42.1204(c).

8 FAR 42.1203, 42.1204.

9 See Appendix 6 for a copy of the Standard Novation Agreement set forth in the FAR.

. . . ordinarily provide in part[:]

1. The transferee assumes all the transferor's obligations under the contract;
2. The transferor waives all rights under the contract against the Government;
3. The transferor guarantees performance of the contract by the transferee (a satisfactory performance bond may be accepted instead of the guarantee); and
4. Nothing in the agreement shall relieve the transferor or transferee from compliance with any Federal law.

When there is some type of asset transfer, and a determination that recognition of a successor in interest to a contract is in the government's interest, contracting officers are directed to use the novation agreement for such recognition.[10]

The regulation contains an exception to the use of the novation agreement when there is a "change in ownership" of a contractor as a result of a stock (or equity) purchase.[11] There are three conditions before the exception can apply: (a) there must be no "legal change" in the contractor entity itself, (b) the contractor remains in control of its assets, and (c) the contractor remains the party responsible for performance of the contract. Even when not required, the FAR provision recommends use of an agreement in which "issues related to the change in ownership" may be addressed.

The examples of asset transfers appearing in FAR 42.1204(a) that trigger the novation process are not exhaustive. There may be other forms of acquisition to which a contractor is a party that may or may not require a novation of its contracts. Discussion with the contracting officer is warranted in these cases.

Companies frequently change their form of business. Described as "conversions," a corporation may convert its form into a limited liability company, or vice versa. These changes are recognized under state conversion statutes. For example, the conversion of a Delaware corporation to a Delaware limited liability company is governed by Section 266 of the Delaware General Corporation Law[12] and Section 18-214 of the Delaware Limited Liability Company Act.[13] The Delaware statute provides that the converted entity is a continuation of the converting entity and that the conversion occurs by operation of law. The conversion does not affect the obligations and liabilities that the corporation incurred prior to the date of conversion.[14] The FAR does not as yet adequately address such conversions. As a result, the government may seek a novation agreement to recognize the new form of entity. However, an abbreviated process may be sufficient to deal with this situation.[15] Another option for the government is a Change of Name Agreement, following the procedures at FAR 42.1205, when the legal entity in privity with the government remains the same post-closing.

---

[10] FAR 42.1204(i).

[11] FAR 42.1204(b).

[12] 8 Del. C. § 101.

[13] 6 Del. C. § 18-101.

[14] 6 Del. C. § 18-214.

[15] See Appendix 7 for a sample of a Truncated Novation Agreement for a Limited Liability Corporation (LLC).

Only "contracts" may be novated from one entity to another. Instruments such as Blanket Purchase Agreements (FAR 13.303) and Basic Ordering Agreements (FAR 16.703) are not contracts and are not transferred or assigned pursuant to FAR Part 42.12, "Novations." Purchase orders issued under these instruments, however, may be transferred to a third party, using the FAR contract novation procedures.

✓ **Best Practice Tip:** Before the closing date, take the following actions:

- Where multiple contracts and agencies are involved, identify a lead "responsible contracting officer" or officers who will review and approve the novation package in order to streamline the process, if possible.
- Depending on the relationship with the government customer, a "draft" novation package with copies of as many available documents as required in FAR 42.1204(e) may be provided to the contracting officer in advance of closing to expedite the novation process.
- A "draft" novation package may also include a draft subcontract pending novation agreement for the contracting officer's review, and if consent to subcontract is required, approval.
- Review the Target's subcontracts, if planned for continuation by the Acquirer, for any assignment-related provisions.

✓ **Best Practice Tip:** After the closing date, take the following actions:

- Provide to the contracting officer a complete novation package with all documents required in FAR 42.1204(e) in both hard copy (as required by the FAR) and electronic versions.
- Any specific agreement between the Acquirer and Target regarding the contracts to be transferred, such as assumption of liabilities, costs, and noncompliances, may be referenced in the novation agreement.[16]

2. Transition Arrangements Pending Novation

Notwithstanding the closing of the transaction, from the government's perspective any contracts to be novated remain in the name of the Target, and contract payments are made to the Target until the novation agreement is signed. While novation agreements are effective as of the closing date of the transaction, the novation package cannot

16 *See* FAR 42.1203(e).

be completed and ready for review and execution by the government until after the transaction has closed. It is essential, therefore, that the parties negotiate transition arrangements and, when possible, have those arrangements approved by the responsible contracting officer who is managing the novation process on behalf of the Target's government customers.

Depending on the circumstances and contract requirements, the contracting officer may insist on more or less formal transition arrangements. These arrangements could include entering into subcontracts under which the work or a portion of the work is subcontracted by the Target to the Acquirer, pending approval of the novation. Pre-novation subcontracts frequently include a form of guarantee by the prime contractor, under which the prime contractor guarantees payments of all liabilities and performance of all obligations assumed by the subcontractor under designated contracts. The subcontract may also include an indemnification by the subcontractor to indemnify and hold the prime contractor harmless for any damages, costs, or charges incurred by the prime contractor as a result of the subcontractor's failure to perform in accordance with the subcontract agreement or designated contracts.

The acquisition agreement should provide that the parties shall cooperate by providing all information necessary for the government to execute the novation. The agreement could provide further details on interim financial and other arrangements (i.e., invoicing, allocating expenses, interacting with customers, etc.) governing the parties' ongoing relationship while the novation request is pending. The parties may also consider provisions for renegotiating the purchase price or even unwinding the deal post-closing in the event the government does not execute the novation agreement.

✓ **Best Practice Tip:** Identify and consult as early as possible with the responsible contracting officer(s) who will be managing the transition. Engaging the contracting officer early can facilitate the novation process, especially if the parties can provide assurance that the proposed deal will not jeopardize, but rather enhance, performance of the contract and the ability to meet the government's requirements. Contracting officers may be more inclined to work with the parties on transition arrangements and may not insist on certain formalized arrangements if they are included early in the process.

E. Change of Name Agreements

Corporate transactions often result in name changes for the entities involved, even if the transaction does not require novation. FAR 42.1205 requires that the parties execute a "Change of Name Agreement" when a company with government contracts files with a state jurisdiction to change its legal name. The agreement's purpose is to change the name of the contractor as it appears on all its existing government contracts. Each contract is modified to reflect the name change. FAR 42.1205(a) explains the circumstances under which an Agreement is necessary:

> If only a change of the contractor's name is involved and the Government's and contractor's rights and obligations remain unaffected, the parties shall execute an agreement to reflect the name change. The contractor shall forward to the responsible contracting officer three signed copies of the Change of Name Agreement, and one copy each of the following:
> (1) The document effecting the name change, authenticated by a proper official of the State having jurisdiction.
> (2) The opinion of the contractor's legal counsel stating that the change of name was properly effected under applicable law and showing the effective date.
> (3) A list of all affected contracts and purchase orders remaining unsettled between the contractor and the Government[.]

Where only the name—not the legal identity of the company—changes, the Anti-Assignment Act is not implicated. A change of name does not constitute a transfer or assignment of a contract within the purview of the Act.[17]

✓ Best Practice Tip:

- A name change to the legal entity of the contractor requires only a Change of Name Agreement. Other changes such as to a "doing business as" (dba) name, which are not filed with a state jurisdiction, do not require an agreement. However, a dba or similar change that alters the Target's name on the contract may cause payment or other problems, and it is thus advisable to contact the contracting officer in advance of such a change.
- When creating a plan of action for ensuring name changes are properly reflected in SAM and other government databases, remember that these changes cannot take effect until the contracting officer has signed the Change of Name Agreement. An agreement signed by the contracting officer is required to properly effect the change.

F. Effect of Acquisition on Bids and Proposals

In addition to reviewing the Target's current government contracts during diligence, Acquirers should also ask Targets to identify their current and pending bids and proposals. A number of bid protests in the last several years have highlighted the risks presented by pending proposals, which could impact, among other issues, revenue projections and the Target's ability to maintain critical customer relationships. When the Target has submitted a bid or proposal in a pending procurement, and a change of ownership will occur before the award is made, the transaction may impact the agency's evaluation of the Target's submission.

---

[17] *See Dickman Builders, Inc.*, ASBCA No. 32612, 89-3 BCA ¶ 22,206.

As a preliminary matter, the parties must decide *when* to notify the procuring agency of the acquisition. Depending on the stage of the procurement process, the procuring agency may reject a pending proposal outright or refuse to allow proposal revisions. Also, a subsequent contract award to the Target may be overturned in a bid protest proceeding for reasons relating to the acquisition. This section discusses various factors the parties should consider in deciding when and how to notify procuring agencies of a forthcoming transaction.

Though the Anti-Assignment Act generally prohibits the transfer of a government contract or order to another party,[18] the Government Accounting Office (GAO) has long held that the assignment of a bid or proposal is not precluded if the transfer occurs "by operation of law" and no harm results to the government.[19] Specifically, the GAO has long recognized that "the transfer or assignment of rights and obligations arising out of a bid or proposal is permissible where the transfer is to a legal entity which is the complete successor in interest to the bidder or offeror by virtue of merger, corporate reorganization, the sale of an entire business or the sale of an entire portion of a business embraced by the bid or proposal."[20] The essential requirement is that the original offeror remains intact, with access to the same resources, and honors the commitments set forth in its technical and price or cost proposal.[21]

The GAO has held that where an offeror is the Target of a transaction that is "imminent and essentially certain," the procuring agency must consider the impact of that transaction on the procurement before making an award.[22] This standard sets the mark for when notice is required to avoid potential disqualification from a pending procurement. Indicia of a transaction being imminent and essentially certain include "whether the timing and manner of the spin-off were within the control of the offeror," such that

---

18 *See* 41 U.S.C. § 6305(a).

19 *See McNeil Techs., Inc.*, B-254909, Jan. 25, 1994, 94-1 CPD ¶ 40; *J.I. Case Co.*, B-239178, Aug. 6, 1990, 90-2 CPD ¶ 108 (agency properly awarded contract to successor-in-interest where the original bidder, a wholly owned subsidiary of the parent-successor, merged with the parent company after bid opening); *see also* Seaboard Air Line Ry. v. United States, 256 U.S. 655, 657 (1921) (Anti-Assignment Act does not restrict assignments where there is no probability that the United States could suffer injury); 48 C.F.R. § 14.404-2(l) ("After submitting a bid, if all of a bidder's assets or that part related to the bid are transferred during the period between the bid opening and the award, the transferee may not be able to take over the *bid*. Accordingly, the contracting officer shall reject the bid unless the transfer is effected by merger, operation of law, or other means not barred by 41 U.S.C. 6305 or 31 U.S.C. 3727.").

20 *Harnischfeger Corp.*, B-224371, Sept. 12, 1986, 86-2 CPD ¶ 296; see also *Sunrise Int'l Grp., Inc.*, B-266357, Feb. 12, 1996, 96-1 CPD ¶ 64; *Numax Elecs., Inc.*, B-181670, Jan. 16, 1975, 75-1 CPD ¶ 21; L-3 Commc'ns Integrated Sys., L.P. v. United States, 84 Fed. Cl. 768, 777 (Fed. Cl. 2008) (holding that following the sale of a Raytheon business unit to L-3, assignment of claim for bid and proposal costs to L-3 was not precluded by the Anti-Assignment Act).

21 *Consortium HSG Technischer Serv. GmbH*, B-292699.6, June 24, 2004, 2004 CPD ¶ 134 (entity remained intact, retained same location and office, and promised to honor its previous commitments); *see also* Lyons Sec. Servs., Inc. v. United States, 38 Fed. Cl. 783, 787 (1997); *Enter. Servs., LLC et al.*, B-415368 et al., Jan. 4, 2018, 2018 CPD ¶ 44.

22 *Lockheed Martin Integrated Sys., Inc.*, B-410189.5, B-410189.6, Sept. 27, 2016, 2016 CPD ¶ 273 (holding that "an agency should analyze the effect of a possible corporate restructuring on an offeror's proposal when the transaction at issue is 'imminent and essentially certain.'").

the acquisition agreement could be signed in the near term without significant interruption or delay, and "whether the offeror had disclosed detailed plans to the SEC, including the anticipated time frame for closing the transaction."[23] Where a transaction involving the original offeror is "at best, only a possibility"—for example, only summary-level information has been provided to prospective purchasers and/or potential terms exchanged in preliminary discussions—the agency is afforded greater discretion by the GAO in considering the transaction's possible impact on the procurement.[24] Accordingly, in such circumstances, the Target may defer providing notice to the agency.

When the procuring agency is required to, or otherwise elects to, consider the impact of a potential transaction involving the offeror, the agency will consider one central question: will the transaction have a "material effect" on the offeror's proposed method or manner of performance of the contemplated contract?[25] This inquiry is fact-specific and will turn on the circumstances surrounding the nature and terms of the proposed transaction, as well as its timing and impact on the Target and, specifically, on its proposal. To complete its evaluation, the procuring agency will generally consider a variety of factors.

First, the agency will consider whether the resultant company will have access to the same corporate and technical resources, such as cleared facilities, equipment, and intangible assets, such as intellectual property.[26] Key corporate assets identified in a proposal must be transferred as part of an acquisition, or the bid or proposal may be rejected. The agency will also consider whether the manner in which the contract will be performed, as detailed in the bid or proposal, will remain unchanged after the transaction.[27] Postacquisition, the successful awardee must intend to and have the proposed resources to execute the same technical approach.[28] Where the solicitation places no restrictions on subcontracting, the resultant company may consider subcontracting performance to the original offeror in order to limit or eliminate altogether any potential impact. The GAO

---

23 *Lockheed Martin Integrated Sys., Inc.-Recon.*, B-410189.7, Aug. 10, 2017, 2017 CPD ¶ 258 n. 3; see also *Nat'l Aeronautics & Space Admin.-Recon.*, B-408112.3, May 14, 2014, 2014 CPD ¶ 155.

24 *Trailblazer Health Enters., LLC*, B-406175, B-406175.2, Mar. 1, 2012, 2012 CPD ¶ 78 (denying protest challenging agency's failure to take into account in its evaluation the awardee's possible divestiture where protester failed to establish that the agency "knew" prior to contract award that the divestiture was "either certain or required").

25 *Wyle Labs., Inc.*, B-408112.2, Dec. 27, 2013, 2014 CPD ¶ 16 ("Where an offeror's proposal represents that it will perform the contract in a manner materially different from the offeror's actual intent, an award based on such proposal cannot stand, since both the offeror's representations, and the agency's reliance on such, have an adverse impact on the integrity of the procurement process.").

26 Universal Prot. Serv. LP v. United States, 126 Fed. Cl. 173, 194 (2016) (holding that, where proposal relied on original offeror's software license that was specifically excluded from the asset purchase agreement, protester's claims that it could obtain a similar license commercially did not afford it a "substantial chance" to be awarded the contract and therefore, protester lacked standing).

27 *FCi Fed., Inc.*, B-408558.7, B-408558.8, Aug. 5, 2015, 2015 CPD ¶ 245 ("In these circumstances, where the record indicates that the sale of USIS PSD materially and significantly altered the approach to contract performance as set forth in USIS PSD's proposal, it was unreasonable for the agency to generally confine its review to PAE/USIS PSD's responsibility, and we sustain the protest on this basis.").

28 *IBM U.S. Fed.*, B-409806 et al., Aug. 15, 2014, 2014 CPD ¶ 241; *Lockheed Martin Integrated Sys., Inc.*, B-410189.5, B-410189.6, Sept. 27, 2016, 2016 CPD ¶ 273.

has specifically held that an intent to subcontract for this purpose is not a basis to sustain a protest challenging the contract award.[29]

The agency may also consider whether the past performance references cited by the original offeror remain relevant after the transaction. If the Target included in its proposal (and was afforded credit by the agency for) work completed by its former corporate parent or affiliate, its reliance is misplaced if the parent or affiliate company is not also acquired as part of the transaction.[30] Even stray references to the offeror's former parent company may be interpreted by the procuring agency (or the GAO or US Court of Federal Claims) as "designed to bolster the proposal" and therefore irrelevant to a proper evaluation of the Target's proposal.[31] The procuring agency is also likely to consider the impact of a potential transaction on the various resources available to the resultant company as compared with the original offeror. This includes organizational resources and support functions, such as contract and subcontract administration, finance, facility services, research and development resources and capabilities, quality assurance, security, staffing and training, and legal and compliance resources. The more heavily a bid or proposal relies on such resources and functions of the original offeror (or its parent or affiliate companies), the more susceptible it is to challenge or disqualification as a result of a transaction.[32]

The agency will also consider whether the offeror retains management resources and contractor personnel, including key personnel specifically named in the bid or proposal. Where specific individuals are named or resumes provided in the proposal, the Acquirer should confirm that such personnel will be available postacquisition to perform the contract.[33] "Bait and switch" case law is plentiful at the GAO and requires as a general matter that "offerors are obligated to advise agencies of changes in proposed staffing and resources, even after submission of proposals."[34] Failure to do so may constitute a

---

[29] *IBM U.S. Fed.*, B-409806 et al., Aug. 15, 2014, 2014 CPD ¶ 241 (denying protest where Leidos's intent to subcontract performance of task orders to "new" SAIC "does not appear to reflect a significant change in the technical approach contemplated by the quotation" and "solicitation placed no restriction on subcontracting").

[30] *FCi Fed., Inc.*, B-408558.7, B-408558.8, Aug. 5, 2015, 2015 CPD ¶ 245 (sustaining protest where "past performance evaluation confirmed the substantial role USIS LLC [parent company] was proposed to have in USIS PSD's [original offeror] performance").

[31] *Universal Protection Serv. LP*, 126 Fed. Cl. at 193.

[32] *FCi Fed. Inc.*, B-408558.7, B-408558.8, 2015 CPD ¶ 245 (sustaining protest challenging award where proposal relied on the corporate resources and back-office support of its former parent, and agency's technical evaluation report stated that "the Offeror on this contract will be substantially supported by the same infrastructure"); *AIU N. Am., Inc.*, B-283743.2, Feb. 16, 2000, 2000 CPD ¶ 39 (sustaining protest where agency's evaluation failed to consider the "availability of corporate resources" as required by the evaluation criteria, where proposal described corporate resources of prior parent company not transferred to acquirer).

[33] *Universal Prot. Serv. LP*, 126 Fed. Cl. at 194 (proposal listed seventeen key personnel, at least six of whom were employees of the offeror's former parent company and not employed by the acquirer at the time of the protest); *CBIS Fed., Inc.*, Mar. 27, 1992, 92-1 CPD ¶ 308 (sustaining protest where awardee proposed key personnel in its final proposal whom it could not reasonably expect to be available for contract performance).

[34] *General Revenue Corp., et al.*, B-414220 et al., Mar. 27, 2017, 2017 CPD ¶ 106.

material misrepresentation and may render the bid or proposal unacceptable.[35] In the same vein, the agency may consider whether the resultant company has access to the same financial resources. For instance, in *Wyle Laboratories, Inc.*, the original offeror made references to its then-parent company's "over 40,000 employees and $10.6 billion in annual revenue," a substantial portion of which was left behind in the transaction.[36] To limit the impact of this, where circumstances permit, the Target should consider submitting its own financial statements where required by the solicitation, rather than a consolidated statement that reflects the assets and revenues of its corporate parent.[37] This way, the agency's evaluation of the bid or proposal is more likely to reflect the financial resources of the Target alone.

Finally, as the procuring agency considers the impact of a potential transaction involving the Target, it is likely to consider whether the transaction would result in any changes to the pricing and evaluated costs set forth in the Target's proposal. Here, the contract type is particularly important. For instance, where the procurement is for a fixed-price contract, the contractor bears the risk of overruns, regardless of which entity performs under the contract. In *IBM U.S. Federal*, the GAO denied a protest challenging an award on account of a corporate restructuring because the award was based on submission of fixed labor rates by the original offeror that would be binding on the resultant company and, thereby, would not likely have any significant cost or technical impacts.[38] The GAO reached a different conclusion in *National Aeronautics and Space Administration-Reconsideration*, where the contract at issue was cost reimbursable, the entirety of the agency's cost evaluation was premised on performance by the original offeror, and the government assumed the risk and responsibility of paying for performance by a different entity.[39] In this regard, the same transaction involving the same Acquirer and

---

35 *Patricio Enters. Inc.*, B-412738, May 26, 2016, 2016 CPD ¶ 145; *Greenleaf Constr. Co., Inc.*, B-293105.19, Jan. 17, 2006, 2006 CPD ¶ 19 ("An offeror's material misrepresentation in its proposal can provide a basis for disqualification of the proposal and cancellation of a contract award based upon the proposal."); *Dual, Inc.*, B-280719, Nov. 12, 1998, 98-2 CPD ¶ 133 (holding that an award based on the offeror's representation that it owned a particular division and employed certain personnel was improper where the awardee had signed an agreement to sell that division and transfer those personnel before the contract was awarded); but see Unisys Corp., B-242897, June 18, 1991, 91-1 CPD ¶ 577 (holding that "where the offeror provides firm letters of commitment and the names are submitted in good faith with the consent of the respective individuals (that is, the offeror is not proposing personnel it has no intention of providing), the fact that the offeror, after award, provides substitute personnel does not make the award improper").

36 *Wyle Labs., Inc.*, B-408112.2, Dec. 27, 2013, 2014 CPD ¶ 16.

37 *Universal Prot. Serv. LP*, 126 Fed. Cl. at 193-94 (offeror's submission of consolidated financial statements could be viewed as reliance by the offeror on its former parent company to its advantage in the evaluation of its proposal).

38 *IBM U.S. Fed.*, B-409806 et al., Aug. 15, 2014, 2014 CPD ¶ 241 (explaining that "the solicitation did not contain an express provision for price realism analysis, nor did it advise vendors that their quotations could be rejected on the basis of low prices; accordingly, a price realism analysis was neither required nor permitted"); see also *Enter. Servs., LLC et al.*, B-415368 et al., Jan. 4, 2018, 2018 CPD ¶ 44 (holding that "protesters have not shown that Leidos will not be bound by the fixed labor rates proposed by Lockheed").

39 *Nat'l Aeronautics & Space Admin.-Recon.*, B-408112.3, May 14, 2014, 2014 CPD ¶ 155 ("Under a cost-reimbursement contract, it is the government that bears the risk and responsibility to pay the contractor's

Target may impact two separate procurements differently, depending on the type of contract to be awarded.

In addition to the foregoing factors, which a procuring agency will consider when evaluating the impact of a proposed transaction on the Target's pending bid or proposal, additional considerations may arise under various circumstances. For instance, where the Target is a small business, the agency will consider whether the offeror will lose its size status as a result of the acquisition. The Small Business Administration (SBA) determines a contractor's size status based on annual receipts or number of employees. Under the SBA rules on affiliation, the receipts or employees of the Target's future domestic and foreign affiliates may count toward the relevant total depending on factors such as stock ownership, common management, and contractual relationships, each of which informs whether the affiliates have control or the power to control the Target after the acquisition.[40] Thus, the acquisition may impact whether the Target remains eligible for small business set-aside contracts. The Target may also be required to recertify its size status while its proposal is pending.[41]

An additional consideration arises when the Target performs government contracts requiring access to classified information. Not only does this make it difficult for the Acquirer to review the Target's current contracts during diligence review, but depending on the potential for foreign ownership, control, or influence of the Acquirer, the acquisition may impact the Target's ability to retain necessary facility security clearances and employees with personal security clearances necessary for the performance of current and future contracts in accordance with its pending proposals. The Acquirer will need to ensure that the Target's facility security clearances will continue to meet the NISP Operating Manual requirements on foreign ownership, control, and influence or, alternatively, implement appropriate restrictions and mitigation measures. Similarly, the procuring agency will consider whether the acquisition may present an organizational conflict of interest (OCI) or violates any exclusivity provisions precluding award to the Target or requiring mitigation measures. An Acquirer should therefore evaluate whether the Target's work could create a conflict with regard to present and future business opportunities of the Acquirer, its subsidiaries, or affiliates, and vice versa.

When and how the agency learns about the various factors bearing on its analysis of the Target's bids or proposals may also be significant. Procuring agencies may learn of potential or pending transactions through press releases, SEC filings, news reports, etc., and often with unwelcome consequences. The preferable method of disclosure is through the Target, which affords the parties the opportunity to frame the discussion and provide assurances to the agency that performance will not be impacted (or may, in fact, be enhanced) by the transaction. As the GAO has held, agencies may reasonably

allowable costs, regardless of the costs set forth in the offeror's proposal."); *Wyle Labs., Inc.*, B-408112.2, Dec. 27, 2013, 2014 CPD ¶ 16.

40 *See* 13 C.F.R. § 121.103.

41 13 C.F.R. § 121.404(g)(2)(ii)(D) (requiring recertification "[i]f the merger, sale or acquisition occurs after offer but prior to award, the offeror must recertify its size to the contracting officer prior to award."); *see also* 81 Fed. Reg. 34243, 34253 (May 31, 2016) (adopting final rule revising the SBA's regulations).

rely on "assurances" by the offeror that "certain resources and functions will continue to be provided . . ., which would provide a seamless transition and continuity of operations to fully meet the contractual obligations without disruption."[42] Ultimately, if the agency concludes that a corporate transaction or restructuring "does not appear likely to have significant impact on cost or technical impact on contract performance, and the offering entity remains intact and retains the same resources reflected in its proposal, the subsequent acquisition of that offeror does not render the agency's evaluation and award decision improper."[43] If, however, the agency concludes that contract performance will be materially affected by the transaction, the bid or proposal may well be disqualified.

The adequacy of the procuring agency's consideration of—or failure to consider—the impact of an "imminent and essentially certain" transaction on contract award and performance is most often tested in bid protest proceedings. Protests may be filed by unsuccessful offerors challenging an award to an offeror that has been involved in a corporate transaction during the pendency of the procurement, or by a Target that has been excluded from a procurement or not selected for award of a contract.

Protests may also be filed by a "complete successor-in-interest to the actual offeror."[44] The postacquisition surviving company has standing to challenge an agency's evaluation of the original offeror's pretransaction bid or proposal submission and award decision. However, disappointed offerors will not be successful in challenging a subsequent contract assignment following an acquisition, where there is no evidence that the agency awarded the contract with intent to assign it to another firm. In such instances, the assignment from the original offeror to the resultant company is considered to be a matter of contract administration and, therefore, is not subject to the GAO's review.[45] A bid protest is available to challenge an award when it is "clear at the time of the award that [the agency] knew that it would have to accept performance of the contract by an entity that was fundamentally different from the one presented in [the awardee's] technical proposal."[46]

---

42 *Enter. Servs., LLC et al.*, B-415368 et al., Jan. 4, 2018, 2018 CPD ¶ 44.

43 *Id.*

44 *L-3 Comm'ns Integrated Sys., L.P.*, 84 Fed. Cl. at 778-79; accord *Enter. Servs. LLC*, B-415517, B-415517.2, Jan. 18, 2018, 2018 CPD ¶ 83 (explaining that the GAO "routinely recognizes complete successors in interest as interested parties to protest").

45 *Acepex Mgmt. Corp.*, B-283080 et al., Oct. 4, 1999, 99-2 CPD ¶ 77 ("This case clearly involves a preexisting contract, and because there is no evidence that the agency awarded the contract to Kleen-Tech with the intention of allowing its assignment to KTBS, the assignment relates not to the award of the contract but to contract administration."); *Bosma Mach. & Tool Corp.*, B-257443, Oct. 17, 1994, 94-2 CPD ¶ 143 ("Where a contract has been awarded, we generally will not review a protest that the assignment of the contract to a different firm was improper.").

46 *Nat'l Aeronautics & Space Admin.-Recon.*, B-408112.3, May 14, 2014, 2014 CPD ¶ 155.

✓ **Best Practice Tip:** The following factors should be considered during diligence review of the Target's current and pending bids and proposals, including anticipated changes following the closing:

1. Corporate and technical resources, including intellectual property
2. Method of contract performance, including changes in technical approach
3. Past performance references
4. Organizational resources and support functions
5. Management resources and key personnel
6. Financial resources and lines of credit
7. Differences in pricing and evaluated costs, including changes in indirect rates
8. Small business size status
9. Classified contracts and security clearances
10. Organizational conflicts of interest and exclusivity provisions

✓ **Best Practice Tip:** Once the acquisition is "imminent and essentially certain," the Target should notify the procuring agency of the planned change in ownership. Open communication will facilitate the agency's evaluation of the pending bid or proposal and afford the Target an opportunity to provide assurances that performance will not be affected by the transaction.

CHAPTER 12

Issues for the Combined Company

OUTLINE

A. Guarantee of Performance of an Acquired Subsidiary
   1. Existing Guarantees
   2. Future Guarantees—General Considerations
      a. Respecting the Organizational Structure
      b. Financial Accounting Standards Board Interpretation No. 45
         1. Disclosure
         2. Liability in the Financial Statements
      c. Tax Concerns
      d. First Demand Guarantees and Revenue Recognition Policy
   3. Alternatives to a Guarantee
      a. When Unnecessary
      b. Comfort Letters and "Keep Well" Commitments
      c. Performance Bonds
      d. Letters of Credit or Bank Guaranty
   4. Government Contract Considerations
   5. Legal Issues in Negotiating Guarantees
      a. Allow the Guaranteeing Party to Assert the Defaulting Party's Defenses
      b. Permit the Guaranteeing Party to Set Off or Net Amounts Owed by the Beneficiary
      c. Require Exhaustion by the Beneficiary of All Remedies Against the Defaulting Party
      d. Limit Guarantee Payment
      e. Require Notice of Default from the Beneficiary and Allow for a Cure Period before Triggering the Guarantee
      f. Limit the Guarantee to a Specified Term
      g. Specify Obligations Covered by the Guarantee
      h. Ensure that the Guarantee Is Not Assignable by the Beneficiary
      i. Governing Law

B. Restructuring
   1. Allowability of Restructuring Costs
   2. Capturing Restructuring Costs
   3. Restructuring Agreements
C. Cost Accounting Issues
   1. Cost Accounting Standards
      a. Cost Disclosure Statements
      b. Cost Accounting Changes
      c. Cost Impacts
      d. Quantifying Cost Impact of Changes
   2. Effect of Acquisition on Cost-Reimbursement and Incentive Contracts
   3. Stepped-Up Basis and Goodwill
      a. Allowability of Step-Ups/Downs
   4. Other Costs—Acquisition of Intangible Capital Assets
   5. Intercompany Transfers
   6. Pension Costs

A. Guarantee of Performance of an Acquired Subsidiary

When novations are required, the Acquirer should anticipate that it will have to deal with demands to guarantee performance by the Target on the Target's government prime contracts. Prime contractors may also have the right to insist on guarantees of performance of the Target's subcontracts. These guarantees involve not only government contract law considerations but corporate and tax considerations as well.

1. Existing Guarantees

The Target's customers who are parties to existing guarantees with the Target may request guarantees due to the structural change of the Target from parent company to subsidiary of the Acquirer as a result of a reverse triangular merger, a customary form of acquisition in which the Target merges with and into an acquisition subsidiary of the Acquirer, such that the Target survives as a wholly owned subsidiary of the Acquirer. When the transaction closes, the Target becomes controlled by the Acquirer and, while the contractual obligations of the Target cannot be abrogated by the Acquirer, the Acquirer is free to shift capital and resources away from the Target, absent some other limitations on doing so, such as requirements in the Target's credit facilities or loan documents.

As a result, third parties, including government customers, that have contractual relations with acquired companies may determine that they are less comfortable dealing with a controlled subsidiary than with a parent company, especially in situations where the Target is handling mission critical applications of the customer or may be liable for significant amounts payable to the customer. In those situations, customers may request that the existing guarantee be replaced with a new guarantee from the new parent company. The issue is eliminated in cases where the contract is assumed by the parent, where the parent is novated into the contract or where the Target merges upstream into the Acquirer. In such cases, the Acquirer takes on all the rights and obligations of the Target.

2. Future Guarantees—General Considerations

Customers may request guarantees any time they are dealing with a performing subsidiary. This may occur in or out of the acquisition context. Parent companies have several reasons for having subsidiaries enter into and perform their own contracts, including (a) tax reasons, where the parent does not wish to be taxed within the jurisdiction of performance; (b) capital and employee locations, and (c) liability insulation if the subsidiary is working in high-risk, high-liability areas.However, parent company guarantees give customers comfort knowing parent company resources are behind the performing subsidiary. Customers typically argue that they cannot afford to worry about an undercapitalized subsidiary's inability to perform. Further, customers often assert that they should not be forced to look behind the corporate wall to determine the party with whom they are dealing.

a. Respecting the Organizational Structure

Most multinational companies have an elaborate organization structure that is populated with well-capitalized operating subsidiaries that routinely perform service and product contracts regionally and in certain countries. The organization of those subsidiaries and holding companies is influenced by tax and operational considerations that enable the consolidated company to operate efficiently given the multitude of laws, customs, and logistical considerations that impact a company's ability to deliver products and services globally in various theaters. A principal purpose of a subsidiary is to insulate the parent company and other affiliated companies from the liabilities of the subsidiary. A parent company guarantee pierces the insulation and exposes the parent company to added subsidiary liabilities. This is often unnecessary since the delivering subsidiary will be well capitalized and fully capable of delivering the products and services on its own.

b. Financial Accounting Standards Board Interpretation No. 45

Financial Accounting Standards Board Interpretation No. 45 (FIN 45), released in November 2002, is an interpretation of "SFAS 5: Accounting for Contingencies," and applies to a guarantor's accounting and disclosure requirements for guarantees, including indirect guarantees of the indebtedness of others.

1. Disclosure

Under FIN 45, parent companies that are guaranteeing the performance of a wholly owned subsidiary need not disclose such guarantees specifically. Such guarantees may require benign footnote disclosure of their existence on an aggregate basis, depending on their materiality to the consolidated company. However, guarantees of third-party performance (i.e., a non-owned partner performing as a subcontractor to the company) require specific disclosure about the guarantee, including the terms, triggers, and potential exposure, if material.

2. Liability in the Financial Statements

FIN 45 does not require the recording of a liability in the financial statements of the guarantor, if the guarantee is of a wholly owned subsidiary's performance. However, guarantors of third-party performance are required to record a liability for any material obligations it has undertaken in issuing the guarantee, namely the ongoing obligation to stand ready to perform during the term of the guarantee.

c. Tax Concerns

US companies must avoid permanent establishment status in foreign jurisdictions. Failure to do so may cause US companies to be perceived as doing business in foreign jurisdictions and, therefore, subject to taxation in such jurisdictions. US parent companies that issue guarantees of the performance of foreign subsidiaries run the risk of challenge by foreign taxing authorities that the parents themselves are operating in such jurisdictions and are therefore subject to taxation of their income in such jurisdictions.

✓ **Best Practice Tip:** If guarantees of foreign subsidiaries must be given, the guarantee language should require only that the guarantor assure performance if necessary, through another subsidiary or a third party; it should not require that the US parent actually perform if the foreign subsidiary fails to perform.

d. First Demand Guarantees and Revenue Recognition Policy

A first demand guarantee generally requires that the guarantor pay the amounts in dispute upon demand and then claim the amounts back, if the payment of such amounts is ultimately determined to have been unjustified. With such guarantees, some companies take the view that they should not declare the full amount of their contract revenues until the guarantee expires.

✓ **Best Practice Tip:** There is no one accounting view on this analysis. The risk profile of the contract and the existence of any historical defaults by the performing subsidiary would impact the ultimate decision to defer a portion of the company's revenue.

3. Alternatives to a Guarantee

a. When Unnecessary

Guarantees should be deemed to be unnecessary if the performing subsidiary is well capitalized and has a long history of meeting its performance obligations. While theoretically a parent company could drain assets from any of its controlled subsidiaries, thus making a parent guarantee seem necessary, in reality several considerations such as tax effects, transfer pricing, workers council, contractual limitations, and reputational issues may likely reduce the likelihood of a parent draining the assets of a large, established, and well-capitalized subsidiary. In most cases, after appropriate due diligence and assurances from the vendor, customers should be comfortable that the subsidiary is contractually liable for the performance of the contract and able to stand on its own merits.

✓ **Best Practice Tip:** If already publicly filed (i.e., certain Europe, Middle East, and Africa (EMEA) jurisdictions), or where the parties agree on confidentiality, consider furnishing the performing subsidiary's balance sheet and other financial information to the customer as evidence of the subsidiary's viability and ability to perform.

b. Comfort Letters and "Keep Well" Commitments

Comfort letters for performance take various forms, but the general theme is that the parent commits to using commercially reasonable efforts to cause its subsidiary to perform its obligations to the customer. "Keep well" commitments also take many forms, but their general theme is a commitment from the parent company to ensure that the subsidiary stays appropriately capitalized and/or maintains sufficient resources and expertise to perform its obligations under the relevant contract.

✓ **Best Practice Tip:** Comfort letters and "keep well" commitments may be treated as guarantees by courts in some jurisdictions, particularly in EMEA. To guard against this result, comfort letters and "keep well" commitments should explicitly state that they do not constitute guarantees. A law that respects the difference between comfort letters, "keep well" commitments, and guarantees should govern these instruments (in the United States, Delaware or New York law is advisable).

c. Performance Bonds

A performance bond is a surety bond typically issued by an insurance company or a bank to guarantee satisfactory completion of a project by a contractor. If the contractor fails to perform according to the specifications in the contract (often due to the bankruptcy or insolvency of the contractor), the customer is guaranteed compensation for any monetary loss up to the amount of the performance bond. This is a commonly used technique in certain types of outsourcing and construction contracts. There are many factors that go into determining the cost of a performance bond, such as (but not limited to) the amount, contract type, state, the surety company's filed rate, the performing company's credit and/or financial standing, past history and other underwriting factors, as well as any fees charged by the agent or broker. The average rates and costs can range from 1 percent to 5 percent.

d. Letters of Credit or Bank Guaranty

Another alternative would be a letter of credit or guarantee provided by a bank. Banks usually require a fee ranging from 0.5 percent to 1.0 percent per year for such instruments.

4. Government Contract Considerations

The government may only award contracts to entities that are presently responsible. Present responsibility includes having adequate financial resources or the ability to secure such resources to be able to perform the contracts.[1] An inadequately financed subsidiary will not meet this requirement. Therefore, the government will insist on some sort of financial assurance, usually in the form of a guarantee. A properly negotiated guarantee from the corporate parent will provide the necessary assurance for both current and future contracts.

The Defense Contract Management Agency (DCMA) has published Form 1620, entitled "Guarantee Agreement for Corporate Guarantor," that is designed for an identified contract, or set of contracts (See Appendix 8.)

5. Legal Issues in Negotiating Guarantees

Certain issues arise in each negotiation of a guarantee by a parent of its subsidiary's contracts.

a. Allow the Guaranteeing Party to Assert the Defaulting Party's Defenses

This should be acceptable to the customer, as the customer should not care about a parent's ability to stand in the shoes of its defaulting subsidiary. The customer simply wants prompt performance from the consolidated entity.

b. Permit the Guaranteeing Party to Set Off or Net Amounts Owed by the Beneficiary

Setoff rights are an extension of the guarantor's right to assert defenses. Such rights permit a level playing field between the contractor and customer and should not be objected to by a reasonable customer requesting a guarantee.

c. Require Exhaustion by the Beneficiary of All Remedies Against the Defaulting Party

This is often a negotiated provision. Usually, common ground is found somewhere between the obligation of the customer to exhaust all contractual and judicial remedies concluding with a final, nonappealable judgment on the one hand, and the obligation of the guarantor to incur first demand, primary liability on the other hand.

> ✓ **Best Practice Tip:** Often the underlying contract will contain detailed dispute resolution and escalation provisions that can be used to govern the exhaustion of remedies clause in the guarantee.

[1] FAR 9.104-1.

d. Limit Guarantee Payment

Limits of liability typically either take the form of a specific negotiated numeric amount, including payment and performance obligations, or will take the form of a limitation that is co-extensive with, and not in excess of, the liability of the performing subsidiary.[2]

e. Require Notice of Default from the Beneficiary and Allow for a Cure Period before Triggering the Guarantee

This provision imposes restraint on the customer to work with the company to find a solution to a possible default under the main contract. Often these guarantee provisions can reference or track the dispute resolution and escalation provisions in the main agreement.

f. Limit the Guarantee to a Specified Term

Often, the guarantee will co-terminate with the main agreement. Customers may sometimes request that the guarantee extend beyond the term of the main agreement to cover any periods in which claims may survive, but such extensions are unusual.

> ✓ **Best Practice Tip:** Have the guarantee terminate upon the earlier of the satisfaction of the underlying obligations or the termination of the underlying agreement containing the guaranteed obligations.

g. Specify Obligations Covered by the Guarantee

Ensure that the guarantee covers only the obligations within the main agreement and nothing more. Ensure that the guarantee cannot be enlarged by changes to the underlying agreement, unless specifically agreed to by the parties.

h. Ensure that the Guarantee Is Not Assignable by the Beneficiary

This provision is routinely agreed to, except in limited circumstances where the beneficiary has a justified rationale for assignment.

i. Governing Law

As noted above, prime government contracts are governed by federal law (see chapter III, section B.1). Thus, a guarantee directly in favor of the government would be subject to federal law. A government subcontract, however, may be subject to state law (see chapter II, section B.2). If the guarantee covers a subcontract that specifies state law, the guarantee should be subject to the law of the same state.

---

2 In jurisdictions where Shariah principles prevail, the parties cannot agree to liability caps, but guarantors are protected by the principle that special and consequential damages are not permitted.

B. Restructuring

1. Allowability of Restructuring Costs

When an acquisition is completed, the Acquirer might undertake a reorganization or restructuring of its business. This typically entails the integration of the new entity into its corporate structure, involving measures such as consolidation or dissolution of one or more business units. This in turn may cause facility closures, asset dispositions, and employee-related expenditures. The goal of postacquisition restructuring is increased efficiency and lower operational costs. Consequently, the performance costs of the Acquirer's current and future contracts that are affected by restructuring should be reduced.

Statutory and regulatory provisions authorize companies with DOD contracts to treat the costs of restructuring activities as an allowable cost. Under 10 U.S.C. § 2325, defense agencies may pay restructuring costs "associated with a business combination" when:

a. The amount of projected savings for DOD will be at least twice the amount of the costs allowed; or
b. The amount of projected savings for DOD will exceed the amount of the costs allowed, and the business combination will result in the preservation of a critical capability that otherwise might be lost to DOD.

The term "business combination" is defined in the statute as including a merger or acquisition. Implementation of 10 U.S.C. § 2325 is contained in DFARS 231.205 70, which provides a more refined definition of "business combination: "Business combination means a transaction whereby assets or operations or two or more companies not previously under common ownership or control are combined, whether by merger, acquisition, or sale/purchase of assets."

The regulation permits reimbursement of restructuring costs only for so-called "external restructuring activities"—those that occur after a business combination that affect the operations of both the acquiring and acquired companies, not just one of them. As a "direct outgrowth" of a business combination, external restructuring activities normally will be initiated within three years of the combination.[3]

The recognition by the government of restructuring costs is subject to four conditions: (a) the costs are allowable under FAR Part 31 and DFARS Part 231, (b) DCAA performs an audit of projected costs and savings, (c) the contracting officer negotiates an advance agreement with the contractor on the proper treatment of restructuring costs, and (d) the cognizant government official makes a written determination that the audited projected savings (on a present value basis) due to restructuring meet the statute's 2:1 "savings:cost" ratio. The latter three conditions do not apply if the costs associated with external restructuring that is to be allocated to DOD contracts are less than $2.5 million.

---

[3] DFARS 231.205-70(b)(2).

Contractors seeking reimbursement of restructuring costs must submit to the contracting officer a restructuring proposal containing the overall plan of restructuring activities and projects. The proposal should also include an annual breakdown of the various cost elements that shows projected costs and projected savings.[4] Furthermore, a copy of the novation agreement resulting from the acquisition (if one was required), should be submitted. The contractor may also provide a proposed advance agreement for review and discussion with the contracting officer.

✓ **Best Practice Tip:** Companies with both DOD and NASA contracts should be aware of a special provision to be used in the novation agreement when a novation of contracts is required under FAR Subpart 42.12. As the "transferee" in the novation agreement, an Acquirer who intends to restructure should request inclusion of the substitute provision found at DFARS 242.1204 in the agreement with the government. This provision replaces the (b)(7) clause in the standard FAR novation agreement, FAR 42.1204(i), which prohibits increased costs on novated contracts. The DFARS provision exempts restructuring costs from the prohibition, as they pertain to the contracts transferred to Acquirers, subject to compliance with the restructuring rules in DFARS 231.205-70.

2. Capturing Restructuring Costs

Following the acquisition, the contractor who plans to restructure should begin to identify and document the various costs associated with restructuring. Pursuant to DOD Procedures, Guidance and Information (PGI) 231.205-70, the contracting officer will direct the contractor to segregate restructuring costs and to suspend them from billings, until the approval for their payment is received from the government.

Care should be taken to distinguish between restructuring costs that are allowable and those that may be unallowable under the FAR Part 31 cost principles. As stated in DFARS 231.205-70, only costs allowable under the FAR may be paid as restructuring costs. To illustrate, "Organization Costs" are expressly unallowable under FAR 31.205-27 and thus would not be included in the restructuring proposal.

The costs for each planned restructuring activity should be estimated and provided with supporting data. These costs, along with the estimated savings to be achieved, form the basis for the restructuring proposal to be submitted to the government. The costs may be direct or indirect, as defined in FAR 2.101. The DFARS does not state the time period over which the costs may be incurred and be eligible for reimbursement. However, CAS 406, "Cost Accounting Period," provides guidance in this area.

CAS 406-61, "Interpretation," addresses the assignment of restructuring costs to cost accounting periods. It permits treatment of the costs either as an expense of the current period or as a deferred charge that is amortized over future periods. If a deferred charge method is used, the Interpretation states that the amortization period shall not exceed five years.

---

[4] *See* PGI 231.205-70.

The contractor should assure that individual restructuring actions qualify as such under DFARS 231.205-70, which defines them in part as:

> nonroutine, nonrecurring, or extraordinary activities to combine facilities, operations, or workforce, in order to eliminate redundant capabilities, improve future operations, and reduce overall costs. Restructuring activities do not include routine or ongoing repositionings or deployments of a contractor's productive facilities or workforce (*e.g.*, normal plant rearrangement or employee relocation).

Corporate restructuring initiatives will vary, but the following activities and their related costs illustrate those covered by the statute and regulation:

- Employee early retirement incentives and severance payments
- Retention pay (*but see* FAR 31.205-6(l) on unallowable "golden handcuff" pay)
- Employee relocation
- Recruitment costs
- Employee training
- Bonuses (but for DOD contracts, DFARS 231.205-6(f)(1) disallows compensation exceeding normal salary that is part of restructuring relating to an acquisition)
- Idle facilities
- Asset disposition or relocation, such as facilities, equipment
- Lease cancellation
- Depreciation for capital expenditures
- Information technology consolidation or reconfiguration
- Professional services for restructuring planning and/or implementation

Under the CAS clause at FAR 52.230-6, the contractor is required to provide advance notice to the government of any change in its accounting practices. Also, a cost impact statement must be submitted if the changed practice may result in an increase or decrease to the contract cost or price. Adjustments to contract costs or prices may then be necessary. There is an exception to the need for such adjustments for accounting changes due to external restructuring activities. Under FAR Part 30, CAS Administration the contract price and cost adjustment rule is inapplicable to accounting practice changes that are "directly associated" with external restructuring and which meet the requirements of 10 U.S.C. § 2325. The advance disclosure of the change, however, is still required.[5]

3. Restructuring Agreements

Once the contracting officer's review of the restructuring proposal and the audit by the DCAA have taken place, DFARS 231.205-70 requires that an advance agreement be

[5] FAR 30.603-2(e).

negotiated (Agreement). The Agreement contains all terms and conditions with respect to the type and amount of restructuring costs to be paid and the savings to be achieved. This unexecuted Agreement, together with the DCAA audit report, restructuring proposal, novation agreement (if required), and other pertinent information, is forwarded to the cognizant government official identified in DFARS 231.205-70. The contracting officer prepares a recommendation to that official for use in his or her determination of whether restructuring costs will be paid. If the determination is affirmative, the Agreement is executed by the company and the contracting officer.

The Agreement is tailored to the type of acquisition that occurred and the restructuring activity resulting from it. PGI 231.205-70 requires, as a minimum, two provisions in the Agreement: (a) a cumulative cost ceiling for restructuring projects and (b) when necessary, a cost-amortization schedule. The PGI also reaffirms that the costs may not exceed the amount of projected restructuring savings on a present value basis.

Some basic elements to include in the Agreement are:

- Classification of the costs as either direct or indirect
- The time period during which the costs are chargeable to contracts, for example, 2009–2014
- Recognition that only allowable costs under the FAR are recoverable
- The dollar estimate of DOD's share of restructuring costs and the dollar estimate of DOD's share of restructuring savings over the time period selected; the ratio must at least be 2:1 of savings to costs
- The negotiated cost ceiling amount required by the PGI and acknowledgment that any excess amount is an unallowable cost
- Identification of each restructuring activity and when commenced
- An attachment showing, by year, the projected cost and savings amounts for each restructuring activity
- An attachment with a cost amortization schedule
- Retention of records by the contractor for periodic government review of actual restructuring costs as incurred and actual savings as achieved
- Submission of a cost and savings impact analysis for any major changes to the restructuring plan as contained in the restructuring proposal
- How restructuring costs and savings will factor into contract billing rates on current contracts and forward pricing rates for future contracts
- Contracts covered by the Agreement, for example, current, future, fixed-price, cost-type, contract modifications.

✓ **Best Practice Tip:** Where restructuring is planned after the acquisition, and before a novation agreement is signed with the government, request inclusion of the special DFARS 242.1204 provision in the agreement, which will permit payment of restructuring costs on contracts transferred to the Acquirer, subject to the criteria in DFARS 231.205-70.

C. Cost Accounting Issues

1. Cost Accounting Standards

Chapter IV, section C contains a detailed discussion of CAS and its applicability and requirements; this section of the manual considers post-closing issues in greater detail.

a. Cost Disclosure Statements

In an acquisition or divestiture, the management structure of an organization may be materially affected based on the magnitude of the transaction. If the activity results in a change to the structure contained in the CAS Disclosure Statement, a revision may be required for both the Acquirer and the Target (if it remains in existence). As a result of a merger or acquisition, Disclosure Statements may need to be revised to address various issues, including:

1. Corporate or business unit name/address changes
2. Harmonizing or changes of accounting practices
3. Creation, elimination, or consolidation of home offices
4. Creation, elimination, or consolidation of any segments
5. Creation, elimination, or consolidation of layers of intermediate corporate management (e.g., intermediate home offices or group home offices)
6. Creation, elimination, or consolidation of benefits or insurance plans

b. Cost Accounting Changes

If a company performs under modified or full CAS-covered contracts and a cost accounting change is made, the company is obligated to notify the US government of the change, as well as any cost impact associated with making the change. The definition of a cost accounting change encompasses a change in measurement of a cost, the allocation to cost objectives, or the assignment of a cost to a cost accounting period. A change in estimate or estimating practices is not a change in accounting practice.

An example of a cost accounting change requiring a cost impact analysis would be a change in practice to allocate General and Administrative expenses (G&A) over a total cost input base versus a value-added G&A base. Also, changing the treatment of a cost or function from direct to indirect would be considered a change. For example, in a manufacturing business, changing "Quality Inspection" from a direct charging function to a function that is allocated through manufacturing overhead would constitute an accounting change. In contrast, an update of the interest rate used for present value pension obligations is not an accounting change. A change in the useful life used to depreciate a class of fixed assets, based on the history of experienced useful lives of similar assets, would not be an accounting change, but instead it would constitute a change in the estimation of depreciation expense. Implementation of a practice that did not previously exist is not a cost accounting change. It is instead regarded as the establishment of a new practice, and a cost impact analysis is not required.

c. Cost Impacts

While all contracts will experience a cost impact by virtue of their presence in the base, the contractor is only obligated to report the cost impact on those contracts covered by CAS. When cost accounting practices are changed by a contractor in connection with a merger or acquisition, they would normally be considered "voluntary" or "unilateral" changes which can only result in downward price adjustments to CAS-covered contracts. If the new method would result in the contract price being higher, then the price will not be increased, but if the price decreases, the contract price would be adjusted downward.

d. Quantifying Cost Impact of Changes

To quantify the cost impact of changes, CAS requires the impact of each change to be determined separately. FAR Part 30.6 requires cost impacts to be resolved based on contract type—fixed vs. flexible—without combining different changes (i.e., desirable vs. unilateral vs. noncompliance vs. required). More than one unilateral or more than one noncompliance change can be combined only if the cost impacts all result in downward price adjustments. Moreover, the contractor and the government can agree to adjust some or all affected contracts or use an alternative method such as an actual cash payment.

2. Effect of Acquisition on Cost-Reimbursement and Incentive Contracts

As prescribed in FAR 52.215-19 (Oct. 1997), "Notification of Ownership Changes," the Target is to notify the contracting officer of any change in its ownership that could result in changes in the valuation of its capitalized assets. Asset valuations are used in the capitalization and depreciation of contractor assets utilized during contract performance and charged to the government. The clause applies to contracts for which cost and pricing data were required at the time of award, or for which any postaward cost determination is subject to the FAR Part 31 cost principles. For both the pre- and postacquisition periods, records are to be maintained on the assets, their capitalized values, accumulated depreciation, and remaining useful lives.

3. Stepped-Up Basis and Goodwill

a. Allowability of Step-Ups/Downs

While FAS 141 (R) dictates GAAP treatment for business combinations, FAR 31.205-52, "Asset valuations resulting from business combinations," discusses the allowability of acquired assets for government contracting purposes. For many years, the subject of "stepped-up basis" in acquisitions treated under the purchase method of accounting was a hotly debated subject and resulted in numerous court and board of contract appeals cases, some of which still linger today. However, in light of the current cost principles and the revisions made to CAS 404, there is now clear guidance. CAS 404-50(d) states:

> The capitalized values of tangible capital assets acquired in a business combination, accounted for under the 'purchase method' of accounting, shall be assigned to these assets as follows:
>
> (1) All the tangible capital assets of the acquired company that during the most recent cost accounting period prior to a business combination generated either depreciation expense or cost of money charges that were allocated to Federal government contracts or subcontracts negotiated on the basis of cost, shall be capitalized by the acquirer at the net book value(s) of the asset(s) as reported by the target at the time of the transaction.
>
> (2) All the tangible capital asset(s) of the acquired company that during the most recent cost accounting period prior to a business combination did not generate either depreciation expense or cost of money charges that were allocated to Federal government contracts or subcontracts negotiated on the basis of cost, shall be assigned a portion of the cost of the acquired company not to exceed their fair value(s) at the date of acquisition. When the fair value of identifiable acquired assets less liabilities assumed exceeds the purchase price of the acquired company in an acquisition under the 'purchase method,' the value otherwise assignable to tangible capital assets shall be reduced by a proportionate part of the excess.

Therefore, unless the Target did not include depreciation or cost of money in its government contracts, the Acquirer would continue to use the book value on its books.

4. Other Costs—Acquisition of Intangible Capital Assets

Under FAR 31.205-52, the cost of acquired intangible capital assets is limited to the amount of amortization and cost of money that would have been allowed had the acquisition not taken place. However, if intangible capital assets acquired had not been previously recorded and amortized, amortization and cost money associated with these acquired assets would be allowable.

5. Intercompany Transfers

Often, the evaluation of a transaction includes the value of prospective transfers of goods or services within the combined company. The due diligence team needs to be aware that government contract cost principles contain special requirements for pricing intercompany transfers to the government. Under FAR 32.205-26 (e), in pricing government contracts, transfers among related entities must be at the cost of the transferor, unless: (a) it is the established practice of the transferor to price intercompany transfers at other than cost; or (b) the item being transferred is exempt from cost or pricing data because it is a commercial item or is being procured on a competitive basis.

This requirement creates difficulty if the transferor entity is not in a position to provide cost information for these intercompany transfers. Furthermore, the transferor entity might not wish to disclose that information, even if it could obtain it.

To avoid this problem, and to be able to account for intercompany transfers at price for government contract purposes, the company must have a well-documented and disciplined procedure that describes the process for the intercompany transfers on commercial work.

✓ **Best Practice Tip:** If the intent is to have intercompany transfers between related entities at price (rather than cost) for government contracts, determine whether the transferor: (a) has a standard practice to make intercompany transfers under commercial contracts at price, and (b) monitors compliance with that practice.

6. Pension Costs

For mergers and acquisitions involving a federal contractor, there are two primary areas for consideration with regard to pension plans. These involve CAS 413, "Adjustment and Allocation of Pension Cost," and a related provision in FAR 31.205-6, "Compensation for Personal Services." The acquisition of a contractor with a pension plan subject to CAS 413 will generally trigger the rules for segment closure accounting, involving adjustment and allocation issues. Where surplus pension contributions have been made by the government, it will generally seek reimbursement for its share of any pension plan surplus; the contractor may have an opportunity to recover its share of a pension deficit from the government.

CAS 413 provides for adjustments to pension costs by measuring actuarial gains and losses and assigning gains and losses to cost accounting periods. CAS 413 also provides the bases on which pension cost shall be allocated to segments of an organization. The CAS Board rewrote CAS 413 in 1995. Although the original CAS 413 did not define an event constituting a segment closure, the decisions of the ASBCA and the courts consistently held that the sale of a division constituted a segment closure.[6] In *NI Industries, Inc.*, ASBCA No. 34943, 92-1 BCA ¶ 24631, however, the ASBCA held that a pension plan termination did not constitute a segment closure.

During the 1990s, when contractors began amassing pension surpluses, the government sought to obtain its share of such surpluses. The revised CAS 413 brought additional guidance to and broadened the definition of segment closure, beyond the prerevision decisions. The current CAS 413 defines a segment closure as follows:

> *Segment closing* means that a segment has:
> (i) been sold or ownership has been otherwise transferred,
> (ii) discontinued operations, or
> (iii) discontinued doing or actively seeking Government business under contracts subject to this Standard.[7]

---

6 *See* Teledyne Inc. v. U.S., 50 Fed.Cl. 155, 168 (2001), aff'd, Allegheny Teledyne Inc. v. U.S., 316 F.3d 1366 (Fed. Cir. 2003), cert. denied, Gen. Motors Corp. v. U.S., 540 U.S. 1068 (2003); *Gould, Inc.*, ASBCA No. 46759, 97-2 BCA ¶ 29254, recon. denied, 98-1 BCA ¶ 29469.

7 48 C.F.R. 9904.413-30(a)(20).

Additionally, the CAS Board extended segment closure accounting to plan terminations as well as curtailment of benefits (i.e., freeze in benefits).[8] Either of these events might result from a merger or acquisition.

Consistent with CAS 413, the FAR cost principles provide for contract cost/price adjustments for the same events as CAS 413, and in accordance with the CAS 413 procedures.[9] The FAR also allows for a credit to the government when the contractor "constructively receives" pension assets.[10] For all other situations where assets revert to or are constructively received by a contractor, the government is entitled to a refund for its equitable share of the gross amount withdrawn.[11]

For contractors subject to full CAS coverage, a segment closing in connection with an acquisition triggers an accounting in accordance with CAS 413-50(c)(12). Under the CAS provision, the transferred assets and liabilities are carried forward and recognized in the accounting for pension costs at the successor contractor.[12] The full amount of the government's share of an adjustment is allocable, without limit, as a credit or charge during the cost accounting period in which the event occurred, and contract prices or costs will be adjusted accordingly.[13]

If, however, the parties to a transaction transfer all of the assets and actuarial accrued liability of the plan to the successor, then no adjustment under CAS 413 need be made.[14]

As noted, a segment closing triggers the process for adjustment and asset reversions for pension costs. In some cases, the government has also investigated the broader impact of segment closings. For example, after Raytheon's acquisition of Hughes Aircraft Co., Texas Instruments, E-Systems, and Chrysler Defense in 2001, the DOD Inspector General reviewed the effect of the acquisitions on DOD pension costs and DOD-funded pension assets. DOD was concerned that accrued post-retirement benefit (PRP) costs that had been funded by the acquired contractors may not have been transferred to Raytheon, thus exposing DOD to a double payment for the same PRP costs.[15]

Numerous decisions have been issued on the subject of segment closures by the boards of contract appeals and federal courts. Many of the decisions involve contracts subject to the prior version of CAS 413, when the definition of a segment closing was less certain. For example, in *Teledyne, Inc. v. United States*, 50 Fed. Cl. 155 (2001), *aff'd, Allegheny Teledyne Inc. v. United States*, 316 F.3d 1366 (Fed. Cir. 2003), *cert. denied, General Motors Corp. v. United States*, 540 U.S. 1068 (2003), a contractor sought to apply the CAS 413 rewrite to segment closures occurring before 1995. The court held that the CAS 413 rewrite applied to segment closures occurring after the rewrite became effective, regardless of whether the segment included CAS-covered contracts prior to the CAS 413

---

8 48 C.F.R. 9904.413-50(c)(12).

9 FAR 31.205-6(j).

10 *Id.* at 31.205-6(j)(3)(ii).

11 *Id.*

12 *Id.* at 9904.413-50(c)(12)(v).

13 *Id.* at 9904.413-50(c)(12)(vii).

14 *Id.* at 9904.413-50(c)(12)(v).

15 43 No. 9 Gov't Contractor ¶ 98.

revisions. Thus, contractors with CAS-covered contracts that predate and postdate the change have to engage in two versions of accounting for pension costs.

More recent decisions consider the calculation of the adjustment and allocations resulting from a segment closing. For example, in *General Electric Co. v. United States*, 84 Fed. Cl. 129 (2008), the court held that if a contractor sells a segment but retains part of the pension assets and liabilities, the contractor is required to calculate a segment closing adjustment on the entire segment. Further, in its calculation, the contractor must consider the benefit the government will receive from surplus pension assets that are transferred to the Acquirer.[16]

✓ **Best Practice Tip:** In conducting due diligence on a potential acquisition, a contractor should not overvalue the benefit of a pension plan surplus. Companies often see the surplus as a potential asset after the sale, by terminating the plan and retaining the excess under ERISA. If the contracts are subject to CAS, a plan termination will trigger a segment closure accounting and an adjustment either under the CAS or FAR for constructive receipt. Targets should also consider the ramifications of parceling out plans and assets. Where a Target agrees to retain that portion of a pension plan attributable to retirees, the Target should be certain to retain sufficient assets, as the retained portion of the plan might be subject to segment closure accounting. A transaction may also present an opportunity to seek recovery from the government, if a plan is underfunded.

---

[16] *Id.* at 145-46. *See also* 47 Gov't Contractor ¶ 147 (comprehensive discussion of CAS 413, including development of case law).

APPENDIX 1

Glossary of Acronyms

AAP	Affirmative Action Program
ADR	Alternate Disputes Resolution
AFOSI	Air Force Office of Special Investigations
Army CID	Army Criminal Investigation Division
ASBCA	Armed Services Board of Contract Appeals
CA	Confidentiality Agreement
CAGE Codes	Commercial and Government Entity Codes
CAS	Cost Accounting Standards
CASB	Cost Accounting Standards Board
CBCA	Civilian Board Contract Appeals
CCR	Central Contractor Registration
CDA	Contract Disputes Act of 1979
CERCLA	Comprehensive Environmental Response, Compensation & Liability Act of 1980
CFAO	Cognizant Federal Agency Official
CFI	Court of First Instance
CFIUS	Committee on Foreign Investment in the United States
CID	Civil Investigative Demand
CLIN	Contract Line Item Number
CO(s)	Contracting Officer(s)
COMSEC	Communications Security
COTS	Commercially Available Off-the-Shelf
CSAs	Cognizant Security Agencies
DAEO	Designated Agency Ethics Official
DCAA	Defense Contract Audit Agency
DCIO	Defense Criminal Investigative Organizations
DCIS	Defense Criminal Investigative Service
DCMA	Defense Contract Management Agency
DFARS	Defense Federal Acquisition Regulation Supplement
DG COMP	European Commission's Competition Directorate
DOD	Department of Defense

DOD IG	Department of Defense Inspector General
DOD Task Force	Defense Science Board Task Force on Antitrust Aspects of Defense Industry Consolidation
DOE	Department of Energy
DOJ	Department of Justice
DOL	Department of Labor, Wage and Hour Division
DPAS	Defense Priorities and Allocations System
DS&E	Defense Systems and Electronics Unit of Texas Instruments, Inc.
DSS	Defense Security Service
DUNS Number	Dun & Bradstreet Number (for Identification of Organizations)
EAR	Export Administration Regulations
EC	European Commission
ECMR	European Commission Merger Regulation
EEA	European Economic Area
EEO-1	Employment Information Report (Standard Form 100)
EEOC	Equal Employment Opportunity Commission
EMEA	Europe, Middle East, and Asia
EPLS	Excluded Parties List System
EU	European Union
FAR	Federal Acquisition Regulation
FAS 5	Financial Accounting Standard No. 5
FCA	False Claims Act
FCL	Facility Security Clearance
FERA	Fraud Enforcement and Recovery Act of 2009
FIN 45	Financial Accounting Standards Board Interpretation No. 45
FOCI	Foreign Ownership, Control, or Influence
FOIA	Freedom of Information Act
FSO	Facility Security Officer
FSS	Federal Supply Schedule
FTC	Federal Trade Commission
G&A	General and Administrative Expense
GAAP	Generally Accepted Accounting Principles
GAO	Government Accountability Office
GCA	Government Contracting Agency
GE	General Electric Company
GOCO	Government-Owned, Contractor-Operated
GSA	General Services Administration
GSAM	General Services Administration Manual
HHI	Herfindahl-Hirschmann Index
HSR or HSR Act	Hart-Scott-Rodino Antitrust Improvements Act of 1976
HSR Rules	Rules promulgated pursuant to the Hart-Scott-Rodino Antitrust Improvements Act of 1976
IDIQ	Indefinite-Delivery, Indefinite-Quantity
IFF	Industrial Funding Fee
IG	Inspector General
IP	Intellectual Property

IR&D	Independent Research and Development
ITAR	International Traffic in Arms Regulations
LOI(s)	Letter(s) of Intent
MAS	Multiple Award Schedule
MMIC(s)	Monolithic Microwave Integrated Circuit(s)
MOD	Ministry of Defense (United Kingdom)
NAICS	North American Industry Classifications System
NASA	National Aeronautics and Space Administration
NATO PHM	North Atlantic Treaty Organization Patrol Craft Hydrofoil Missile
NCIS	Navy Criminal Investigative Service
NDA	Nondisclosure Agreement
NID	National Interest Determination
NISP	National Industrial Security Program
NISPOM	National Industrial Security Program Operating Manual
NRC	Nuclear Regulatory Commission
OCIs	Organizational Conflicts of Interest
OFAC	Office of Foreign Asset Control
OFCCP	Office of Federal Contract Compliance Programs
OFPP	Office of Federal Procurement Policy
OFT	Office of Fair Trading
OGE	Office of Government Ethics
OHA	Office of Hearings and Appeals
OIG	Office of Inspector General
OMB	Office of Management and Budget
ORCA	Online Representations and Certifications Application
OSHA	Occupational Safety and Health Administration
PBGC	Pension Benefit Guaranty Corporation
PCL	Personnel Security Clearance
PCO	Procuring Contracting Officer
PGI	Procurement Guidance Information
PIA	Procurement Integrity Act
PNO	Premerger Notification Office
PRB	Post-Retirement Benefit
PRP	Potentially Responsible Party
R&D	Research and Development
SAFETY Act	Support Anti-terrorism by Fostering Effective Technologies Act
SBA	Small Business Administration
SBA OHA	Small Business Administration Office of Hearings and Appeals
SCA	Service Contract Act of 1965
SCIF	Secure Compartmentalized Information Facility
SED	Shipper's Export Declaration
SETA	Systems Engineering and Technical Assistance
SO	Statement of Objections
SOW	Statement of Work
SOX	Sarbanes-Oxley
SSNIP	Small but Significant Nontransitory Increase in Price

T4C	Termination for Convenience
T4D	Termination for Default
TI	Texas Instruments, Inc.
TINA	Truth in Negotiations Act
TRW	TRW, Inc.
VA	Veterans Affairs

APPENDIX 2

Sample Confidentiality Agreement (1)

[Date]

[Name and Address]

Gentlemen:

You have requested information from ______________________________________, a ______________ corporation (the "Disclosing Party"), in connection with your consideration of a possible acquisition of [**insert description of business unit/product line to be divested**] (the "Business"), such acquisition is hereinafter referred to as the "Possible Transaction." In connection therewith, the Disclosing Party is prepared to make available to you certain information concerning the Business. All such information, which may be oral, written or in physical form, together with analyses, compilations, studies or other documents prepared by you or your Representatives (as defined below) which contain or otherwise reflect such information or your review of, or interest in, the Possible Transaction is hereinafter referred to as "Confidential Information."

All Confidential Information shall be subject to the following terms and conditions:

1. Except as otherwise expressly permitted herein, you shall not disclose or otherwise make the Confidential Information available to any other individual, corporation, firm, or person without the prior written consent of the Disclosing Party. You further agree not to use the Confidential Information other than for the exclusive purpose of evaluating the Possible Transaction.

2. Information shall not be considered Confidential Information if such information:

(a) was in the public domain prior to receipt thereof by you or your Representatives from the Disclosing Party other than as a result of any unauthorized act or omission on your or your Representatives' part;

(b) was supplied to you or your Representatives without restriction by a third person under no obligation to the Disclosing Party to maintain such information in confidence;

(c) becomes publicly known after receipt thereof from the Disclosing Party through no fault of yours or your Representatives.

3. You shall limit access to Confidential Information to such of your directors, officers, employees, representatives and advisors (collectively, "Representatives") who need the Confidential Information for purposes of evaluating the Possible Transaction. You shall instruct all individuals who have access to the Confidential Information of the necessity to maintain the confidentiality of the same and shall take reasonable care to prevent the disclosure or use of the Confidential Information other than as permitted in this Letter Agreement. You shall be responsible for any breach of this Letter Agreement by any of your Representatives.

4. You acknowledge that you are aware (and that your Representatives who are apprised of the matters which are the subject of this Letter Agreement have been or will be advised) that the United States securities laws prohibit any person or entity in possession of material non-public information relating to a company from purchasing or selling securities of such company or from communicating such information to another person under circumstances under which it is reasonably foreseeable that such person is likely to purchase or sell such securities.

5. Neither this Letter Agreement nor disclosure of the Confidential Information to you shall be deemed by implication or otherwise to vest in you rights in or to the Confidential Information other than the right to use such Confidential Information solely for purposes of evaluating the Possible Transaction.

6. You understand and acknowledge that neither the Disclosing Party nor any of its representatives, agents or affiliates makes any representation or warranty, express or implied, as to the accuracy or completeness of the Confidential Information. You agree that neither the Disclosing Party nor any of its employees, directors, officers, representatives, stockholders, affiliates or advisors shall have any liability to you or any of your Representatives relating to or resulting from the use of the Confidential Information.

7. At any time, upon the request of the Disclosing Party, you shall return to the Disclosing Party or destroy all Confidential Information (whatever the form or storage medium) including any and all copies, notes or extracts therefrom which is then in your possession and shall deliver to the Disclosing Party the written statement of an authorized officer supervising such return or destruction certifying that such action has been completed.

8. Except as required by applicable law, regulation or legal process, neither you nor your Representatives will disclose to any person that the Disclosing Party is considering a Possible Transaction, that discussions are taking place between the Disclosing Party and you with respect thereto or that the Confidential Information has been furnished to you. You acknowledge that disclosure of any of the information described in the preceding sentence may irreparably damage the Disclosing Party and/or the Business.

9. In the event that you or any of your Representatives are required by applicable law, regulation or legal process to disclose any of the Confidential Information or information discussed in the preceding paragraph, you agree to so notify the Disclosing Party promptly so that the Disclosing Party may seek a protective order or other appropriate remedy or, in its sole discretion, waive compliance with the terms of this Letter Agreement. In the event that no such protective order or other remedy is obtained, or that the Disclosing Party waives compliance with the terms of this Letter Agreement, you agree to furnish only that portion of the Confidential Information or such other information which you are advised by counsel is legally required to be disclosed and to exercise your best efforts to obtain reliable assurance that confidential treatment will be accorded the Confidential Information or such other information.

10. For a period of two years from the date of this Letter Agreement, you shall not, directly or indirectly, solicit for employment any person who is now employed by the Business, whether or not any such person would breach an employment contract in leaving such employment; provided, however, that general solicitations of employment by means of newspaper, periodical or trade publication advertisements not directed at employees of the Business shall not constitute a violation of this provision.

11. You acknowledge and confirm that any information made available to you or your Representatives prior to, in the course of, or for the purpose of negotiations, will not constitute an offer by or on behalf of the Disclosing Party, nor will any such information form the basis of any contract to enter into a Possible Transaction, which contract will be constituted solely by the execution and delivery of a definitive transaction agreement. You hereby waive in advance any claims (including, without limitation, breach of contract) in connection with the sale of the Business unless and until a definitive transaction agreement has been executed and delivered by you and the other parties thereto. You also agree that unless and until a definitive transaction agreement between the Disclosing Party and you has been executed and delivered, neither the Disclosing Party nor its advisors (nor any of their respective affiliates, officers, directors, employees, stockholders or owners) has any legal obligation of any kind whatsoever with respect to any such transaction by virtue of this Letter Agreement or any other written or oral expression with respect to such transaction except, in the case of this Letter Agreement, for the matters expressly agreed to herein.

12. You acknowledge that the Disclosing Party and its advisors shall be free to conduct the process regarding a Possible Transaction as they in their sole discretion shall determine including, without limitation, (i) negotiating with any other party and entering into a definitive transaction agreement with any other party without prior notice to you or any other person and (ii) changing any procedures relating to the sale process at any time without prior notice to you or any other person.

13. No failure or delay by the Disclosing Party in exercising any right, power or privilege under this Letter Agreement shall operate as a waiver thereof and no variation shall be effective unless in writing and signed by an officer of the Disclosing Party on its behalf.

14. It is understood and agreed that money damages would not be a sufficient remedy for any breach of this Letter Agreement by you or any of your Representatives and that the Disclosing Party shall be entitled to equitable relief, including injunction and specific performance, as a remedy for any such breach. Such remedies shall not be deemed to be the exclusive remedies for a breach by you or any of your Representatives of this Letter Agreement but shall be in addition to all other remedies available to the Disclosing Party at law or in equity.

15. During the course of your evaluation, all inquiries to and other communications with the Disclosing Party are to be made solely through [**insert internal personnel and banker contact names**]. Accordingly, you agree not to directly or indirectly contact or communicate with any executive or employee of the Disclosing Party concerning the Possible Transaction or to seek any information in connection therewith from any such person without the prior written consent of the aforementioned.

16. You agree not to discuss with or offer to any third party an equity position in any Possible Transaction or any other form of direct or indirect participation in any Possible Transaction or any joint acquisition by you and such third party without the Disclosing Party's prior written consent.

17. In addition to your other obligations under this Letter Agreement, you acknowledge that certain Confidential Information may be subject to US export control regulations. You agree not to disclose or transfer any Confidential Information to any "foreign person" (as defined in the US ITAR and EAR regulations) without first advising the Disclosing Party in writing of your intention to make such a disclosure or transfer and obtaining all required US government authorizations for such disclosure or transfer.

18. This Letter Agreement shall be governed by and construed in accordance with the laws of ____________________________ without regard to the conflicts of law principles thereof. This Letter Agreement constitutes the entire agreement between the parties hereto with respect to the subject matter hereof and may be changed only by a written agreement signed by the parties hereto.

All references in this Letter Agreement to "you" and "your" shall mean and include you and your affiliates.

Please confirm your agreement with the foregoing by signing and returning one copy of this Letter Agreement to the undersigned, whereupon this Letter Agreement shall become a binding agreement between you and the Disclosing Party.

[DISCLOSING PARTY]

By: ______________________________
Name

Accepted and agreed to as of the date first written above:

[Name]

By :__________________________
Name:
Title:

Sample Confidentiality Agreement (2)

This Agreement is made and entered into this ____ day of __________, 20 __ by and between ___________________, a __________________ corporation ("Disclosing Party"), and___________________, a ______________________corporation ("Receiving Party"). Disclosing Party will provide certain information to Receiving Party with respect to Disclosing Party's business and assets for purposes of evaluating a possible transaction (the "Transaction"). All information for which protection is sought under this Agreement shall be in writing and be identified as confidential by an appropriate stamp or marking on the document disclosed and may include design, marketing, manufacturing, personnel, accounting and/or technical information, and/or other information relating to financial or operational affairs of Disclosing Party and/or its subsidiaries and/or affiliates and is hereinafter referred to as "Confidential Information."

Any Confidential Information acquired by Receiving Party shall be subject to the following terms and conditions:

1. For a period of two years from the date hereof, Receiving Party shall not disclose or otherwise make the Confidential Information available to any other person, firm or corporation without the prior written consent of Disclosing Party, nor shall Receiving Party use the Confidential Information for any purpose other than for evaluating the Transaction.

2. Information shall not be considered Confidential Information if such information is:

(a) Known and in the possession of Receiving Party when received or thereafter developed independently by Receiving Party without the benefit of information disclosed hereunder; or

(b) Rightfully obtained by Receiving Party from a source other than Disclosing Party through no wrongful act on the part of Receiving Party; or

(c) In the public domain when received or thereafter in the public domain through no fault of Receiving Party; or

(d) Released by Disclosing Party to a third party without any restriction as to use or disclosure.

3. In the event that Receiving Party or anyone to whom Receiving Party transmits the Confidential Information pursuant to this Agreement becomes legally compelled to disclose any of the Confidential Information, Receiving Party will provide Disclosing Party with prompt notice before such Confidential Information is disclosed so that Disclosing Party may seek a protective order or other appropriate remedy. In the event that such protective order or other remedy is not obtained, Receiving Party will furnish only that portion of the Confidential Information which it is advised by counsel is legally required and will exercise reasonable efforts to obtain a protective order or other reliable assurance that confidential treatment will be accorded to the Confidential Information. Except in connection with failure to notify Disclosing Party in accordance with the first sentence of this Section 3, Receiving Party shall not be liable for

any damages or loss arising from disclosure of Confidential Information pursuant to judicial action or government regulations.

4. Receiving Party shall limit access to Confidential Information to such of its employees, agents, representatives and advisors who need the Confidential Information for purposes of evaluating the Transaction. Receiving Party shall instruct all employees, agents, representatives and advisors who have access to the Confidential Information of the necessity to maintain confidentiality and shall take reasonable care to prevent the disclosure or use of the Confidential Information other than as permitted in this Agreement.

5. Neither this Agreement nor disclosure of the Confidential Information to Receiving Party shall be deemed by implication or otherwise to vest in Receiving Party any rights in the Confidential Information, other than the right to use such Confidential Information for purposes of evaluating the Transaction.

6. At any time, upon written request of Disclosing Party, Receiving Party shall destroy all Confidential Information and all copies, notes, analyses, or extracts therefrom, which are then in the possession of Receiving Party provided, however, that Receiving Party shall be entitled to retain one copy of all Confidential Information in the Office of its General Counsel, solely for recordkeeping purposes and otherwise consistent with the terms of this Agreement.

7. Except to the extent contemplated by paragraph 4 hereof, without the prior written consent of the other party, neither party shall disclose to any person (including without limitation Disclosing Party's employees) the existence of this Agreement, its terms or the fact that the parties are evaluating the Transaction.

8. The parties agree that their respective rights hereunder are such that immediate and irreparable harm may result from any failure to perform their respective obligations. Accordingly, in addition to whatever other remedies may be available under applicable law, the parties shall be entitled to seek injunctive relief with respect to any actual or threatened breach of the terms hereof.

This Agreement constitutes the entire agreement between the parties with respect to the Confidential Information and supersedes all previous communications, whether oral or written, between the parties relating to the Confidential Information. No modification or amendment of this Agreement shall be effective unless it is in writing and signed by the parties. This Agreement shall be governed by and construed in accordance with the laws of the ______________ without giving effect to the conflicts of law principles thereof.

IN WITNESS WHEREOF, the parties have entered into this Agreement as of the day and year first set forth above.

[NAME]	**[NAME]**
By: ______________________	By: ______________________
Name:	Name:
Title:	Title:

APPENDIX 3

Sample Due Diligence Checklist

[PROJECT ____________________]

LEGAL DUE DILIGENCE

CHECKLIST

[DATE]

In responding to the enclosed due diligence requests, please specify the request or requests (e.g., "Request 3.4") to which a document or information is responsive. If you believe that the Company already has provided documents or information responsive to a particular request, please cross-reference the location of that information in your response. Finally, if a particular request is not applicable to the Company or its business, please so indicate in your response (e.g., "N/A").

TABLE OF CONTENTS

1. General Corporate Information

1.1. The full names, places, dates of incorporation and registered offices of the Company and each subsidiary, including a capitalization table showing the issued and outstanding interests of each.

1.2. Names of all members, managers and officers of the Company and each subsidiary.

1.3. Names of any company which was formerly a subsidiary or affiliate but which has been wound up or sold within the last three years.

1.4. Copies of articles or certificates of incorporation or formation, as amended to date, of the Company and each subsidiary, together with:

a. By-laws, as amended to date, or operating agreements of the Company and its subsidiaries;

b. List of all states and foreign countries in which the Company and/or its subsidiaries are qualified to do business or are otherwise operating and each state or foreign country in which the Company and/or its subsidiaries is licensed by any official or agency, including certificates of authority to do business as a foreign corporation.

1.5. Copies of any:

a. Agreements relating to the purchase, sale or issuance of interests of the Company and each subsidiary;

b. Warrants outstanding with respect to interests of the Company and each subsidiary;

c. Member agreements, voting trust agreements and the like pertaining to the Company or any subsidiary;

d. Reports by investment advisors for the past three years;

e. Documents pertaining to any recapitalization of the Company or any subsidiary; and

f. Agreements or plans for mergers, consolidations, reorganizations, acquisitions or the purchase or sale of assets involving the Company or any subsidiary; or agreements in principle or letters of intent, currently in effect or temporarily suspended, with respect to mergers, consolidations, reorganizations or acquisitions; and all agreements with federal, state and local regulatory agencies entered into in connection with such transactions.

1.6. Copies of minutes of all meetings of (i) the Board of Managers of the Company and each subsidiary; (ii) all committees of the Board of Managers of the Company and each subsidiary; and (iii) the members of the Company and each subsidiary, together with all communications to the members of the Company and each subsidiary during the current and the last three complete fiscal years.

1.7. Copies of member records of the Company and each subsidiary, including membership interest record books and membership interest transfer books for the Company and each subsidiary.

1.8. A list of all corporations, partnerships, associations, joint ventures and other business entities in which the Company owns, directly or indirectly, an interest or any shares of capital stock. Copies of all related partnership and joint venture agreements.

2. Other Liabilities; Contracts; Commitments

2.1. Copies of (i) any contract for rent or (ii) for lease, hire or sale/leaseback or purchase on credit or by installments for personal property, to which the Company or any subsidiary is a party and calling for payments aggregating, in any 12 month period, $25,000 or more.

2.2. Copies of any mortgages (including fixed and floating charges), both on (i) real property and (ii) chattels or other personal property.

2.3. Details of contracts or arrangements which, directly or indirectly, restrict the freedom of the Company or any subsidiary to carry on the business in any part of the world; or the Company's or any subsidiary's ability to transfer the whole or any part of the business.

2.4. Copies of all commitments entered into by the Company or any subsidiary for (i) new buildings; (ii) machinery and equipment; (iii) inventories; and (iv) other matters aggregating, in any twelve-month period, $25,000 or more.

2.5. Sale contracts of the Company (as seller) and each subsidiary in excess of $25,000.

2.6. Purchase contracts of the Company (as purchaser) and each subsidiary in excess of $25,000.

2.7. Long-term service contracts, including any future contracts, which are not terminable within thirty days' notice.

2.8. Letters of credit, performance guaranties and bonds.

2.9. Secrecy, confidentiality, and nondisclosure agreements with employees or third parties. (Indicate any employees not covered by such agreements.)

2.10. Indemnification contracts, change-in-control agreements, and similar arrangements with officers and managers of the Company and each subsidiary.

2.11. Agreements with management or key personnel other than employment or consulting agreements.

2.12. Schedule describing all material transactions involving the Company or any subsidiary and (i) any officer or manager or (ii) any other affiliate of the Company or any subsidiary, and any agreements pertaining to the foregoing, which are not reflected in the items heretofore listed.

2.13. Copies of all agreements not provided in response to any other question which cannot be terminated by the Company or any subsidiary on 30 days' notice or less without payment of compensation or any special fees.

3. Borrowings

3.1. Details of all loan or other financial facilities (including foreign exchange facilities) available to the Company and each subsidiary from any source, including copies of all debentures, charges, guaranties and indemnities relating to any security given and copies of all facility letters, loan and other banking documents relating to the Company and each subsidiary.

3.2. All guarantees, indemnifications, surety relationships and other commitments of the Company and each subsidiary not set out in the answer to paragraph 3.1.

3.3. Compliance letters and notices of default or potential default with respect to any loan agreements, credit agreements or guaranties, including waivers and related correspondence.

3.4. List of all existing or intercompany borrowing or other financial transactions between the Company and its subsidiaries or affiliates.

4. Litigation and Claims

4.1. List and description (including a copy of each judgment, decree, order of court or regulatory agency and settlement of any kind) of all prior litigation, arbitration or investigations involving the Company or any of its subsidiaries or affiliates.

4.2. List and description (including a copy of pleadings, interrogatories, questionnaires, etc. where available) of all other current, pending or threatened litigation, arbitration or regulatory agency action or investigations involving the Company or any of its subsidiaries or affiliates.

4.3. A description of any significant contingent liability relating to the Company or any subsidiary.

4.4. Letters from lawyers to auditors concerning litigation and other legal proceedings involving the Company or any of its subsidiaries during the last five years.

4.5. Any known circumstances that might give rise to any proceedings of the kind mentioned in paragraphs 4.1 or 4.2 above.

4.6. Details of any notifications or requests from any government agency.

4.7. Details of any breach or default under the terms of any agreement or license.

5. Assets and Real Property

5.1. Location, size (acres or square footage, as appropriate) of all owned and leased plant facilities of the Company and each subsidiary.

5.2. Copies of all documents evidencing title to real property owned by the Company, its subsidiaries and any affiliated partnership, and copies of policies of title insurance or title searches relating thereto.

5.3. Leases and related agreements for all "property, plant and equipment" used or owned by the Company or any subsidiary.

5.4. All plans for present and pending real estate development and renovation projects.

6. Intellectual Property Matters

6.1. Identify, describe and give the status of any and all US and foreign intellectual property owned, licensed or used by the Company or any subsidiary, including but not limited to trade names, trademarks, trademark registrations, trademark applications, service marks, service mark registrations, service mark applications, copyrights, copyright registrations, copyright applications, patents, patent applications and any and all other patent rights, trade secrets, proprietary development information and know-how, inventions, inventors' notes, drawings and designs.

6.2. Provide copies of all documents, applications and correspondence relating to the intellectual property described in paragraph 6.1.

6.3. Principal brand names and details of material unregistered intellectual property rights owned by the Company or any subsidiary, or owned by an affiliate of the Company and used in the business of the Company or any subsidiary, including:

a. Unregistered trademarks (including logos);

b. Trade names;

c. Copyright (including rights in computer software and in manuals and other written or graphic materials); and

d. Design rights (including semiconductor topography rights).

6.4. Particulars of any licenses of the above rights to third parties (whether written or oral, formal or informal), including any software licenses.

6.5. List with copies attached of all licensing and royalty agreements running to and from the Company or any subsidiary.

6.6. Particulars of all material intellectual property rights (registered and unregistered) not owned by the Company or any subsidiary but used in the business under a license (formal or informal) or otherwise from any third party, including any licensed-in software.

6.7. Arrangements for the disclosure of confidential information (which includes technical and commercial information and know-how which is not in the public domain) either by or to the Company or any subsidiary.

6.8. Details of agreements with employees and consultants regarding their use of the confidential information of the Company or any subsidiary and/or the assignment of intellectual property to the Company or any subsidiary.

6.9. Details of each employee invention and patent assignment.

6.10. Details of any infringements or alleged infringements by third parties of patents, trademarks, service marks, registered designs, know-how or trade secrets, copyrights or other intellectual property rights or other intellectual property right owned by, or licensed to, the Company or any subsidiary, and of any infringements or alleged infringements of any such intellectual property by the Company or any subsidiary.

6.11. Details of any suspected or alleged infringement by third parties of intellectual property rights owned by the Company or any subsidiary or used in its business.

6.12. Details of any suspected or alleged infringement of third party rights by the Company or any subsidiary.

6.13. Details of any known challenges or disputes relating to intellectual property rights owned or used in the business of the Company or any subsidiary, including any challenges as to the validity, subsistence or ownership of such rights.

6.14. Copies of:

a. Any documentation evidencing the terms of informal arrangements for the use of intellectual property rights;

b. Any agreements relating to the use of confidential information; and

c. Any documentation relating to challenges to, or infringement of, any of the intellectual property rights identified (including copies of any pleadings and counsels' opinions).

7. Competition and Trade Regulation

7.1. Details of any restrictive practices and arrangements (whether or not legally binding), *i.e.*, arrangements that may have the effect of distorting or restricting competition or abusing a dominant market position.

7.2. Details of any communications with or from, or any notifications (including pending notifications) to, any governmental or regulatory authority (including the Federal Trade Commission and the Department of Justice) under any antitrust regulatory or similar legislation in the last five years.

7.3. Details of any judgment, order or any other decision of any antitrust or regulatory authority or of any court binding on the Company or any subsidiary.

7.4. Details of any current or pending investigation by, or proceeding before, any antitrust or relevant regulatory authority or any court, including details of any pending threat by an antitrust or relevant regulatory authority to open any such investigations or proceedings.

7.5. Details of any pending threat by a third party to complain to an antitrust or relevant regulatory authority or to commence antitrust proceedings in any court.

7.6. Details of any grants or other forms of financial assistance received by the Company or any subsidiary from any governmental authority.

8. Insurance

8.1. Copies of all insurance policies in effect at any time during the past five years, providing coverage for:

a. General liability;

b. Products liability;

c. Personal injury liability;

d. Advertising liability;

e. Automobile liability;

f. Workers compensation;

g. Employers liability;

h. Excess/umbrella liability;

i. Fidelity insurance; and

j. Directors and officers liability.

8.2. Loss summaries for the past two years, listing separately the cost for indemnification of claimants or plaintiffs and the cost to defend claims and suits.

8.3. Current insurance budget and self-insurance budget by type of insurance indicating if the cost is for premium, retained losses or self-insurance for each line of insurance coverage. Indicate budgets for at least the categories (a) through (j) of paragraph 8.1.

9. Employees/Employment Matters

9.1. List of all personnel employed by the Company and each subsidiary or engaged in the business, including persons who have accepted but not yet begun employment, showing name of employee, age, date of commencement of employment, number of years of continuous employment (including previous employment when in the same industry), salary or wages and other benefits (including bonus entitlements, if any, and any other arrangements for profit sharing); notice periods; vacation entitlement; other relevant terms.

9.2. Copies of all employment contracts (including consulting agreements) and sales commission agreements for employees, including management and employment contracts, "golden parachute" agreements, severance agreements and agreements not to compete with the Company or any subsidiary upon termination of employment.

9.3. Particulars of any recognized trade unions, any applicable collective bargaining agreements, details of any grievance/disciplinary procedures and details of any labor disputes in the last three years.

9.4. Details of any sickness/disability plans.

9.5. Details of any recent wage or salary awards or increases, frequency of reviews/awards, any current negotiations relating to anticipated awards or interests and next anticipated review date.

9.6. Organizational chart for the Company and each subsidiary broken down by department, division or other appropriate segment.

9.7. Details of all service agreements entered into or proposed which cannot be terminated by the Company or, as the case may be, the relevant subsidiary, on three months' notice or less without payment of compensation.

9.8. Details of any inducement (financial or otherwise) given to any person by the Company, any subsidiary or any manager or employee or associate of such person with a view to, or in connection with, the Company, any subsidiary or any such member entering into any form of contract or other arrangement or obtaining any other benefit whatsoever.

9.9. Receipts by the Company or any subsidiary or any manager or employee of the Company or such member or any associate of any such person of any such inducement.

9.10. Details of any agreements between employees and third parties (such as previous employers) still binding on the employees.

9.11. Details of any secrecy or non-compete agreements between employees of the Company or any subsidiary and other companies.

9.12. Details and/or copies of any agreements or arrangements, not covered by the above questions and whether legally binding or not, made otherwise than in the ordinary course of business of the Company or any subsidiary or on arm's length terms between the Company, any subsidiary or such member and any manager, employee or associate of any such manager or employee.

9.13. Loans and guaranties to or from managers, officers or employees of the Company and each subsidiary.

9.14. Copies of personnel policies, personnel manuals and employee handbooks.

9.15. Copies of all documentation pertaining to plans or programs relating to occupational safety and health, and affirmative action plans.

9.16. Copies of any executive/employee option plans, deferred compensation plans or profit sharing plans and any executive incentive compensation plans, including:

a. Related trust agreements; and

b. Employee descriptive material.

9.17. Interest ownership plans, option and appreciation rights plans, incentive option plans, bonus plans or similar arrangements; a schedule of the salaries of officers of the Company and each subsidiary; and a list of all outstanding options and vesting schedule for such options.

9.18. Pension plans, including qualified defined contribution and defined benefit plans.

a. Copies of all defined contribution and defined benefit plan documents and all amendments thereto.

b. Copy of most recent determination letter for each plan.

c. Copies of Forms 5500, with schedules, for past three years for each plan.

d. Copies of three most recent actuarial valuation reports for each defined benefit plan.

e. Copies of any financial reports for past three years for each plan.

f. Copies of summary plan descriptions, summaries of material modifications and material employee correspondence during the past three years relating to each plan.

g. Copies of trust documents and any investment management agreements for each plan.

h. Copies of Forms 5300, 5310 or 5310-A filed with respect to any of the plans for the past three years.

i. Copies of all material correspondence and filings with the IRS, PBGC, Department of Labor or other agencies within the past three years.

9.19. Welfare plans, including plans providing medical, surgical, health, sickness, accident, disability, death benefits; life insurance, reimbursement plans, group insurance plans, other insured or self-insured arrangements, vacation plans, training programs, daycare programs, scholarship funds, prepaid legal services, severance plans and supplemental unemployment benefit plans, cafeteria plans, dependent care reimbursement programs and retiree health/insurance benefits:

a. Copies of all plan documents and insurance contracts.

b. Copies of all summary plan descriptions, summaries of material modifications and material employee correspondence for past three years.

c. Copies of Forms 5500, with schedules, for past three years for each plan.

d. Copies of any financial reports for past three years for each plan.

e. Copies of the most recent actuarial valuation reports, if any, for each plan.

f. With respect to retiree health/insurance benefits, any other communications to employees regarding benefits.

9.20. Other benefit and employment arrangements, including bonus arrangements; fringe benefit plans; executive benefit policies; executive compensation arrangements; other nonqualified plans, such as incentive compensation, cash and bonus and option arrangements; "golden parachute" arrangements; individual and supplemental executive retirement plans; excess benefit plans; consulting agreements; employment agreements; secrecy agreements; non-compete agreements; and other management agreements:

a. Copies of all plan documents, contracts and agreements.

b. Copies of all summary plan descriptions and summaries of material modifications, if any, and any material employee correspondence for the past three years.

c. Copies of top-hat plan filings with the Department of Labor.

d. Copies of any plan financial reports for past three years.

e. Insurance policies or arrangements.

9.21. Benefit arrangements for employees covered by unions, if any, including:

a. Copies of all collective bargaining agreements.

b. Copies of all multi-employer plans.

10. Environmental Matters

10.1. Description of operations involving use, emissions or discharges of hazardous materials or generation or disposal of waste. Details of relevant hazardous materials and wastes, including methods of handling, storage and disposal. Copies of disposal contracts and contractors' registrations. Description of any situation relating to generation, handling or disposal of solid waste, hazardous waste, hazardous substances or any other contaminants which could require any Company to report such situation to any governmental authority (federal, state or local).

10.2. Copies of environmental licenses and any current applications for licenses. Details of any remediation or other work required to comply with the licenses. Details of any additional or renewed environmental licenses that are required or are likely to be required over the next three years.

10.3. Details of any past or current noncompliance with any conditions of any environmental licenses or any environmental laws. Is any remediation required to prevent recurrence?

10.4. Details of any known spillages or accidental discharges or emissions. Details of any known or suspected soil or groundwater contamination (or potential for contamination by neighbors).

10.5. Details of any investigations outstanding in relation to any notice, claim or requirement of any relevant authority in relation to any matters referred to in paragraphs 10.3 or 10.4 above.

10.6. Details of any known or suspected former use of any site which may have caused soil or groundwater contamination or involved use of hazardous materials or generation of waste.

10.7. Details of any known or suspected landfills, dumps, lagoons, or storage tanks (above ground or underground) or other storage areas for hazardous materials or waste. Details of any other known or suspected underground pipes, drains or other underground structures or equipment.

10.8. Details of any known or suspected Polychlorinated Biphenyls (PCBs), Trichlorobenzene (TCBs) or asbestos.

10.9. Details of any known exposure of employees to hazardous materials, noise, vibration or dust.

10.10. Details of any actual or threatened investigations, proceedings or claims by the relevant authorities or claims by third parties in relation to environmental or health or safety matters (including past investigations or claims). Details of any notice or claim of a violation or that remediation is required in relation to any environmental or health or safety matters.

10.11. Details of any off-site impacts (*e.g.*, noise, dust, odor). Details of any claims, proceedings or complaints relating to alleged off-site impacts.

10.12. Details of any potential liabilities in relation to formerly owned sites or businesses (*e.g.*, where warranties or indemnities have been given by a relevant company to a purchaser or where a relevant company formerly operated a polluting business which has been sold through an asset sale).

10.13. Copies of environmental audits, assessments or other reports relating to any property owned, leased or operated by the Company and subsidiaries.

10.14. Details of insurance policies covering environmental risks and any claims made.

10.15. All decrees, orders, consent decrees or orders, compliance plans, guidelines, agreements, contracts, or financing documents (or drafts of any such documents currently being negotiated) relating to environmental matters.

11. Tax Matters

11.1. Copies of all federal tax returns for the Company and each subsidiary for the last three tax years and all other years that remain open.

11.2. Copies of all foreign, state and local income, franchise, sales, use, and other state and local tax returns for the Company and each subsidiary for the last three tax years and all other years that remain open.

11.3. Copies of all tax auditors' reports and revenue agents' reports (federal, state, local or foreign) for the last five tax years with respect to the Company and each subsidiary.

11.4. Description of any current audit (federal, state or local) of the Company or any subsidiary, and all documentation in connection with such audit.

11.5. Copies of all agreements waiving or extending the statute of limitations for audit of any tax returns.

11.6. All ruling requests made and rulings received, and description of any ruling withdrawn, within past three years.

11.7. All tax-sharing or tax-indemnification agreements entered into by the Company and any subsidiary.

11.8. All unexpired IRS, state or local powers of attorney addressing tax matters with respect to the Company or any subsidiary.

11.9. Copies of all settlement documents, closing agreements and correspondence with the IRS or any state or local tax authorities relating to the Company or any subsidiary within the past five years.

11.10. To the extent not covered above, federal and state income tax returns for all years in which net operating losses arose.

11.11. Description of all changes in ownership of Company and each subsidiary during any period in which net operating losses arose or were carried forward, and documents or other information concerning asset values and tax bases as of dates of change in ownership.

11.12. To the extent not covered above, any business records or files relating to federal, state, local or foreign taxes or any tax attributes (*e.g.*, loss carryforwards or carrybacks, tax credits, tax basis of depreciable assets) of Company or any subsidiary.

11.13. Describe any potential obligations or liabilities of the Company or any subsidiary to pay taxes of or attributable to another person or entity.

12. Government Contractor Information/Export Control Matters

12.1. Details regarding percentage of revenues that are derived from government contracting.

12.2. Copies of any federal procurement law compliance policies and procedures, including any internal compliance audits, monitoring reviews, ongoing internal investigations, management letters and procedures on issues such as billing and time-charging.

12.3. Contract files for all executory government contracts and subcontracts and all contracts closed during the past six years, including but not limited to all correspondence between the Company and the Government, the Company and a prime contractor and the Company and its subcontractors pertaining to any government prime contract or subcontract. For subcontracts, identify standard "flow down" forms and procedures for obtaining required government representations, certifications and other required provisions and consents and approvals. Correspondence should include but should not be limited to any audits, claims or allegations of noncompliance with any statutory or regulatory obligations arising from current or past government contracts. Include documentation of any and all existing or potential Company, government, prime or subcontractor claims and any notices regarding existing or potential threats of default termination, product liability claims or warranty claims.

12.4. Proposal files, if separate from contract files, including all sales, cost, pricing and discount information supporting government recordkeeping, accounting and data disclosure requirements; subcontractor sales, cost, pricing and discount information; and data supporting required representations and certifications (generally set forth in Section K of federal government contracts) pertaining to various business practices, contract performance and socioeconomic requirements. These include, but are not limited to, compliance with gratuities and kickbacks prohibitions, lobbying disclosure requirements, Buy American Act, new material requirements, equal employment and affirmative action requirements, small business subcontracting requirements and any certifications regarding special subcontractor status, including small, small disadvantaged or women-owned business or 8(a) contractor status.

12.5. Copies of any and all pre- and post-award government audit reports by the Defense Contract Audit Agency (DCAA) or any agency Inspector General's office. Such documentation should include but should not be limited to rate agreements submitted to or approved by government agencies pertaining to forward pricing, provisional or final indirect cost rates; advance agreements on independent research and development (IR&D) and bid and proposal (B&P) costs; Cost Accounting Standards (CAS) Disclosure Statements; and any agreements relating to other categories of costs allocated to or charged by the Company to its government contracts.

12.6. Asset lists, including identification of any and all liens, encumbrances, or security interests on assets used by the Company to perform government contracts and subcontracts. Include documents relating to the Company's facilities and equipment, whether leased or owned, which are utilized in the performance of government contracts and subcontracts. Also identify any government-furnished equipment at Company facilities.

12.7. Information relating to any contract appeals or other litigation asserted by or against the Company arising under or relating to its government contracts or subcontracts. In addition to the audits mentioned above, include documentation relating to any contractor purchasing system reviews conducted by the Defense Contract Management Command and other compliance reviews of the Company or any subsidiary being conducted by any governmental agency, including the EPA, OFCCP, EEOC and OSHA.

12.8. Documents relating to any environmental issues that may affect the performance by the Company or any subsidiary of government contracts and subcontracts.

12.9. Documents relating to employment law issues, including but not limited to percentages of employees fully dedicated to government contract or subcontract work; workforce composition (number of full-time, part-time, or temporary employees); any collective bargaining agreements in force; summary plan descriptions relating to employee benefits, pensions and severance; other employment contracts or agreements in effect.

12.10. Copies of any export control policies and procedures, including any internal compliance audits, monitoring reviews and ongoing internal investigations.

12.11. Copies of special licenses issued by the Commerce Department and agreements approved by the State Department authorizing shipments of technical data, goods and services over a multiyear period.

12.12. Corporate export control records and shipping documentation to confirm that exports match the scope of licensing approvals.

12.13. Copies of any denied export license applications and a list of applications pending before the Departments of Commerce and State.

12.14. Communications with export licensing agencies, including but not limited to that concerning (i) commodity jurisdiction; (ii) product or technical data classification under the Commerce Department's Commerce Control List (CCL) or the State Department's ITAR; and (iii) existing or potential export control violations.

12.15. Anti-boycott compliance files, including accident reports or boycott requests and agreements filed with the Department of Commerce.

12.16. Records indicating whether the Company disclosed the known end-user or end-use in applying for export licenses.

12.17. Any internal memoranda or related documents regarding the applicability of export controls to specific products, end-users or end-uses.

12.18. Any internal procedures for the handling, control and storage of classified data.

12.19. On significant contracts, whether any stop work orders have been issued.

12.20. Copies of any cure notices and list of remedial actions taken.

12.21. Indications whether any voluntary disclosures of improper or potentially improper conduct have been made by the Company.

12.22. List of the contracts containing "most favored nation" or "most favored customer" clauses.

12.23. Indication if any former employees have made threats of filing a *qui tam* action against the Company.

12.24. Records confirming compliance with Sections 889(a)(1)(A)&(B) of the John S. McCain National Defense Authorization Act (NDAA) for Fiscal Year (FY) 2019, and any representations or certifications made or submitted by or on behalf of the Company, as a prime or subcontractor, in connection with the Company's compliance with FAR 52.204-24, Representation Regarding Certain Telecommunications and Video Surveillance Services or Equipment, FAR 52.204-25, Prohibition on Contracting for Certain Telecommunications and Video Surveillance Services or Equipment, and FAR 52.204-26, Covered Telecommunications Equipment or Services – Representation.

12.25. Gap analyses or assessments regarding compliance with DFARS 252.204-7012 and NIST Special Publication 800-171, and reporting self-assessment scores in accordance with DFARS 252.204-7018.

12.26. Indication if the Company has experienced any data breach, cybersecurity incident, or unauthorized access to its IT systems during the past ten years, and any related notices provided to any customer or government entity.

13. Compliance with Laws

13.1. Copies of all permits, licenses, approvals, determinations, rulings and orders of, all filings, compliance reports, deficiency notices and applications to, matters pending before, correspondence with and all documents relating to investigations or reviews conducted by, any domestic or foreign governmental or regulatory agency for the past two years, including but not limited to:

a. Department of Defense;

b. Department of Justice;

c. Federal Trade Commission;

d. Environmental Protection Agency, and similar state, local or foreign authority;

e. Securities and Exchange Commission;

f. Equal Employment Opportunity Commission;

g. Occupational Safety & Health Administration; and

h. Internal Revenue Service.

13.2. Any reports, notices or correspondence relating to any purported violation or infringement by the Company or any of its subsidiaries and any suspended or revoked governmental permits or licenses and copies of all other material correspondence with governmental agencies.

APPENDIX 4

Sample Due Diligence Document Request

1.1 Contract Files: Copies of all executory government contracts and subcontracts and all contracts that are currently open or that closed during the past six years, including but not limited to:

1.1.1 Internal documents or correspondence concerning contract performance or administration, including, but not limited to, all records concerning costs incurred, costs billed, estimated costs to complete, requests for progress payments, quality of products or services delivered, timeliness of deliveries, labor, or personnel issues.

1.1.2 All documents relating to the Company's compliance with lobbying disclosure requirements, environmental regulations, procurement integrity requirements (including restrictions on hiring of former government employees), the Buy American Act, the Service Contract Act, and Occupational Safety and Health Administration (OSHA) requirements, as well as documents relating to the administration or performance of any subcontracts.

1.1.3 All correspondence between the Company and the government, the Company and a prime contractor, and the Company and its subcontractors pertaining to any government prime contract or subcontract. Correspondence should include but should not be limited to any audits, claims or allegations of noncompliance with any statutory or regulatory obligations arising from current or past government contracts.

1.1.4 Any change orders that have been proposed or are under consideration by the Company. This includes any requests for equitable adjustment that the Company has filed or is considering filing with the government or a prime contractor under any prime contracts or subcontracts.

1.1.5 For subcontracts, identify standard "flow down" forms and procedures for obtaining required government representations, certifications and other required provisions and consents and approvals.

1.1.6 Documentation of any and all existing or potential company, government, prime or subcontractor claims and any notices regarding existing or potential threats of default termination, product liability claims, or warranty claims.

1.2 Proposal Files (if separate from contract files): Outstanding or pending bids or proposals submitted to any government agency, or prime contractor, including but not limited to:

1.2.1 All sales, cost, pricing, and discount information supporting government record-keeping, accounting and data disclosure requirements.

1.2.2 Subcontractor sales, cost, pricing, and discount information.

1.2.3 Data supporting required representations and certifications (generally set forth in Section K of US government contracts) pertaining to various business practices, contract performance and socioeconomic requirements. These include, but are not limited to, compliance with gratuities and kickback prohibitions; lobbying disclosure requirements; Buy American Act; new material requirements; equal employment and affirmative action requirements; small business subcontracting requirements; and any certifications regarding subcontractor status (*e.g.*, status as a small, small disadvantaged, veteran-owned, woman-owned, or 8(a) contractor).

1.3 Audit Reports: Copies of any pre-award and post-award audit reports issued by the Defense Contract Audit Agency (DCAA) or any agency Inspector General's office. Such documentation should include but not be limited to:

1.3.1 Rate agreements submitted to or approved by government agencies pertaining to forward pricing, provisional, or final indirect cost rates.

1.3.2 Advance agreements on independent research and development (IR&D) and bid and proposal (B&P) costs.

1.3.3 Documents relating to compliance with Cost Accounting Standards (CAS), including submission of CAS Disclosure Statements and any allegations of noncompliance.

1.3.4 Any agreements relating to other categories of costs allocated to or charged by the Company to its government contracts.

1.4 Asset Lists: Asset lists, including identification of any and all liens, encumbrances, or security interests on assets used by the Company to perform prime contracts and subcontracts, and any licenses or similar agreements concerning such assets. This includes documents relating to the Company's facilities and equipment, whether leased or owned, which are utilized in the performance of government contracts and subcontracts.

1.5 Government-Furnished/Customer-Furnished Equipment or Information: Identify any equipment, information, or property provided or furnished by the government or a customer at Company facilities.

1.5.1 All documents related to the company's property control system.

1.6 Contract Appeals/Litigation: Information relating to any contract appeals, bid protests, requests for equitable adjustment, or other claims or litigation asserted by or against the Company arising under or relating to its government contracts or subcontracts. This includes, but is not limited to:

1.6.1 Any existing or potential Company, government, prime contractor, or subcontractor claims.

1.6.2 Any notices regarding past, current or potential threats of default termination; product liability claims or warranty claims, as well as any notices to show cause or to cure, or suspensions of work relating to any government contract or subcontract.

1.6.3 Any notices regarding past, current or potential termination for convenience of the government of any prime government contract or subcontract.

1.7 Contractor Purchasing System Reviews: Documentation relating to any contractor purchasing system reviews conducted by the Defense Contract Management Command and other compliance reviews of the Company or any subsidiary being conducted by any governmental agency, including, but not limited to, the Environmental Protection Agency, Consumer Product Safety Commission, Office of Federal Contract Compliance Programs, Equal Employment Opportunity Commission and Occupational Safety and Health Administration.

1.8 Intellectual Property: All documents relating to intellectual property rights, including any patents, trademarks, or copyrights that have been licensed by or to the Company, and any documents relating to any claim or assertion that the Company has violated the intellectual property rights of any other person or entity, or that any other person or entity has violated the Company's intellectual property rights.

1.9 Environmental Issues: Documents relating to any environmental issues that relate to or may affect the performance by the Company or any subsidiary of government contracts and subcontracts.

1.10 Employment Law Issues: Documents relating to employment law issues, including but not limited to percentages of employees fully dedicated to government contract or subcontract work; workforce composition (number of full-time, part-time, or temporary employees); any collective bargaining agreements in force; summary plan descriptions relating to employee benefits, pensions, and severance; other employment contracts or agreements in effect.

1.11 Foreign/Domestic Government Agreements: Any documents relating to agreements or arrangements with any foreign or domestic government or government agency, including any government-owned entity, and any amendments thereto, to which the Company or any Subsidiary has been a party during the past five years.

1.12 Corporate Compliance Program: Documents pertaining to the Company's compliance program, including any government contract compliance program, including but not limited to:

1.12.1 The company's Code of Business Conduct or Ethics.

1.12.2 All compliance policies and procedures relating to federal procurement law, including any procedures or management letters on issues such as compliance with most favored customer pricing requirements, billing, time-charging, and completion of representations and certifications.

1.12.3 Identification of, and documentation relating to, internal compliance audits, monitoring reviews and ongoing internal investigations.

1.12.4 Any Audit Committee records and any communication between internal auditors and company management or the Board of Directors.

1.13 Handling of Classified Information: All documents relating to the Company's obligations with respect to classified information, including facility clearance documents, personnel clearance documents, documents related to any actual or alleged security violations, and documents requiring the company to possess or utilize classified information,

1.13.1 Any internal procedures for the handling, control, and storage of classified or sensitive data.

1.14 Stop Work Orders: On any prime contracts, identify any stop work orders that have been issued by the government.

1.15 Cure Notices: Copies of any cure notices issued by the government, the company's response(s) thereto, and a list of any and all remedial actions taken.

1.16 Voluntary Disclosures: Identify whether any voluntary disclosures of improper or potentially improper conduct have been made by the Company to any government agency.

1.17 Mandatory Disclosures: Identify whether any mandatory disclosures have been made by the Company to any government agency of credible evidence of a violation of Federal criminal law involving fraud, conflict of interest, bribery or gratuity violations found in Title 18 of the United States Code or a violation of the civil False Claims Act with respect to any government contract or subcontract, as a result of the three (3) year "look back" required by FAR Subpart 3.10.

1.18 Most Favored Customer/Nation Clauses: List of all contracts containing "most favored nation" or "most favored customer" clauses.

1.19 *Qui Tam* Actions: Indication if any former employees have made threats of filing a "qui tam" action against the Company.

1.20 Whistleblower Actions: Any documents relating to any actual or threatened whistleblower actions against the Company.

1.21 Use of Agents, Consultants or Brokers: Any documents relating to the Company's use of agents, consultants, or brokers currently or formerly engaged in assisting the company to obtain sales where the ultimate customer is a foreign entity.

1.22 Cybersecurity: Describe the Company's IT systems and the types of government contract-related information or data the company stores, generates, or accesses on its own IT systems, including whether the Company's IT systems are server-based or cloud-based, or a combination of the two; and if cloud based, which cloud service provider or "gov cloud" versions are used.

1.22.1 Describe the extent to which the company accesses any government IT systems for purposes of its government contracts.

1.22.2 Identify any FedRAMP-certified products or systems.

1.22.3 Identify whether the Company performs any contracts subject to specific cybersecurity standards (e.g., NIST standards, DISA STIG, VA Directive 6500, DOD SRG (IL standards), etc.).

1.22.4 Describe the extent to which the Company stores, generates, processes, or transmits covered defense information or controlled unclassified information?

1.22.5 Is the company currently compliant with the requirements of NIST special publication 800-171 and DFARS 252.204-7012?

1.22.6 Describe the results of any assessment of the Company's compliance with DOD cybersecurity requirements (e.g., DFARS 252.204-7012, Safeguarding Covered Defense Information and Cyber Incident Reporting, any NIST frameworks) performed by the Company or a third party.

1.22.7 Provide a copy of the Company's System Security Plan (SSP) and Plan of Actions and Milestones (POAMs).

1.22.8 Provide the Company's assessment score in the Supplier Performance Risk System (*see* DFARS 252.204-7018, Notice of NIST SP 800-171 DoD Assessment Requirements, and DFARS 252.204-7020, NIST SP 800-171 DoD Assessment Requirements).

1.22.9 Describe the Company's efforts to prepare for certification under the DOD's Cybersecurity Maturity Model Certification (CMMC) program, including the CMMC level at which the Company intends to seek certification and any assessments or gap analyses against that CMMC level.

1.22.10 Describe any data breaches, cybersecurity incidents, or unauthorized access into its IT systems during the past ten years. Describe the systems and processes the Company has in place to detect data breaches, cybersecurity incidents, and/or unauthorized access into its IT systems, and provide any notices provided by the Company regarding any data breaches, cybersecurity incident or unauthorized access into its IT systems to any customer or government entity.

1.23 Supply Chain: Describe the Company's efforts to comply with the requirements of sections 889(a)(1)(A)&(B) of the John S. McCain National Defense Authorization Act (NDAA) for Fiscal Year (FY) 2019.

1.23.1 Provide any representations or certifications made or submitted by or on behalf of the Company, as a prime or subcontractor, in connection with the Company's compliance with FAR 52.204-24, Representation Regarding Certain Telecommunications and Video Surveillance Services or Equipment, FAR 52.204-25, Prohibition on Contracting for

Certain Telecommunications and Video Surveillance Services or Equipment, and FAR 52.204-26, Covered Telecommunications Equipment or Services – Representation.

APPENDIX 5

Government Contracts Representations and Warranties

Article XXX. **GOVERNMENT CONTRACTS**

1) **Definitions**: As used in this Article XXX:

   a) "Active Government Contract" means a Government Contract that, as of the date of this Agreement, has not been closed-out under the procedures of the Governmental Authority responsible for administering the Government Contract.

   b) "Applicable Law" means, with respect to any Person, any domestic or foreign, federal, state, or local statute, law, ordinance, rule, administrative interpretation, regulation, order, writ, injunction, decree, or other requirement of any Governmental Authority applicable to such Person or any of its properties, assets, officers, directors, employees, consultants, or agents (in connection with such officer's, director's, employee's, consultant's, or agent's activities on behalf of such Person).

   c) "Governmental Authority" means any agency of a United States federal, state, or municipal government [or any agency of any foreign sovereign].

   d) "Government Contract" means any contract entered into between Company and an agency of the United States or an agency of any of its respective States, or any municipality, [or an agency of a foreign sovereign or agency of a provincial, regional or metropolitan government thereof] or any intergovernmental agency or quasi-governmental agency. The term "Government Contract" also includes any subcontract (at any tier) of the Company (i) with another entity under a prime contract held by the Company and (ii) with another entity that holds either a prime contract with such a governmental agency or a subcontract (at any tier) under such a prime contract, in each case including any task orders or delivery orders issued under, or any modifications to, any such prime contract or subcontract, whether currently active or subject to an open audit period.

e) "Government Contract Bid" means any offer, proposal or quote for goods or services to be delivered by the Company that if awarded by a Governmental Authority would lead to a Government Contract. The term Government Contract Bid shall exclude task execution plans, delivery order proposals and EBUY submissions and any response requested under previously awarded indefinite quantity contracts or blanket purchase agreements.

f) "Material Amount" shall mean a sum in excess of $ ______________.

2) **Schedules**

a) **List of Schedules**

i) Schedule A sets forth a true and correct list of each Active Government Contract that is in effect as of [date] as to which, in each case, the Company has received written notification of award by such date.

ii) Schedule B sets forth a true and correct list of each Government Contract Bid for which an award has not been made prior to the date of this Agreement.

iii) Schedule C sets forth the exceptions to the representations and warranties in this Article XXX.

iv) Schedule D sets forth the Company's backlog.

v) Schedule E sets forth the Company's active security clearances.

vi) Schedule F sets forth the Company's list of foreign sales of defense articles.

b) To the extent that a security classification precludes disclosure of information in an unclassified schedule, the classified information shall be provided in a classified annex to the appropriate schedule, which annex shall be reviewed only by representatives of Buyer who have the required security clearance. The representations and warranties in this Article XXX shall apply to the items listed in each such annex.

3) **Representations and Warranties as to Government Contracts, Active Government Contracts and Government Contract Bids:**

a) As to each Active Government Contract listed in Schedule A and each Government Contract Bid listed in Schedule B, except as set forth in Schedule C:

i) no such Active Government Contract or Government Contract Bid is based on the Company having §8(a) status, small business status, small disadvantaged business status, protégé status, or other preferential status afforded by statute or regulation; and

ii) the Company has complied with the terms and conditions of each such Active Government Contract and Government Contract Bid.

b) As to each Active Government Contract listed in Schedule A, except as set forth in Schedule C:

i) no termination for default, cure notice or show cause notice has been issued and remains unresolved, and no event, condition or omission has occurred or exists that would constitute grounds for such action;

ii) the Company has not recognized collectively on all Active Government Contracts a Material Amount of revenue in excess of the Government's current contractual obligation;

iii) no money due to the Company pertaining to any such contract has been withheld or set off other than in accordance with the withholding provisions of any such Government Contract; and

iv) each contract constitutes the valid and subsisting obligation of the Company.

c) As to each Government Contract listed in Schedule A and each Government Contract Bid listed in Schedule B, except as set forth in Schedule C:

i) the Company has complied with the requirements of any Applicable Law pertaining to each such Government Contract or Government Contract Bid, including, but not limited to, the Truth in Negotiations Act of 1962, as amended, the Service Contract Act of 1963, as amended (the "Service Contract Act"), the Office of Federal Procurement Policy Act, as amended, the Federal Acquisition Regulation (the "FAR") and any applicable agency supplement thereto, the Cost Accounting Standards, any and all export control laws and regulations, and any other applicable procurement law or regulation or other laws;

ii) all representations and certifications made by the Company with respect to such Government Contract or Government Contract Bid were accurate as of their effective date, and the Company has complied with such representations and certifications;

iii) neither the United States Government nor any prime contractor, subcontractor, vendor or other third party has notified the Company in writing that the Company has breached or violated, or is alleged to have breached or violated, any Applicable Law pertaining to such Government Contract or Government Contract Bid;

iv) the Company has not received any adverse or negative past performance evaluations or ratings within the past three (3) years; and

v) no reasonable basis exists to give rise to a claim for fraud (as such concept is defined under the state or federal laws of the United States) in connection with any Government Contract or Government Contract Bid under the United States civil or criminal False Claims Acts, the United States Procurement Integrity Act or other laws adopted by any other Government Authority, as applicable.

4) **Representations and Warranties as to Compliance**: Except as set forth in Schedule C, within the past six [FCA statute of limitations] years:

a) neither the Company, nor any of its officers, employees, nor, to the Knowledge of Sellers, consultants, agents or representatives (collectively, "Representatives") of the Company has been under any administrative, civil or criminal investigation or indictment by any Governmental Authority with respect to the conduct of the business of the Company;

b) no audit has resulted in costs being challenged by any government agency or auditor in an amount greater than the Material Amount;

c) there has not been any audit or investigation of the Company, or any of its officers, employees, or (to the Knowledge of the Company) Representatives that resulted in any adverse finding with respect to any alleged unlawful conduct, misstatement or omission arising under or relating to any Government Contract or Government Contract Bid;

d) the Company has not made any mandatory disclosure under FAR 52.203-13(b)(3)(i) or any voluntary disclosure to any Governmental Authority with respect to any alleged unlawful conduct, misstatement or omission arising under or relating to any Government Contract or Government Contract Bid, and there are no facts that would require mandatory disclosure under FAR 52.203-13(b)(3)(i);

e) neither the Company nor any of its officers, employees, nor (to the Knowledge of the Company) Representatives, is or has been suspended or debarred from doing business with any Governmental Authority or is or has been the subject of a finding of noncompliance, non-responsibility or ineligibility for contracting with any Governmental Authority. The Company is not aware of any circumstances that would likely become a basis for the suspension or debarment of the Company, or any of its officers, employees, Affiliates or, to the Knowledge of the Sellers, Representatives from bidding on contracts or subcontracts for or with any Governmental Authority;

f) there are no facts that could reasonably be expected to result in an "organizational conflict of interest" as defined in the FAR. The Company is unaware of any such "organizational conflict of interest" that might result from the execution of this Agreement;

g) the Company has conducted its operations in compliance with all requirements of all statutes, laws, rules and regulations of any Governmental Authority and all orders pertaining to all Government Contracts, and the Company has not had any determination of noncompliance nor entered into any consent order or undertaken any internal investigation pertaining to any Government Contract;

h) no statement, representation or warranty made by the Company in any Government Contract, any Government Contract Bid or any exhibit thereto or in any certificate, statement list, schedule or other document submitted or furnished to any Governmental Authority in connection with any Government Contract contained on the date so furnished or submitted contained any untrue statement of material fact, or failed to state a material fact necessary to make the statements therein contained, in light of the circumstances in which they are made, not false or misleading;

i) no payment has been made by the Company or by a Person acting on the Company's behalf, to any Person [other than to any bona fide employee or agent (as defined in subpart 3.4 of the FAR) of the Company] that is or was contingent upon the award of any Government Contract or that would otherwise be in violation of any Applicable Law;

j) the Company's cost accounting system is in compliance with Applicable Law, and has not been determined by any Governmental Authority not to be in compliance with any Applicable Law.

5) **Representations and Warranties as to Claims and Disputes**: Except as set forth in Schedule C, as of the date of this Agreement:

a) there are no outstanding claims against the Company, either by a Governmental Authority or by any prime contractor, subcontractor, vendor or other third party arising under or relating to any Government Contract or Government Contract Bid to which the Company is a party;

b) there are no outstanding disputes between the Company, on the one hand, and any Governmental Authority, on the other hand, under the Contract Disputes Act or any other federal statute or between the Company, on the one hand, and any prime contractor, subcontractor or vendor, on the other hand, arising under or relating to any such Government Contract or Government Contract Bid;

c) the Company has no interest in any pending or potential claim under the Contract Disputes Act against the United States Government or any prime contractor, subcontractor or vendor arising under or relating to any Government Contract or Government Contract Bid;

d) the Company has not, on all Active Government Contracts, individually or collectively, incurred or currently projects annual cost overruns in excess of price in a Material Amount;

e) the Company has not assigned, granted a security interest in, or otherwise conveyed or transferred to any Person any account receivable or other right of the Company arising under any Government Contract;

f) the Company is not subject to any financing arrangement or assignment of proceeds with respect to the performance of any such Government Contract; and

g) the Company is not using any Intellectual Property developed under any Government Contract for purposes outside of the scope of that Government Contract without having obtained the necessary and appropriate prior permission of the Governmental Authority involved;

h) Schedule D sets forth for each Government Contract having backlog as of [date] the dollar amount of backlog of the Company thereunder as of such date (calculated by the Company consistent with past practice), the name of the customer, a brief description of the products and services to be provided, and any dollar amounts included which are unfunded by any Governmental Authority or any customer in respect of undelivered orders. All of the contracts constituting the backlog of the Company (i) were entered into in the Ordinary Course of Business of the Company and based upon assumptions believed by the management of the Company to be reasonable and (ii) subject to such assumption being fulfilled, would be capable of performance in accordance with the terms and conditions of each such contract by the Company without a total program loss.

6) **Representations and Warranties as to Security and Facility Clearances**

a) Schedule E sets forth as of the date of this Agreement a true and complete list of all facility security clearances held by the Company and all personnel security clearances held by the Company, any officer, director, or employee of the Company (listed by category only).

b) The clearances set forth on Schedule E are all of the facility and personnel security clearances reasonably necessary to conduct the business of the Company.

c) The Company is in compliance with all national security obligations, including, without limitation, those specified in the National Industrial Security Program Operating Manual, DOD 5220.22-M (January 1995) (as amended).

d) Other than routine audits by the Defense Security Service, there has been no audit relating to the Contractor's compliance with the requirements of the National Industrial Security Program that resulted in material adverse findings against the contractor.

7) **Representations and Warranties as to Export Controls and Foreign Sales**

a) Schedule F sets forth a true and correct list of the contracts under which, during the period from five years prior to the date of the Agreement to the date of this Agreement, the Company has manufactured "defense articles," exported "defense articles" or furnished "defense services" or "technical data" to foreign nationals in the United States or abroad, as those terms are defined in 22 C.F.R. 120.6, 120.9 and 120.10, respectively.

b) Except as listed in Schedule C:

i) The Company has at all times been in compliance with all requirements of Applicable Law relating to export control and trade embargoes. No product or service provided by the Company, without explicit approval from the United States Government during the last six (6) years has been, directly or indirectly, sold to or performed on behalf of Cuba, Iraq, Iran, Libya, North Korea, Sudan, Syria, or any other country against which the US maintains economic sanctions or an arms embargo.

ii) the Company is unaware of any facts that could from the basis for a claim that the Company, or its officers, employees, and Representatives, have violated the Foreign Corrupt Practices Act.

8) **Representations and Warranties as to Cybersecurity**

a) The Company has complied with all data security, cybersecurity, and physical security terms and conditions and procedures required by its Government Contracts and by all applicable Law. Except as set forth in Section [XXX] of the Disclosure Schedule, in the past ten years, the Company has not had or experienced any breach of data security or cybersecurity, whether physical or electronic. Any data security, cybersecurity or physical security breach related to any Government Contract has been reported to the necessary Governmental Authority or higher tier contractor, as required by the terms of the Government Contract.

APPENDIX 6

Basic Novation Agreement, FAR 42.1204(I)

NOVATION AGREEMENT

The ABC Corporation (Transferor), a corporation duly organized and existing under the laws of _______________ *[insert State]* with its principal office in ________________ *[insert city]*; the XYZ Corporation (Transferee), *[if appropriate add "formerly known as the EFG Corporation"]* a corporation duly organized and existing under the laws of ___________________ *[insert State]* with its principal office in ________________ *[insert city]*; and the United States of America (Government) enter into this Agreement as of _______________ *[insert the date transfer of assets became effective under applicable State law]*.

(a) The parties agree to the following facts:

(1) The Government, represented by various Contracting Officers of the _______________ *[insert name(s) of agency(ies)]*, has entered into certain contracts with the Transferor, namely: ______________________ *[insert contract or purchase order identifications]*; *[or delete "namely" and insert "as shown in the attached list marked 'Exhibit A' and incorporated in this Agreement by reference."]*. The term "the contracts," as used in this Agreement, means the above contracts and purchase orders and all other contracts and purchase orders, including all modifications, made between the Government and the Transferor before the effective date of this Agreement (whether or not performance and payment have been completed and releases executed if the Government or the Transferor has any remaining rights, duties, or obligations under these contracts and purchase orders). Included in the term "the contracts" are also all modifications made under the terms and conditions of these contracts and purchase orders between the Government and the Transferee, on or after the effective date of this Agreement.

(2) As of __________, 20___, the Transferor has transferred to the Transferee all the assets of the Transferor by virtue of a ______________________ *[insert term descriptive of the legal transaction involved]* between the Transferor and the Transferee.

(3) The Transferee has acquired all the assets of the Transferor by virtue of the above transfer.

(4) The Transferee has assumed all obligations and liabilities of the Transferor under the contracts by virtue of the above transfer.

(5) The Transferee is in a position to fully perform all obligations that may exist under the contracts.

(6) It is consistent with the Government's interest to recognize the Transferee as the successor party to the contracts.

(7) Evidence of the above transfer has been filed with the Government. [*When a change of name is also involved, e.g., a prior or concurrent change of the Transferee's name, an appropriate statement shall be inserted (see example in paragraph* (8) *of this Agreement*)].

(8) A certificate dated ____________, 20____, signed by the Secretary of State of ___________ [*insert State*], to the effect that the corporate name of EFG Corporation was changed to XYZ Corporation on ____________, 20____, has been filed with the Government.

(b) In consideration of these facts, the parties agree that by this Agreement—

(1) The Transferor confirms the transfer to the Transferee and waives any claims and rights against the Government that it now has or may have in the future in connection with the contracts.

(2) The Transferee agrees to be bound by and to perform each contract in accordance with the conditions contained in the contracts. The Transferee also assumes all obligations and liabilities of, and all claims against, the Transferor under the contracts as if the Transferee were the original party to the contracts.

(3) The Transferee ratifies all previous actions taken by the Transferor with respect to the contracts, with the same force and effect as if the action had been taken by the Transferee.

(4) The Government recognizes the Transferee as the Transferor's successor in interest in and to the contracts. The Transferee by this Agreement becomes entitled to all rights, titles, and interests of the Transferor in and to the contracts as if the Transferee were the original party to the contracts. Following the effective date of this Agreement, the term "Contractor," as used in the contracts, shall refer to the Transferee.

(5) Except as expressly provided in this Agreement, nothing in it shall be construed as a waiver of any rights of the Government against the Transferor.

(6) All payments and reimbursements previously made by the Government to the Transferor, and all other previous actions taken by the Government under the contracts, shall be considered to have discharged those parts of the Government's obligations under the contracts. All payments and reimbursements made by the Government after the date of this Agreement in the name of or to the Transferor shall have the same force and effect as if made to the Transferee, and shall constitute a complete discharge of the Government's obligations under the contracts, to the extent of the amounts paid or reimbursed.

(7) The Transferor and the Transferee agree that the Government is not obligated to pay or reimburse either of them for, or otherwise give effect to, any costs, taxes, or other expenses, or any related increases, directly or indirectly arising out of or resulting from the transfer or this Agreement, other than those that the Government in the absence of this transfer or Agreement would have been obligated to pay or reimburse under the terms of the contracts.

(8) The Transferor guarantees payment of all liabilities and the performance of all obligations that the Transferee—

(i) Assumes under this Agreement; or

(ii) May undertake in the future should these contracts be modified under their terms and conditions. The Transferor waives notice of, and consents to, any such future modifications.

(9) The contracts shall remain in full force and effect, except as modified by this Agreement. Each party has executed this Agreement as of the day and year first above written.

UNITED STATES OF AMERICA,

By ____

Title ____

ABC CORPORATION,

By ____

Title ____

[*Corporate Seal*]

XYZ CORPORATION,

By ____

Title ____

[*Corporate Seal*]

CERTIFICATE

I, __________________________, certify that I am the Secretary of XYZ Corporation, that ________________________, who signed this Agreement for this corporation, was then ______________ of this corporation; and that this Agreement was duly signed for and on behalf of this corporation by authority of its governing body and within the scope of its corporate powers. Witness my hand and the seal of this corporation this day of ______________ 20___.

By ____

[*Corporate Seal*]

CERTIFICATE

I, __________________________, certify that I am the Secretary of ABC Corporation, that ________________________, who signed this Agreement for this corporation, was then ______________ of this corporation; and that this Agreement was duly signed for and on behalf of this corporation by authority of its governing body and within the scope of its corporate powers. Witness my hand and the seal of this corporation this day of ______________ 20___.

By ____

[*Corporate Seal*]

APPENDIX 7

Sample Truncated Novation Agreement

Bravo Corporation (BRAVO Corp.), a corporation that was duly organized and existing under the laws of Delaware with its principal office in Hometown, North Dakota; Bravo, LLC (BRAVO LLC), a limited liability company duly organized and existing under the laws of Delaware with its principal office in Hometown, North Dakota; and the United States of America (Government) enter into this Agreement as of January 2, 2009.

(a) The parties agree to the following facts:

(1) The Government, represented by various Contracting Officers, has entered into certain contracts with BRAVO Corp., as shown in the attached list marked "Exhibit A" and incorporated in this Agreement by reference. The term "the Contracts," as used in this Agreement, means the above contracts and purchase orders and all other contracts and purchase orders, including all modifications, made between the Government and BRAVO Corp. before the effective date of this Agreement (whether or not performance and payment have been completed and releases executed if the Government or BRAVO Corp. has any remaining rights, duties, or obligations under these contracts and purchase orders). Included in the term "the Contracts" are also all modifications made under the terms and conditions of these contracts and purchase orders between the Government and BRAVO LLC, on or after the effective date of this Agreement.

(2) As of January 2, 2009, BRAVO Corp. was converted to BRAVO LLC by virtue of a Certificate of Conversion from a Corporation to a Limited Liability Company Pursuant to Section 18-214 of the Limited Liability Act of Delaware. BRAVO LLC is a wholly owned subsidiary of Alpha Corporation, a Delaware Corporation (Alpha).

(3) BRAVO LLC has retained all the assets of BRAVO Corp. by virtue of the above conversion.

(4) BRAVO LLC has retained all obligations and liabilities of BRAVO Corp. under the Contracts by virtue of the above conversion.

(5) BRAVO LLC is in a position to fully perform all obligations that may exist under the Contracts.

(6) It is consistent with the Government's interest to recognize BRAVO LLC as the successor party to the Contracts.

(7) Evidence of the above conversion has been filed with the Government.

(b) In consideration of these facts, the parties agree that by this Agreement—

(1) BRAVO Corp. confirms the conversion to BRAVO LLC and waives any claims and rights against the Government that it now has or may have in the future in connection with the Contracts.

(2) BRAVO LLC agrees to be bound by and to perform each of the Contracts in accordance with the conditions contained in the contracts. BRAVO LLC also assumes all obligations and liabilities of, and all claims against, BRAVO Corp. under the contracts as if BRAVO LLC were the original party to the contracts.

(3) BRAVO LLC ratifies all previous actions taken by BRAVO Corp. with respect to the Contracts, with the same force and effect as if the action had been taken by BRAVO LLC.

(4) The Government recognizes BRAVO LLC as BRAVO Corp.'s successor in interest in and to the Contracts. BRAVO LLC by this Agreement becomes entitled to all rights, titles, and interests of BRAVO Corp. in and to the Contracts as if BRAVO LLC were the original party to the Contracts. Following the effective date of this Agreement, the term "Contractor," as used in the Contracts, shall refer to BRAVO LLC.

(5) Except as expressly provided in this Agreement, nothing in it shall be construed as a waiver of any rights of the Government against BRAVO Corp.

(6) All payments and reimbursements previously made by the Government to BRAVO Corp., and all other previous actions taken by the Government under the Contracts, shall be considered to have discharged those parts of the Government's obligations under the Contracts. All payments and reimbursements made by the Government after the date of this Agreement in the name of or to BRAVO Corp. shall have the same force and effect as if made to BRAVO LLC, and shall constitute a complete discharge of the Government's obligations under the Contracts, to the extent of the amounts paid or reimbursed.

(7) BRAVO Corp. and BRAVO LLC agree that the Government is not obligated to pay or reimburse either of them for, or otherwise give effect to, any costs, taxes, or other expenses, or any related increases, directly or indirectly arising out of or resulting from the conversion or this Agreement, other than those that the Government in the absence of this conversion or Agreement would have been obligated to pay or reimburse under the terms of the Contracts.

(8) ALPHA has provided to the Government a guarantee of the performance by BRAVO LLC of the contracts. A copy of that guarantee is attached hereto as Exhibit B.

(9) The Contracts shall remain in full force and effect, except as modified by this Agreement. Each party has executed this Agreement as of the day and year first above written.

UNITED STATES OF AMERICA,

By ____

Title ____

BRAVO CORPORATION,

By ____

Title ____

[***Corporate Seal***]

BRAVO, LLC,

By ____

Title ____

[***Seal***]

CERTIFICATE

I, William Shakespeare, certify that I was the Assistant Secretary of Bravo Corporation; that John Doe, who signed this Agreement for this corporation, was then President and Chief Executive Officer of this corporation; and that this Agreement was duly signed for and on behalf of this corporation by authority of its governing body and within the scope of its corporate powers. Witness my hand and the seal of this corporation this ____________day of ________________ 20_____.

By ____

[Corporate Seal]

CERTIFICATE

I, William Shakespeare, certify that I am the Assistant Secretary of Bravo, LLC; that John Doe, who signed this Agreement for this limited liability company, is the President of this limited liability company; and that this Agreement was duly signed for and on behalf of this limited liability company by authority of its governing body and within the scope of its powers. Witness my hand and the seal of this limited liability company this _____________ day of __________________ 20 ____.

By ____

[Corporate Seal]

APPENDIX 8
GUARANTY AGREEMENT

(Applicable to One or More Government Contracts)

The undersigned ________________________________(Guarantor's legal name) whose principal office is located at ______________________________ ________________________________ (address) for itself, its successors and assigns, hereinafter referred to as the Guarantor, hereby issues its Guaranty Agreement to Defense Contract Management Agency, acting on behalf of the US Government, for the benefit of ________________________________ (bidder or contractor's name), doing business at ______________________________ ______________________________ (address of bidding entity or contractor), hereinafter called the Contractor. The undersigned Guarantor agrees to guarantee to the Government they will provide the required resources, to include financial support, to the contractor to ensure full, complete and faithful performance of the Contractor on such contracts, according to the terms and conditions thereof and at the time and in the manner provided therein.

In consideration for the Government taking the following action (i.e. award of contract; novation of existing contract; contract financing; granting debt deferment; foregoing financial information on the contractor in conjunction with existing contracts)__________ ____ ______________, the undersigned Guarantor agrees as follows:

1. *Guaranty.* The Guarantor absolutely guarantees the full, complete and faithful performance by the Contractor of such contracts, as such contracts may be from time to time amended as authorized by its terms, according to the terms and conditions of such contract as so amended, and at the time and in the manner provided therein. The Guarantor agrees to provide the Contractor all necessary and required resources including financing, which are necessary to assure the full, complete and satisfactory performance of such contract.

2. *Extension of Time of Performance.* Any extension of the time of performance of such contract as so amended shall not release the undersigned Guarantor from liability hereon.

3. *Assignment.* This instrument shall bind the undersigned Guarantor, its successors and assigns. If any person, firm, corporation, or entity (a "Successor") other than the prospective contractor becomes obligated to perform the contract, or any part thereof, as a result of a novation of the Contracts or under operation of law, the rights and obligations of the Government and the Guarantor shall remain in effect. If the Successor provides a guaranty which protects the Government's interests with respect to the assigned Contracts, the Government will seek to enforce this Guaranty only if, and to the extent, it is unable to enforce the guaranty of the Successor.

4. *Default.* In the event of termination for default under the terms of covered contract, or in the event of failure, insolvency, default, bankruptcy, arrangement, appoint of receiver of the Contractor or other liquidation of the Contractor, the Guaranty herein shall become absolute.

5. *Waiver of Notice.* The Guarantor waives notice of default on the part of the Contractor and agrees that its Guaranty shall become absolute without necessity for the giving of such notice.

6. *Continuation of Guaranty.* Subject to paragraph #10 hereof, the Guaranty herein shall continue until full, complete and faithful performance of such contract(s) as it may be from time to time amended as authorized by its terms.

7. *Default Liability.* In the event that the Government terminates a Contract for default and awards the uncompleted portion of such contract to another source at a fair and reasonable price, the Guarantor shall be liable for any excess costs incurred by the Government as a result of such procurement and for the repayment of any unrecouped payments (e.g., partial payments, Progress Payments, or Advance Payments) paid to the Contractor by the Government. In addition, the Guarantor shall be liable for all costs and expenses paid or incurred by the Government in enforcing this Guaranty. The Contracting Officer representing the Government in connection with such contract shall determine the total costs and expenses, if any, incurred by the Government.

8. *Enforcement.* This Guaranty Agreement shall inure to the benefit of and may be enforced by the Government. This Guaranty shall be construed and interpreted in accordance with the substantive laws of the United States of America. If Guarantor is a non-US entity, by the execution of this Guaranty, the Guarantor expressly agrees to waive any rights to invoke the jurisdiction of their local national courts and agrees to accept the exclusive jurisdiction of the United States Armed Services Board of Contract Appeals and/or the United States Court of Federal Claims for the hearing and determination of enforcement and any and all disputes that may arise under this Guaranty.

9. *Construction.* Nothing in this Guaranty Agreement shall be construed to obligate the Government to take any aforementioned action as it pertains to the Contractor.

10. *Coverage, Termination, Waiver, and Expiration.*

a. The following contracts are covered by this guaranty (initial, as applicable. Mark "N/A" for those not applicable):

_____ 1) This Agreement applies to all contracts already in existence between the Contractor and the Government on or before the Agreement date

_____ 2) This Agreement applies only to the following solicitation(s) and/or contract(s): _______

____

_____ 3) This Agreement applies to all solicitations and/or contracts entered into on or after the date of the Agreement.

_____ 4) This Agreement applies only to Debt Deferment requests on the following contract(s) and/or debt identified in Demand Letter(s) or Contracting Officer's Final Decision(s) dated:

____

b. The Guaranty Agreement is a continuing guaranty and shall remain in full force and effect until the later of (1) the performance in full of the guaranteed obligations, or under the guaranteed contracts. (2) the termination of all continuing obligations and commitments of the Contractor under the guaranteed contracts. In the case of termination of the continuing commitments of the Contractor on any guaranteed contract, the termination notices must be given in writing citing the affected contracts.

c. In the event that all of the contracts covered by this Guaranty Agreement have been satisfactorily completed by the Contractor including all continuing commitments of the Contractor under the contracts, the Guarantor may request the cognizant Government Contracting Officer for this Guaranty Agreement to issue a written notice which states that this Guaranty Agreement is considered to have expired.

d. Failure on the Government's part to acknowledge this Guaranty has no effect on its legal status -- the Guaranty is binding and enforceable upon delivery to the US Government.

Executed on ____________________ [date].

On behalf of: ____ (Guarantor name)

By _____________________________________
(Signature)

____
(Printed Name & Title)

____
(Business Address)

Witness ______________________________ ___________________________ (printed name and title)

Witness ______________________________ ___________________________ (printed name and title)

If the Guarantor is a corporate entity, complete the following:

I, ____, certify that I am a duly appointed Secretary of the Corporation named as Guarantor herein; that __________________ who signed this Agreement on behalf of the Guarantor, was then _______________________ (identify position title) of said Corporation; and that said Agreement was duly signed for and on behalf of said Corporation by authority of its governing body, and is within the scope of its corporate powers.

{Corporate Seal, if applicable}

____

(signature)

Receipt of a copy of the above Guaranty Agreement is acknowledged.

THE UNITED STATES OF AMERICA

By ____

(signature)

____

(Printed name of Government official accepting the Guaranty)

____

____

(address of Government official)

INSTRUCTIONS

This form can be used for either business guarantors or personal guarantors and for US entities or non-US entities. It can be modified to reflect the identity and relationship of the parties. The substantive parts (Paragraphs 1-10) should not be modified without review by DCMA General Counsel (GC).

Preamble portion –

In this portion, the guarantor needs to identify themselves, who they are issuing a guaranty for, and for what reason the guaranty is being proffered. The blank lines in the preamble section allow for all of these matters to be addressed.

Paragraph 10 –

This is the next section which requires modification. The guarantor selects each applicable choice by initialing next to it and indicating which ones are not applicable by placing "N/A" in the line preceding the statement. More than one option may be applicable.

So let's look at each statement more in depth:

1) This Agreement applies to all contracts already in existence between the Contractor and the Government on or before the Agreement date

If the guarantor initials this statement, it means that the guaranty applies to ALL contracts already in existence. This would be the desirable choice if the guaranty is not intended to cover any future contracts. This would be a common choice in novation reviews, debt deferments, contract financing reviews. It is not anticipated that this would be the only selection when conducting a pre-award analysis since this language would not address contracts entered into after the date of the Guaranty.

2) This Agreement applies only to the following solicitation(s) and/or contract(s):

____

____

By initialing only this choice, the guarantor is limiting their guaranty to the solicitation/contract numbers specifically listed in blank space. This would appropriately be used if the guarantor is seeking to only guaranty specific solicitations/contracts. Though possible to see this choice in almost any situation where a guaranty is sought, it will be most common in the pre-award guaranty situation.

3) This Agreement applies to all solicitations and/or contracts entered into on or after the date of the Agreement.

By choosing this option, the guarantor is indicating that they want to guaranty any solicitations/contracts that the named contractor will enter into from the date of signing forward. This choice would be most common in the case of a contractor who is doing ongoing business with the government and a parent company wants to guaranty their performance from this point forward. This would also be an appropriate selection in a pre-award situation, though not necessary. It would also be common in a contract financing situation.

4) This Agreement applies only to Debt Deferment requests on the following contract(s) and/or debt identified in Demand Letter(s) or Contracting Officer's Final Decision(s) dated:

____

This option would be used when the only thing being considered is a debt deferment package. When a contractor requests a debt deferment, the cognizant contracting officer must determine whether it is in the government's best interest to grant such a deferment, pending outcome of a dispute. The two considerations are 1) will requiring a contractor to pay at this time cause a significant financial hardship on the contractor, potentially damaging the industrial base for the government, or 2) if we grant the deferment, will the contractor still be viable at the time of dispute resolution in order for the government to collect. The guaranty could be sought if the contractor's financials are unavailable or if they indicate a concern for any of the aforementioned considerations. The guaranty would then allow the government to consider the debt deferment request with the confidence they will be able to collect the amounts due at a future date.

Other miscellaneous considerations –

Corporate Seals – if the guarantor is a corporation and uses a corporate seal, they should "seal" the document. If not, remove the placeholder.

Acknowledgement by the Government – the Guaranty is legally binding once the Guarantor signs it. Failure by Government official to acknowledge receipt of the document does not alter the enforceability of the Guaranty. While the signature of a Contracting Officer is preferred, any Government employee can acknowledge receipt.

Table of Cases